"*Candy is a feisty little lady and that, tog*
faith, allowed her to fight her disease, recurren
and thankful for what she has and not giving in to depression about what she lost.
"*Candy is a force to be reckoned with. The sheer wonder of her personality in the
face of all she has gone through is almost magical.*"

Ian T. Jackson, MD, Sc (Hon) FRCS, FACS, FRACS (Hon)
Director, The Institute for Craniofacial and Reconstructive Surgery,
Providence Hospital, Southfield, Michigan

"*Candy has a remarkable ability to focus on God's grace despite multiple adversities.
Her honest and unshakable faith in the midst of trauma is an encouragement to
anyone who has faced life's terrifying 'what ifs.'*"

Sandra P. Aldrich
Speaker and author

"*Candy's trauma may not be all that different from other courageous souls
who have battled cancer and survived. But what makes her story so unique is a
dynamic, unwavering faith in God. In this modern age when supernatural is so easily
dismissed, Candy's fascinating struggle is not just candid and heroic, but is most of
all … inspiring! Her life was dramatically changed by amazing lessons of life learned
through almost impossible physical agony and intense spiritual suffering.*"

Joe Musser
Author of *Joni*

"*I first met Candy while writing* When Cancer Comes *for Moody Press. I've seen
her deal with multiple adversities with grace and persistence, while maintaining
a strong commitment to the Lord and a love for people. Candy has a message of
hope, perseverance and trust, and God has given her the personality and skill to
communicate it effectively.*"

Don Hawkins
President, Southeastern Bible College
Radio Host of Life Perspectives,
Author of *Never Give Up, How to Beat Burnout* and *When Cancer Comes*

"*Candy's Southern hospitality will speak to your hearts as she shares her testimony
of tragedy, turmoil and triumph through a life in Christ. Her inner beauty will radiate
from the inside out bringing new definition to what it means to be truly beautiful.*"

Florence Littauer
Speaker and author, Personality Plus series and *Silver Boxes*

"*Candy's testimony and life have motivated me to keep my faith in the Lord and to
allow Him to lead and direct my life through the good and bad times.*"

Jay Barker
Quarterback, University of Alabama's National Championship team, 1991
Quarterback, National Football League, Quarterback, Canadian Football League
***In Due Time: The Struggles and Triumphs of Alabama Quarterback Jay Barker* by Wayne Atcheson**

"Never have I been more moved and more aware of God's presence on this earth than I was when I first heard the words of Candy. While the stories of her past personal trials were heart wrenching, the story of the grace that saved her and saves all of us each day was the most inspiring. Speaking directly from God's Word, Candy shared with me the message of salvation through Christ's blood alone, and gave me a big nudge in my walk with my Lord and Savior!"

Carrie Colvin
America's Junior Miss 2002

"Having known Candy for more than twenty years, it was my privilege to observe her heroism through the numerous medical crises she endured. Her story is a wonder testimony of God's faithfulness and grace. True stories are always inspiring when, in the struggle of overcoming terrible misfortunes, one's personal faith is renewed and reinforced by that struggle. Candy's conquest of that adversity is particularly inspiring. This woman's extraordinary response to her illness not only transformed her life, but it has given her a message of hope and courage that God continues to effectively use to inspire others. When strong faith carries the day, that story must be shared. This is such a story."

Linda Bachus
Wife of U.S. Congressman Spencer Bachus
6th District of Alabama

"The story of Candy's courageous struggle with what was thought to be an incurable cancer is an inspiration both to other patients and treating physicians, such as myself."

Edward R. Laws, Jr., MD, FACS

"As a participant of the local scholarship program in Jefferson County in 1997, I first came to know Ms. Candy's story. Her story speaks of triumph, tenacity, and resilience. It was a story that I would remember for the rest of my life, a story that would propel me to new heights throughout my lifetime. She loved me and forty-one other young women enough to share the truth of her testimony."

Tyrenda J. Williams
America's Junior Miss 1997

"Candy is a penetrating, knowledgeable speaker concerning her own journey with cancer and living life itself. Her stories are real, warm, and instructive. Candy is considered the most sought out speaker by UAB Medical School students each year for the Medical Ethics series. She is so effective, we have to give her two weeks!"

C. Earle Carpenter, Director
Christian Medical Ministry of Alabama

"Candy's mature faith in Jesus with her childlike view of life has brought life to so many. She is a true vessel being used by God to make a real difference in this world. I rejoice in knowing her."

Jodi Benson,
Broadway Actress/Voice of The Little Mermaid

"Candy is one of God's heroes! She has displayed what it means to trust God in all circumstances and bring glory to Him through unbelievable pain and suffering. With a background in theatre and dance, she herself has become a 'stage' upon which the main actor, Jesus Christ, demonstrates His triumphant grace. Through her book one will get a glimpse of what genuine faith in God looks like in daily experience."

Barbara B. Barker, Director
The Briarwood Ballet
Birmingham, Alabama

"A beautiful young mother has her face changed by cancer in exchange for a vibrant life of healing, health and happiness against impossible odds. Her extraordinary courage and faith will amaze you. It's likely that you will never read a story like this one, a must read you won't forget."

Wayne Atcheson
Director, Billy Graham Library

"Hers proved to be a difficult diagnostic problem, the tumor being in a location that most surgeons would consider impossible to completely remove ... the surgeons were able to effect a satisfactory and nearly miraculous result."

David C. Dahlin, MD
Emeritus Staff
Surgical Pathology, Mayo Clinic

"I had the pleasure of meeting Candy when the ASPS honored Candy with the Patients of Courage Award. Her story has a powerful impact on people."

Brian Hugins
Staff, American Society of Plastic Surgeons

"Candy is one of the most vivacious speakers that CMDA has ever had at their annual convention. Her passion for life and compassion for others is evident in every word she speaks. She will be a blessing to any audience."

Melinda Mitchell
Meeting Manager
Christian Medical and Dental Associations

"Candy Wood Lindley has shared more than just her face of faith, she shares her heart. Face of Faith will renew your spirit and give you a newfound courage to face life today and more importantly the courage to face the future."

First Lady Patsy Riley
Wife of Alabama Governor Bob Riley

"I have found Candy to be one of the most courageous and beautiful human beings that I have ever met as a reporter. Just being with her and listening to her poignant story gave me a spiritual lift. More power to her—if she stills needs any."

Evelyn Holst
***Stern* magazine**
Hamburg, Germany

"Candy's story is amazing! God's providence is so clear and her learning to depend on Him is very instructive. As she has shared her story across the nation in many different venues, life after life has been impacted! So will yours!

Frank M. Barker, Jr., Pastor Emeritus
Briarwood Presbyterian Church
Birmingham, Alabama

"With grit and determination and her faith in the Lord, she has succeeded in living her life to the fullest. She has become a role model for others who have suffered a similar tragedy."

Charles A. Boswell
World War II Hero
Blind Golf Legend and author, *Now I See*

"Her testimony [as a guest on this Canadian television program] is stirring and inspiring. Her steadfast faith in Jesus Christ was so clearly evident through all the circumstances she faced with her health and with her difficult family situation. Candy radiated the 'joy of the Lord' and her joy was (and continues to be) infectious. When I think of Candy and what she's been through, what comes to mind is a verse from Job: But He knows the way that I take; when He has tested me, I shall come forth as gold."

Johanna Webster
Associate Producer *100 Huntley Street* telecast
Ontario, Canada

FACE OF FAITH

discovering a
different kind of makeover

FACE OF FAITH

discovering a
different kind of makeover

CANDY WOOD LINDLEY

WITH KATHI MACIAS

Knoxville, Tennessee

Paperback ISBN-13: 978-0-9820435-1-6
Hardcover ISBN-13: 978-0-9820435-0-9
Library of Congress Control Number: 2008936420
Cataloging in Publication Data on file with publisher.

Exclaim Publishing
publisher@ExclaimPublishing.com
www.ExclaimPublishing.com
www.FaceofFaith.com

Cover Photo: Liesa Cole, Tony Rodio, Omni Studios, Birmingham, Alabama
Makeup Artist: Julie Taylor
Wedding Photographer: Frank Carnaggio
Production and Marketing: Concierge Marketing Inc.
        www.ConciergeMarketing.com

Printed in the United States of America
10 9 8 7 6 5 4

To Momma,
who epitomizes a mother's sacrificial love,
and Daddy,
who exemplifies my heavenly Father's unconditional love

ACKNOWLEDGMENTS

◇　　◇　　◇

WITH HEARTFELT GRATITUDE AND APPRECIATION, FOR EVERYONE WHO —

Smiled a smile at me

Cried a tear for me

Sent expressions of love to me

Thought a thought of me

Prayed a prayer on my behalf

Laughed with me

This is your story, too! Some of you, I know. Many I don't. Thank you for being a part of it!

Special thanks to the "Magnificent Seven," as I like to call you: Dr. Edward Creagan, Dr. John Gerwin, Dr. Morton Goldfarb, Dr. Ed Laws, Dr. John Poynor, Dr. Doug Tilt, and Dr. Ian Jackson. Thank you,

Dr. Jackson and his wife, Marjorie, for giving me a home away from home and making me feel like "family."

Several doctors in Birmingham have followed me through all these years. To Dr. Jim Belyeu, Dr. Jim Gewin, and Dr. Bert Walker and their office staffs, thank you for taking such good care of me and for responding to all 564 telephone calls even in the middle of the night.

If I was going to have a crooked face, I was determined to have straight white teeth. Thanks for my smile, Dr. Bruce Spink.

Thank you Bob and Marianne Turnbull for being there when I needed you.

Looking good is a challenge! Here's my creative team: makeup artists, Leslie Christin, Sharon Myers, and Julie Taylor; William Winslett, friend and hairdresser, and the gang at Oak Street Hair Group; and Rosa at Natural Hair Designs.

In addition to my immediate family, thank you to my extended families.

With so so much love to my Briarwood Church family, my Thursday night Bible study at the Barkers (save my floor cushion!), my Mountain Brook Community Church friends, and Don Richards and Tom Caradine.

To Eddie Macksoud and the entire Junior Miss family, you have been such a huge part of my life for thirty years.

Thank you for the support of my Red Mountain Theatre Company family and especially the RMTC kids for the privilege of working with you and for your excitement over this project.

With thanks to my dance family, especially Lola Mae Coates, who taught me to strive to do everything excellently, and Deanny and the Steeple Arts Academy of Dance "troopers."

To Jan and Tom Hatchett who, when they got Colley, got me too. And to Janice Hill, who is finally happy this book is finished. Now what are we going to talk about? To Elizabeth Ray, my friend and prayer warrior.

If you're not thanked here, it's probably because you're mentioned in the book.

Twenty years ago after reading Corrie ten Boom's book *The Hiding Place*, I called its authors John and Elizabeth Sherrill. I presumptuously asked Mr. Sherrill if he would write my book, too! He said he was unable to write the book for me, but he very graciously offered to help. He said he was happy to be involved even if just as a "stepping stone" to the final product. Thank you, Mr. Sherrill!

Well, here it is—the final product! Thank you to other "stepping stones" along the way who have personally contributed to the writing of this book: Sandra Aldrich, Wayne Atcheson, Dan Benson, Don Hawkins, Jerry Jenkins, Joe Musser, Peg Short, Les Stobbe, the late Van Varner, Bill Watkins, and Terry Whalin. To Debra Watkins—thank you for the perfect title and for checking to make sure I was writing. To Sherri Ash who would drop everything to help me move from no-tech to low-tech. To Teri Page who provided seed money to get this book planted. To Sherle Adams for your excitement in spreading the Gospel and encouraging others to do so. Happy 87th birthday. To my new Knoxville girlfriends for your encouragement and support. To Lisa Pelto, Sandra Wendel, Gary Withrow, and the Concierge Marketing team for taking my manuscript, dozens of my photographs, and (at least) seventy-eight cover ideas to create a book that looks like me.

And to my coauthor, my friend Kathi Macias who took 500 pages of my words and cut it in half and said twice as much. Now that's an editor!

Much love to my children, Elliott and Colley. We lived this story together. You have and always will be a joy. To Elliott's wife, Sara, and Colley's husband, Gilder, you are all I have prayed for for my children. Thank you for my grandchildren: Nathan, Calvin, and Mallie Tate. And to my husband, John. My best friend, my soul mate. You've always been encouraging me to finish this book. I'll let you know when it happens.

As you read my story, you may wonder how I remembered all the details. It was easy. From that first day in the hospital, I told my momma that I wanted to write a book. So she kept a detailed record in spiral-bound notebooks. As she sat by my bedside, she noted every visitor, every bouquet of flowers, every drug I was given, and the names of the multitude of well wishers who phoned me. She wrote down what doctors said, what I said, and even noted her own thoughts at the time.

Momma also carried her camera everywhere. She'd pop it out of her purse frequently, so we have a photographic record, of over 500 pictures. And that's why I can describe so many of these scenes with such vivid detail. Some of those photos are included in this book.

In addition, I kept, and still do keep, my personal thoughts in my prayer journals and on random pieces of paper, notecards, and calendars—all stored in a box for when the time came to use them. We were determined to record it all for that book I intended to write—and now you are holding it in your hands.

May God richly bless you and encourage you as you read it! "I hold you in my heart." Philippians 1:7.

Candy!

1

◇　　◇　　◇

BY THE TIME WE PULLED UP TO THE ENTRANCE OF THE HOSPITAL THAT
Tuesday in May 1982, the afternoon sky was nearly as dark as midnight.
The wind whipped the trees into a near frenzy, and the rain came down
in sheets, as thunder rolled and lightning zigzagged across the heavens.
Despite my forced optimistic demeanor, the weather matched my mood,
and I was having a hard time maintaining my usual sunny disposition.

Of course, I really had no choice. I wasn't about to let my mother or
my one-year-old daughter—or anyone else, for that matter—know how
absolutely terrified I felt as I climbed out of the car and turned back to say
goodbye. Instead I smiled wide and, in my typical upbeat manner, said to
my mom, "I can go in by myself. Ya'll don't need to get out in this rain."
Then I turned my attention to my daughter, who sat in the back seat.

"I love you, Colleybug," I said, using the nickname we'd attached to her because she was so tiny. "I'll see you in a few days." I leaned in to kiss her goodbye, struggling against the tears that rose up at the thought of how much I already missed her.

"Thanks for everything, Mom," I said, my confident smile still in place. "I'll call you later. Oh, and don't forget to pick up Elliott from the birthday party."

As I watched the yellow Camaro pull out of sight, I tried to ignore the growing sense of loneliness that threatened to overwhelm me. *No,* I thought. *I can't let this get the best of me.* I turned and pushed my way through the rotating doors and walked across the lobby to the admissions desk. I would never be the same again.

After smiling through the admissions process and various scheduled tests, I was encouraged when the nurse on duty took me to a brand new, sparkling clean room. I climbed onto the bed, propped myself up on the pillows, and, still in my clothes, gazed out the window at the Birmingham skyline, hidden now by a bleak, black blanket of clouds. The May thunderstorm that seemingly obliterated the heavens was nothing compared to the storm of emotion that was about to break loose inside me.

Now that I was by myself, I sat, entranced, listening to the slapping sound of the raindrops like tiny pebbles hitting the window pane. A sick feeling ran through my stomach as I finally let my defenses down, and a deep sense of sadness washed over me.

I'd been playing games for a year. I wanted to believe the doctors when they told me nothing was wrong. But I knew there was. Now the game-playing was over, and it was time to face reality. I sat on the bed and pent-up tears rolled down my face.

Two hours lapsed, as I waited, staring out the window, alone at last with my fears. Then my husband, Lee, arrived. I was glad Dr. Goldfarb, one of my surgeons, didn't make his rounds until after Lee was there. The two of us were watching television when Dr. Goldfarb came in—or at least, Lee was. I stared in the TV's general direction, but nothing was registering.

"Hello," the doctor said, walking into the room and holding out his hand to Lee. "I'm Mort Goldfarb."

"You don't look very cheerful," I said, watching the two men shake hands and trying to keep my tone light, even though somewhere deep inside I already knew why Dr. Goldfarb wasn't smiling. "Have you had a bad day?"

He turned to me, his words as somber as the expression on his face. "After looking over your tomogram, it looks like the growth is larger than we thought."

His words sliced through my chest and into my heart. I'd been right in thinking something was wrong, though I hadn't wanted to be. The doctors' previous assurances that it was just a pea-sized growth that needed to come out faded to the back of my mind. Still, I did my best to ignore the implications of his statement by quickly responding, "So you just take out a larger growth."

He began to explain to me about a tumor "the size of a golf ball in your sinus cavity," but I cut him off.

"What's the bottom line?" I asked. "What's the worst that could happen to me?"

Without hesitation, he looked me in the eyes and replied, "You could lose the right side of your face."

Stunned, I asked the question that no one ever wants to ask: "Why? It couldn't be cancer, could it?"

Compassionately, yet again without hesitation, he answered, "Yes, Candy, it could. But remember, you asked for the worst. Let's just hope for the best."

◊   ◊   ◊

My greatest fears, those I'd tried to bury for so long, were finally beginning to surface. And there was nothing I could do about it.

I felt crazy and confused. The melodramatic part of me (which, by nature, is huge!) thought, *This is dramatic!* But the part of me that had been hidden in denial for so long quickly gave way to the reality of what I'd just heard, while another part of me was glad there really was something wrong. I wanted to prove to anyone who'd doubted me that I wasn't making up the way I'd felt for a year, and that I wasn't just some hypochondriac. I wanted to say, "See, I told you so"—especially to Lee. I wanted him to feel badly that he didn't believe me and got mad at me for not feeling well, and for making me go places and do things I didn't feel like doing.

For months, I'd chosen to believe that I or someone else could fix things. I was an only child, and I'd always been able to use the art of persuasion or stubborn persistence to get what I wanted or needed. Quite obviously, that wasn't going to work this time.

I decided to call my parents, as well two of the ministers of our large Presbyterian church, and they all agreed to come right away. Then I called our doctor and friend Doug Tilt, who'd run tests on me the previous week. Within an hour, they were all assembled in my room, doing their best to cheer and encourage me.

"Candy, you don't know what it is yet."

"Try not to worry."

"Try to be optimistic."

"They said it *could* be cancer, but you don't know that for sure."

I fixed my eyes on Doug and asked, "You're positive all my tests were all right last week?"

Carefully guarding his words he answered, "Candy, the tests we took were all right." The words he didn't say echoed as loudly in my mind as the ones he did.

Felix, one of our pastors, suggested we pray. We all agreed, though I don't remember what was said, and to be honest, praying didn't seem to help either. The truth was, I wanted an instant solution, and nobody had one.

Lee and I were from church-going families. We were financially secure, and I was able to stay at home to raise our two healthy children, just like my momma had for me. Suddenly, I realized all that security could change in a moment.

What about Elliott and Colley? They're only five and one! What if I die? What if I can't raise my children? Colley won't even remember me. She won't remember asking me at bedtime to "Rock a baby." Tears stung my eyes as I thought of how she sucked her thumb and held her little pink blanket while I rocked her to sleep. *Who will rock her to sleep if I die? Will Elliott remember that each night I read nursery rhymes to him?*

I spent a sleepless night waiting for the surgery that was scheduled for seven-thirty Wednesday morning. Dr. Poynor and Dr. Goldfarb would be performing what was described as a simple procedure, which amounted to cutting across the top of the teeth under the lip on the right side and removing the tumor from the sinus area. By the time I was wheeled into surgery that morning, I was starving for words of hope and reassurance.

Dr. Goldfarb was the last person I saw before I was put to sleep. Mary, his nurse, held my hand, as the doctor stood beside the operating table. Pleading with my eyes as well as my words, I looked at him and, as if I could change the circumstances by begging, said, "Dr. Goldfarb, what do you think?"

In an obvious attempt to encourage me, he repeated his words from the night before: "Let's just hope for the best." But his half-smile and the concern in his deep brown eyes gave him away.

Before either of us could say anything more, I heard the anesthesiologist's voice. "Candy, count to ten."

Obediently, I responded. "One, two, three, four..." And I was asleep.

When I awoke, I looked up to see a nurse wheeling me on a gurney back to my room. I opened my mouth and voiced the first thought that popped into my mind: "Did they get the tumor?"

"Your doctor will talk to you about that later."

I'd seen enough television to know what that meant—and it wasn't good.

Back in my room, I soon heard Dr. Goldfarb's voice, penetrating the lingering haze of my anesthesia.

"The mass was larger than we'd anticipated. We didn't try to remove it; we just took a small section to biopsy. The frozen section has the correct characteristics of being malignant, but the pathologists aren't sure." Then he apologized for not knowing more.

I heard Lee ask, "When will they know?"

"Possibly tonight, but probably tomorrow."

I drifted back into my haze and dozed some more—until the pain woke me up. The anesthetic was wearing off, and the floor I was on, though shiny, clean, and new, was understaffed. No one answered my calls when Momma or I pressed the button. Escalating stabs of pain pierced my face, and my tongue felt thick with thirst. Momma finally went to the desk, insisting someone bring me a pain shot and some water.

Later that afternoon my face began to swell. Momma pressed my call button and asked if an icepack would help.

"We'll need to check her chart to see if her doctor has authorized one," the nurse replied over the intercom.

The nurse never came, and Momma called again.

"I'm sorry," was the reply. "We can't find her chart, and we can't do anything without her chart."

By the time the fugitive chart was located, my face was too swollen for ice to do any good, though pain medicine helped a little.

When Dr. Poynor made his rounds that evening, he and Daddy went out into the hall to talk privately. The doctor explained that there was some confusion about the biopsy report, and we'd have to wait awhile longer before receiving it.

Daddy didn't take that news very well. He naturally wanted to protect me, as he had when I was a child, but he was helpless to fix this situation. All he could do was pace back and forth at the end of my bed.

Momma, on the other hand, continued to be optimistic—at least, she acted like it. When Daddy slept in the waiting room down the hall and Lee went home to spend the night, Momma and I had some quiet time, which I really needed. Many nights when I was growing up, she'd sat at the end of my bed, listening to me think things out, and it was natural for us to fall back into that pattern at such a critical time in my life.

As I lay there that Wednesday night, I silently prayed and begged God to hurry things up, to let me know the biopsy results, whatever they were. But deep inside I already knew.

"Momma," I said, as the truth of what lay ahead permeated my thoughts in a way I didn't understand and couldn't explain, "I'm going to go through something so horrible that people won't believe it, but it's going to be okay in the end. I'm not going to die." Though a dramatic statement, I spoke it somberly, but also with assurance. I wouldn't have used the word *prophetic* at the time, but that was the tone of my pronouncement.

My mother appeared puzzled, examining my face as if to see how I could seem so sure of what I'd said. "How do you know that, Candy?"

I shrugged. "I just know." I couldn't explain it because I'd never experienced that kind of feeling. It didn't bring fear with it—though maybe some dread—but it was as if the Lord chose to give me some knowledge of what lay ahead, as well as some assurance and relief at the same time.

"I wanted to say it out loud," I told Momma, "so when it happens, people will know I didn't make it up."

For my mother, that statement immediately took root and sustained her through the months ahead. I, on the other hand, drifted off to sleep, wondering how I could feel so sure about such a thing.

2

◇ ◇ ◇

THURSDAY BEGAN WITH STILL NO NEWS. IT WAS, HOWEVER, A SPECIAL day—Lee's and my tenth wedding anniversary. I could hardly believe I was spending it in a hospital bed, awaiting news about a biopsy report that could change my life. Lee was doing his own reminiscing and looking at me with deep sadness. When I asked how he was doing, his only remark was, "Our lives will never be the same again."

Though I refused to follow that thought to its logical conclusion, I did allow my mind to drift back to our wedding day, ten years before. That evening, as the light shone through the stained glass windows into the candlelit church, everything seemed perfect. Large arrangements of pink and white flowers decorated the church, and our friends and family, including all four grandmothers, were gathered together to watch us stand before them and the Lord and to vow to love one another for better or worse, in sickness and health, until death…. Now, I shuddered at the impact of those vows and the somewhat macabre way we were "celebrating" them.

Of course, few people knew about what really went on behind our "perfect marriage" façade, but I knew only too well about the seemingly fruitless hours we'd spent with a marriage counselor. I knew that Lee, like me, had regrets. Looking back, it was obvious we'd had them almost from the beginning—not to mention serious misgivings about the wisdom of our getting married in the first place.

Our parents had cautioned us to wait, but we'd stubbornly plowed ahead with our plans. I remembered standing in the narthex of our old stone Methodist church. Our wedding party of fourteen had already gone down the aisle. My two cousin flower girls had just made their way to the front, delicately tossing pink rose petals along the deep red carpeted aisle. Behind the large double doors, I waited at my father's side with my arm tucked into his and holding a bouquet of orchids and sweetheart roses.

As he prepared to walk me down the aisle, he made one last plea: "We can turn around right now and walk out that front door." But I couldn't do that—not then. So Lee and I had made the commitment to stick together, no matter what, a commitment that was now being tested like never before.

I couldn't let myself dwell on it. No longer on strong pain medication, I was able to think clearer, and I was determined to sort things out in my mind. I knew I'd done all the right things, everything a patient could do. I'd seen some of the best doctors in Birmingham. I'd checked all the possibilities for the headaches: Was it hormones? I saw a gynecologist. Was it my eyes? I saw an ophthalmologist. Teeth? I saw a dentist. I even saw two internists, an allergist, and five ear, nose, and throat specialists before Dr. Goldfarb and Dr. Poynor. Did I miss something? Was there something else I should have done, someone else I should have seen? Surely there was something….

Though it was natural for me to wonder why no one had discovered the problem before this, the question I really wanted answered was, *How have I gotten to this place in my life?*

It was the first time I'd slowed down enough even to ponder that question. First, I questioned why I hadn't listened to my misgivings about marrying Lee. It wasn't like I hadn't seen the red flags, but I'd been like an obstinate child, ignoring all warnings. Now we were celebrating our tenth anniversary, and Lee was sad because my illness meant that our lives would never be the same. I, on the other hand, questioned if our life together had ever been what others thought it was, what we tried so hard but failed to make it. True, we were committed, but we weren't connected. There was no bond, and that made me sadder than anything Lee was concerned about losing, as we faced the strong possibility that I might have cancer.

Cancer. There it was again—that word I'd tried so hard to ignore, the word that had haunted and plagued me, that had tried to chase me down no matter how hard and how fast I ran to escape it. It was a word that had forced me into a depth of denial I never thought possible. And yet, the biopsy report wasn't in. There was still hope…wasn't there?

If I learned anything during that time, it was that I couldn't rely on symptoms, resources, machines, or my own medical knowledge to diagnose and fix the problem. Neither could I put my faith and trust in doctors and nurses. As concerned, knowledgeable, and gifted as they were, and even with their reviewing my symptoms and tests constantly, the problem wasn't detected. There were so many unanswered questions that it was impossible to figure it all out, and I was too tired to keep trying.

Spiritually, there were questions as well. Where was God in all of this? I was sure He was with me, but where was I with Him? Several incidents had occurred in the past two months that continued to nag at me.

First, there was the time I was in my car, stopped at a light. Turning the dial on my radio, I caught the title of a minister's sermon: "Is God in Control of Your Life?"

The minister spoke those words as the background music began to play, and I wondered, *Why do people always ask that question? If God is God, He's in control of everyone's life. I'm obviously missing something about that statement.*

Out loud, I said, "I want You in control of my life, God, but You'll have to show me what that means." Then I changed stations and never heard the sermon.

◇   ◇   ◇

A couple of weeks later, in March 1982, Lee and I were on a ski trip in Steamboat Springs, Colorado, with our friends Barbara and Ben. Lee and Ben had left for the slopes ahead of us. As we girls enjoyed a leisurely morning, still in our pajamas and basking in the warmth of the fire, Barbara sat on the sofa, drinking her morning coffee and reading her Bible and a little devotional book. I sat on the floor, drinking my coffee while surrounded with various magazines and catalogues. I was circling all the things I wanted: clothes, jewelry, things for the house. I liked pretty things and always had an ongoing wish-list. But I was curious about Barbara and her Bible.

"Do you do that every morning?" I asked, glancing up at her.

She didn't preach or lecture. She simply answered, "Uh-huh," smiled, and went back to her reading.

"That's nice," I said and returned to my wish-list circling.

Later that morning, Barbara and I skied from our ski-in-ski-out condominium to the chair lift. At the top of the mountain Barbara peeled off to meet Ben on the slopes, while I continued on by myself. I didn't pair up to ski with Lee because he liked the hard runs, as did Barbara and Ben, but I wasn't that advanced.

After a few brief moments of skiing down the hillside, I noticed I was the only skier using that particular run. I stopped, relishing the pristine privacy of my surroundings and realizing how very long it had been since I'd experienced such peace and solitude—and how desperately I needed it. Life at home was full of non-stop activities, many of them self-imposed. But at that moment, the sky stretching out above me was as blue as my shiny new ski suit, and the crisp, fresh air whispering against my face seemed to speak of a relatively problem-free life. In my naiveté and denial, I dared to believe it.

At that particular moment on that picture-postcard day, I meditated on how wonderful it was to be alone in such a quiet and peaceful place. I stood on the mountainside, looking out at the snow-capped Rockies in front of me and the towering evergreens that surrounded me, their boughs heavy with white powder, and I was captivated by the beauty of God's creation.

I unhooked my skis from my boots and stuck them in the snow, toes pointed skyward, smiling as I realized I'd never become an expert skier but content to have learned enough to enjoy the sport with my husband and friends. With the sun warming my face, I removed my jacket and rolled it up to use as a pillow. Then I lay back in the feather-soft snow and listened. The only sound was the clicking of the ski lift in the distance and the occasional fall of too much snow from one of the tree limbs. The thought suddenly occurred to me that if I could reach high enough, I could touch heaven.

"God," I whispered, stretching my arm upward and offering a rare but much-needed prayer to the One I'd believed in since I was a child, "You're so close. I feel like I could almost touch You." Then I paused, thinking suddenly of my friend back home whose six-month-old baby had just died. "God, why doesn't anything bad ever happen to me?" I mused, then quickly added, "I'm glad nothing bad ever happens to me, of course, but I don't understand. All I have to deal with are these crazy headaches."

I sighed. "Okay, God, maybe that's what I should pray for—patience to deal with the headaches. Other than that, I really don't need anything." I smiled heavenward, truly grateful for my many blessings. "Thanks for everything, God."

There didn't seem to be anything else to pray about, so I "signed off," as I often did when I managed to find time for a brief talk with my Creator. For the most part, my life was under control—or so I chose to believe. Little did I know that nothing could be further from the truth.

Then, just two weeks before my surgery, we had a get-together at our house. While the men went to the living room to talk, we girls went to the playroom for our own visit. We were all young moms, discussing various church mother's-day-out programs, when one of the girls remarked, "Ever since I moved back to Birmingham, I've backslidden in my walk with the Lord and missed my time in Bible study."

Walk with the Lord? What does that mean? Instead of asking, I said, "Oh, Molly, you make everything so complicated. Don't you know that all you have to do is believe in Jesus and forget it?" I thought that would take care of the discussion, but instead I found myself wondering why she looked so puzzled by my remark.

As these memories drifted through my mind while I lay in my hospital bed, still waiting for the biopsy results, Lee, Momma, and Daddy walked in. The sight of Lee's sad but resigned face brought a stab of pain to my heart as I remembered how he'd looked ten years before. He'd been a handsome groom, with a baby-faced but hesitant smile, who was, no doubt, every bit as unsure of what he was doing as I was.

With that thought in mind, another stab of pain sliced through me as I considered that neither of us had met the other's expectations, and I truly regretted that. At that moment, I silently resolved that if I recovered from my illness, I'd become the best wife any woman could be.

Meanwhile, I lay there, my face swollen so tight that it shone. My right eye was blue and throbbed with each heartbeat, and the incision across the top of my teeth stung with pain. My nose was packed, and blood still drained slightly onto my lip and down my throat, leaving a metallic taste in my mouth.

With my dinner tray in front of me, I tried to make light of the situation, eyeing my untouched, unappetizing soft-diet hospital meal. "This is not exactly what I had in mind for our anniversary. And look at me!"

I was such a pitiful sight that Momma and I got tickled at the humor of it, but Daddy and Lee didn't think it was funny.

"Let's take a picture," Momma suggested, getting out her camera. She'd made anniversary cupcakes that afternoon, enough for us and all the nurses, too. Momma was famous for her cupcakes, made with real butter and confectioner's sugar, and it was her effort at keeping things as normal as possible.

Later that evening Lee's parents, Hayden and "Trickle" (her nickname), came to see me. They'd been visiting Lee's sister, Tracy, who'd just had a baby and was still in the hospital across town.

"Have your doctors been by yet?" Trickle asked.

"No, and we don't know a thing," I said, stubbornly clinging to hope that an official report would soon arrive, negating what my heart already knew. "There's still a chance that it isn't malignant."

Throughout the remainder of our visit, we all clung to that fragile hope. Momma later told me that when she walked the Woods to the door, Trickle sadly remarked, "I've always thought Candy was one of the prettiest girls I've ever seen." That statement said a lot about the situation and its ominous possibilities.

By the time Dr. Gerwin, Dr. Goldfarb's and Dr. Poynor's partner, came into my room to check on me, it was late, and everyone had gone home. I'd never met Dr. Gerwin, but I immediately attacked him with a barrage of questions.

"Do you know anything yet?"

"About what?" he asked.

"About the biopsy report."

He shook his head. "I don't see an official report in your chart yet."

"So they still don't know whether it's malignant or not?" My frustration was tinged with relief; there was still a ray of hope.

Dr. Gerwin's brows drew together. "Well, I don't think there's any question about that."

"Dr. Goldfarb says there's a possibility that it isn't," I argued. Actually, no one really knew, but Dr. Goldfarb had used the word *possibility*. I guess I took that the way I wanted to, but Dr. Gerwin's next statement hit me hard.

"I certainly would never go so far as to tell you that," he said, and then changed the subject, informing me he was going to remove the packing from my nose.

Now I'd had packing before—a square gauze pad rolled up that easily slid out of the nostril. I wasn't at all prepared for the excruciating procedure that was about to occur.

Taking hold of the protruding tip of gauze with his instrument, he pulled inches of the bloody packing out of my right nostril, along with what felt like my entire nasal membrane. It took my breath away and brought tears to my eyes. When he took hold again, I squeezed my eyes shut.

"No! There can't be more," I cried. But there was.

As he ripped out another section and the tears streamed down my face, my pitiful whimpers turned into pleading. "Please, Dr. Gerwin, don't take out anymore!" When I realized he was indeed going to take more, I bargained for time. "Please. Wait. Let me get my breath. May I have a sip of Coke?"

"Sure," he agreed, smiling empathetically. "Whenever you're ready."

After my little "break," I told him to go ahead. With every muscle in my body tensed, I closed my eyes, held my breath, and clutched the side rails of the bed. He pulled one more section, and then another and another—seventy-two inches in all. By the time that last inch of gauze was removed from my nose, I was exhausted and trembling.

"I'm sorry that hurt you so badly," he said.

"That's okay," I whispered, though it really wasn't.

His concern was evident. "Are you all right?"

I didn't want to make him feel bad; he'd been so nice. "I'm fine," I lied.

After he left, I couldn't contain my emotions any longer. Turning my swollen, aching face into the pillow, I began to sob, uncontrollably and long into the night, until it seemed I had no more tears to cry.

Then I lay there in the quiet. Now what? Physically drained from the ordeal earlier, and now beaten down mentally and emotionally, my thoughts turned back to God. I'd prayed to receive Jesus Christ as my Savior when I was fifteen, but as so many things in my life, I simply checked it off my list of things to do.

Nothing really changed in my life, but the minister of the Baptist church I attended as a teenager said that if we'd just recognize we were sinners, repent, and accept Jesus as our Lord and Savior, asking Him into our heart, we'd be saved and spend eternity in heaven. As much as I could understand what that meant, I did it. But I'd never even read the Bible, except as an assignment for a class in college, where it was treated as a historical account. I sometimes went weeks without thinking to pray. I tried hard to be moral and good, and Lee and I were both involved in our USA Presbyterian Church. I worked with the church's camp for underprivileged children, Lee and I had taught junior high Sunday school, and I was president of the ladies' organization the year before. But spiritually, I realized I was missing something.

I thought about Barbara reading her Bible every morning, about the preacher on the radio asking if God was in control of our lives, about Molly saying she'd backslidden in her walk with the Lord by missing her time in personal Bible study. I also remembered telling God on the mountain that He'd given me a wonderful life and that I didn't need anything—then. How could I have been so blind?

As the reality of my desperate need for God came crashing in upon me, I imploded. "Lord, I'm so sorry," I cried. "I was wrong. I do need You—for everything. I don't want to deal with this. I don't want to make any more decisions. I'm just so, so…tired. You're going to have to do it for me, God. I don't even know how You do that, but You just do it. Whether I live or die, I'm totally Yours to do with whatever You want." I meant every word. I surrendered everything—my hopes, my dreams, my desires, and my very life to the Lord.

It took being at the absolute end of Candy—emotionally, mentally, physically, and spiritually—to finally begin with God. After a lifetime of trying to be religious and morally good, I'd finally given up and surrendered my life to God.

And so I was changed forever…though I didn't truly understand that at the time.

3

◇　　◇　　◇

Born in Montgomery, Alabama, on August 29, 1951, I was the adored, cherished, first, and only child of Bill and Bette Colley. From the time I was a little girl, I knew I wanted to be a dancer some day. In fact, one of my earliest and most beloved memories is that of standing on my daddy's feet, my tiny right hand clasped in his large left one and his right arm encircling and holding me while we danced.

It wasn't surprising, then, that I was taking dance lessons by the time I was five. The tiniest girl in my class, I knew when we danced to "Winter Wonderland" at Christmas that I wanted to dance for the rest of my life. I also wanted to grow up to be a dance teacher, just like my instructor, Miss Carol. I couldn't wait for the annual recital in May. This was the first time I'd performed on a real stage in front of a large audience. A huge painted backdrop hung behind us, my first introduction to a real theater with bright lights and curtains that pulled. Once onstage, I was so excited I felt like I could burst. I knew this is what I'd been born to do. I wanted to smile the biggest, dance the best, and entertain the most.

It wasn't the first time I was attracted to bright lights, though. When I was two years old, I stuck a rolled up piece of toilet paper in my nose. It was nighttime and the doctor's office was closed, so Momma and Daddy took me to the emergency room where the toilet paper was removed. When we got back in the car, we didn't even make it out of the parking lot before I did it again. This time my momma turned around to the back seat, put her finger against my nostril, and told me to blow. The toilet paper flew out, and I didn't get to go back to the lights and attention of the emergency room.

I danced in my first of many school talent shows when I was in the first grade at Mary B. Austin Elementary School in Mobile, Alabama, where we moved when I was five. But I didn't limit myself to wearing my gold sprayed ballet shoes to performances. I wore them every chance I got, not minding one bit if I drew attention to myself. In fact, I enjoyed it—a lot.

Strong-willed. High-spirited. Persistent. Persuasive. Precocious. Tenacious. Stubborn. Creative. Determined—and certainly not timid or shy. Those were the terms that described me as a child and, for the most part, carried over into my adulthood. I was more than a bit of a challenge for my parents, but that strong personality was to serve me well later. Much like the "Unsinkable Molly Brown," I've always had that "I ain't down yet" and "I ain't givin' up" attitude. I believe God designed me that way, tailor-made for His plans, and I know I was created for the part God gave me in this drama called life.

◇   ◇   ◇

This sort of optimistic tenaciousness and adventuresome spirit was already evident throughout my grammar school and junior/senior high school years. I was a star looking for every possible opportunity to shine. True to my "Miss Dramatica" nickname even before it was bestowed upon me, I didn't have a bashful bone in my body. And I wasn't content to limit my flair for the dramatic to the stage.

When I was in the second grade, each individual wooden desk had a place to store books underneath and a two-inch-wide circular hole in the right-hand corner, made to hold a bottle of ink back in the pre-ballpoint-pen days. Of course, we were too young to be trusted with ink bottles, so the round holes were empty—except for the day I decided to stick my right hand inside the hole and keep it there.

I immediately raised my left hand. "Mrs. Mullins, my hand is stuck in the hole."

Now that wasn't really true. I'd situated my thumb under the desktop in such a way that it was impossible for anyone to pull my hand out, but no one knew that except me. I just wanted to cause a little excitement—and it worked. When Mrs. Mullins couldn't budge my hand, she excused herself and went to the restroom to get some soap. While she was gone, the rest of the class came and surrounded me. *Center-stage!* I saw then that I had the ability to cause some excitement and drama.

As everyone watched, Mrs. Mullins soaped my hand until it was slippery, but it still wouldn't come out. My poor teacher then excused herself again. When she came back with the principal and a can of Crisco, they were sure they had the remedy. They were wrong. When they mentioned calling a carpenter to saw his way through the wooden desktop—miracle of miracles, my hand slid right out of that hole! I raised it high in the air for everyone to see, and the entire class, teacher and principal included, broke into applause. Grinning from ear to ear, it was all I could do not to stand and take a bow.

It was during those grammar school years in Mobile that I was introduced to the music of my generation. Teenagers screamed to the music of the groups performing every Saturday morning on Dick Clark's *American Bandstand.* I stood in front of our black and white TV in the corner of the living room of our small house and learned how to rock and roll. My Davy Crockett doll was as tall as I was and danced the slow songs with me.

In addition to having a flair for dancing and the dramatic, I had a problem with talking back to my momma. It seemed I just had to have the last word. One day I'd received a much-deserved "switching" on the back of my legs, and so I leaned out the open window of my upstairs bedroom and wailed at the top of my lungs, "Somebody, help me! Please don't let my momma beat me again! I'll be good, I promise!" Momma was not swayed by the possibility of a damaged reputation in the neighborhood, and she continued to deal with my antics in the manner they deserved.

My dear daddy wasn't exempt from my dramatic exploits just because he was gone during the day. By this time we'd moved to Birmingham, where we lived until I grew up. Daddy was an agent with Allstate Insurance Company and worked at a booth in the Sears and Roebuck store. Often he didn't get home from work until ten at night, which was past my bedtime. As a result, I seldom got to see him during the week, except when he took me to school in the morning. My momma knew how much I missed him, so she sometimes took me to town in the afternoons so I could visit him at work. I loved wandering around the Sears store and knew most of the employees by name.

One afternoon, as I roamed the store, I heard an announcement over the intercom: "Will Joe White please come to customer service?" When I realized everyone in the store had heard Joe White's name, I wanted them to hear mine too. I wandered over to the bedding department where the mattresses were displayed, making sure no one saw me along the way, and slid under one of the beds, completely out of sight. Then I waited.

It wasn't long before I had my reward and the intercom crackled to life: "Will Candy Colley please come to customer service?"

I stayed under the bed, suppressing giggles of excitement as I waited to hear the announcement again. Sure enough, the request was repeated, and I felt like I was famous.

By the time I got to customer service, Momma was so relieved to see me and to know I hadn't been kidnapped and dragged away down the streets of Birmingham that she didn't even punish me for causing such a scare. (I admit the thought of being kidnapped sounded exciting, too!)

Like many girls my age, I was infatuated with the stars of my favorite TV shows and the big movie screen. Like most families, we had one black and white television with three channels. I was glued to shows like *The Patty Duke Show, Donna Reed*, and *Father Knows Best*. The big screen offered Tammy, Gidget, and Beach Blanket Bingo, with such stars as Debbie Reynolds, Sandra Dee, and Annette Funicello.

I didn't just admire those teenage actresses; I wanted to be them. I created drama of my own, often dressing like my favorite stars. Momma made me a spaghetti strap dress like Hayley Mills wore in *The Parent Trap*. She didn't mind letting me express myself, even if I did look silly—especially the day in fifth grade when I put my hair up in a French twist with silk flowers bobby-pinned in the back. A long, lavender silk scarf was tossed dramatically over one shoulder, like Donna Reed's daughter, Mary, had worn in a recent episode.

When my friends gave me curious looks or asked why I was dressed that way, I answered, "Didn't you see the *Donna Reed* show?" Many of them had, but apparently I was the only one who felt compelled to dress and act accordingly.

Growing up in the fifties and sixties, when dancing was more about "doing your own thing" than leading or following a partner, Daddy wanted me to understand how to *really* dance—with someone else in control, leading, while I gracefully and effortlessly followed. I was in junior high when he decided to teach me about that type of dancing.

"You call that dancing?" he'd say, when he'd see how the young people danced opposite one another without even touching, doing the twist or the jerk or the watusi. "Why, you don't even know who your partner is!" Then he'd place a record on the console record player in the living room and say, "Let me show you how to dance with some real music."

From grammar school on, I took advantage of every opportunity to be on the stage. In the seventh grade, when most students were battling self-consciousness and trying to stay out of the limelight, I looked for every chance I could get to bask in it.

Some of my happiest memories are of my junior high years, a time some people would like to forget. For me, it was a time of…well, just being me. I liked that! There were, however, two distinct exceptions, both of which occurred in the eighth grade.

The first was when Momma agreed to take me shopping for some new shoes—black and white rah-rahs, like the other girls wore. They looked like cheerleading shoes, and it took some serious persuasion to convince my mother they were necessary.

When we finally got to Calhoun's Shoes, Mr. Calhoun measured my feet and then looked at my momma and delivered the most awful announcement: "Your daughter's foot is turned in slightly, and she needs corrective shoes."

Corrective shoes? Surely he wasn't serious! It would be social suicide to show up at school in those awful black and white clodhoppers with the thick red soles that he held out for my momma's inspection and then slipped on my feet.

I stared at them in disbelief, horrified at the implications. When he finally took them off, I ran out of the store in humiliation. With tears streaming down my face, I trudged down the sidewalk on the main street of Homewood. When I heard the honk of a car's horn, I turned to see Momma driving alongside me with the window down.

"Candy, get in the car," she said, seemingly unaffected by the life-changing incident that had been inflicted upon us.

I kept walking.

"Candy," she repeated, "get in the car."

This time I grudgingly obeyed, begging her not to make me wear those ugly shoes. My crying and pleading had no effect. Momma never changed her mind easily.

I'd no sooner survived that horrendous episode than another descended upon me. I was informed I needed braces.

"I don't want braces," I insisted. "If ya'll make me wear them, I'll never smile again until they're off!"

Once again, my threats and complaints fell on deaf ears.

"You'll be glad when you have pretty, straight teeth," Daddy said in an obvious attempt to persuade me to his way of thinking.

It didn't work. "Cheerleading tryouts are in two weeks," I wailed. "How will I get cheerleader if I don't smile?" I accused them of being mean, but they held their ground, and I finally gave in and smiled again, braces and all—and I even made the cheerleading squad.

Apart from those two events, I had little trauma during my junior high years. I had confidence in my dancing ability, and I never lacked for friends—boys or girls. I liked everybody. I set my own standards and stuck to them, regardless of what others did, which probably helped make those otherwise emotionally volatile years so pleasant.

The spring of my eighth-grade year stands out as a life-changing time. I went to church camp on the Gulf coast of Mississippi for spring break, my first ever away-from-home-on-my-own time—and I met Robert.

Two weeks later, Robert was my boyfriend. I was thirteen, and he was fourteen. We didn't have a clue what love was, but we said we loved each other, and he was the best boyfriend I ever had. He was cute. He was fun. He made me laugh—and he made me feel special.

Then came ninth grade, which turned out to be the best of times... and the worst. There were pep rallies and football games, homecoming corsages, spend-the-night parties with my girlfriends, the county fair, my best friend, Kim, and Saturday night street parties on Windsor Boulevard, which is where Robert, as well as a lot of other junior high students, lived.

A bunch of us got together there once a week and hung out—all very innocent fun. Robert and I also sat together and held hands at church, and I imagine the grown-ups thought we were cute but silly. We left our initials everywhere—"CC + RP"—on notebooks, napkins, notes to each other, and anywhere else we could. At night, just before ending our every-evening phone calls, we tuned in to our favorite radio station to listen to their regular rendition of "Goodnight, My Love." Life was good—and I had a huge silver I.D. bracelet with Robert's name on it to prove it.

Then, one night after a football game, we went to Melrose, a small ice cream parlor in downtown Homewood, packed with junior high students. Our parents sat in their cars in the parking lot, waiting for us. Robert and I found a little table in the corner. I sat there in my red and white cheerleading uniform, with a big white mum corsage that had a red H for Homewood made out of a pipe cleaner in the center.

Robert took my hand and turned it over. "I'll read your palm."

He smiled slightly, and it was so romantic.

"This is the line," he said, and etched the line in the palm of my hand with his finger, "that says how much I love you."

I didn't even hear the celebration noise in the background. My eyes were locked on my hand.

"This is the line that shows how much I'll always love you." He paused and looked me in the eyes. "Even in Daytona." He then explained that his dad was being transferred to Ormond Beach, Florida, and they'd be moving at the end of December, just two months away.

My eyes filled with tears. He tried to reassure me that he'd come to visit and he'd love me always, but I got up, tears rolling down my cheeks, and pushed my way through the gathering of loud, smelly football players still in their uniforms and other laughing, noisy people and out the door where I could run away and sob. The cheerleaders and some other girls saw me crying and followed. They consoled me when I told them what had happened and that my life was over. And I truly believed it was.

I was crushed. If a fourteen-year-old's heart can be broken, mine certainly was. When the day came for Robert to leave, my parents took me to his house so we could say goodbye. Until that day, I'd never let him kiss me, but as we stood face-to-face, he kissed me on my cheek. I never wanted to wash that cheek again. (I saw that in a movie one time.)

For months afterward, I rushed home from school to find a letter from Robert waiting for me in the mailbox, written on notebook paper, each in the same type of plain envelope and each smelling of English Leather and bearing the letters "LNSG," after the song "Lovers Never Say Goodbye." I saved each and every one of those letters in a box, and I wrote to him every day as well, usually on pink stationery with Wind Song or Shalimar on the pages. I spent hours missing him and listening to the music of the Beach Boys and The Lettermen, and when Sonny and Cher sang "Baby, Don't Go," I cried.

I don't know if we ever really broke up. After all, I never returned his I.D. bracelet! I guess he just came back to Birmingham less frequently as time passed, and I got caught up in other activities.

◇   ◇   ◇

I'd just turned fifteen when I entered Shades Valley High School. Daddy took me to school in the morning, and Momma picked me up.

"What a good day to be alive!" Daddy would proclaim as I sat half asleep on the way to school. He'd shift the gears of his cream-colored Volkswagen and say, "Listen to that motor. This is a fine car. Do you have all your pencils and paper? You're a swell little lady, Candy. I wouldn't pass up taking you to school in the morning for anything."

Daddy was always like that. Sometimes it got on my nerves that he could be in such a good mood so early in the morning. "Right on time!" he'd say, looking at the big red clock on the side of the school's tower. "Are you going to give your dear ol' dad a kiss goodbye?"

Then he'd pull around the circled drive in front of the school, which had a big magnolia tree right in the center. It was embarrassing, but I never wanted to hurt his feelings. Besides, I liked getting to school a little early so I could socialize with my friends in the lobby before the bell rang.

With my entry into the senior high school scene came the opportunity to take two speech classes, something that came naturally for me. That's when

I first began to develop my own speaking style. Shades Valley High was one of the few in the district to have a working theater. In fact, it was ahead of its time, since few schools had a totally separate theater; most used a basketball gym with a stage, where chairs were set up on the court for performances. Shades Valley was the real thing, with all the mechanics of a theater and the seating capacity for approximately 1,000 people. They also had dressing rooms, and their shows were accompanied by the school's orchestra.

Few girls took dance lessons then, at least not seriously. If they did, the classes were considered just another after-school activity. There were only a handful of us who were known as dancers, and we choreographed the show *Music Man.*

High school was also my introduction to a semi-professional community theater in Birmingham, the Town and Gown Theatre, known for bringing in Broadway stars for special appearances or Broadway choreographers. When I was chosen to be a dancer in the musical *Funny Girl* in my junior year, that sealed it. If there was any doubt that I was destined to be on stage, it was erased with that performance.

The show included a huge, rousing red, white, and blue patriotic World War II tap number in the show. By the time the orchestra played the opening notes to "Rat Tat Tat Tat" and I was on stage singing, I couldn't contain my excitement. I wanted to scream to the audience, "I love this! Can you tell I love this?" But instead I squealed under the clatter of twenty-four tap shoes and the sound of the instruments from the orchestra pit. It brought the house down, with a roar of applause and whistles from the audience. While holding our pose for the cheering and clapping, my smile stretched from ear to ear, and again I let out a squeal. It was like an adrenaline rush, and I didn't want it to end.

All in all, my high school years were exciting and fun, with only one real trauma, which occurred in my sophomore year. My left eye tooth was still a baby tooth, and it wasn't even loose. At one of my dental checkups, my dentist announced that in order for the permanent one to come in, the baby tooth had to be removed. I was devastated.

Just as with the braces and corrective shoes, however, my protests were to no avail. The tooth was taken out on a Thursday, and the hole was sewn up with black thread. I had a blind date on Friday night with a boy in the grade ahead of me who was probably one of the cutest boys—ever. How could I possibly go?

I repeated my vow from my eighth-grade braces days: "I will never, ever smile again until my new tooth comes in!"

Once again, I broke the vow. Not only did I go out on the blind date and smile again, I also survived with no eye tooth until the middle of my senior year. Two years! I did roll up a piece of toilet paper to put in the space during one show, but that was too risky; it might have fallen out.

Despite the traumatic missing tooth experience, I somehow managed to be voted cutest in Who's Who. I suppose even then I was learning an important lesson—that as important as looks are to most people, including myself at the time, I didn't have to let them govern how I felt about myself or how others felt towards me. It was a lesson that was to serve me well later.

◇　　　◇　　　◇

As high school blended into college, everything seemed to be going according to the script. I did well in school, was involved in all sorts of activities and social events, and had a boyfriend at home in Birmingham. It was the best of both worlds. I was well suited for Huntingdon, a small Methodist college, where I met one of my favorite professors, Mrs. Parker, who influenced me to major in speech and drama.

I took two classes with her and performed in the musical Oklahoma, and I sang and danced to "I'm Just a Girl Who Can't Say No" from that musical when I participated in the Miss Alabama Pageant that year. By the end of my freshman year, I knew I wanted a bigger social life with a little more excitement.

Then, that summer, I met Lee at a fraternity party in Birmingham. We quickly hit it off, and before long, we were an item—so much so that, completely on my own, I took all the necessary steps to change schools to the University of Alabama in Tuscaloosa, where Lee attended. I quickly declared my major in speech and drama and began my course work for a Bachelor of Arts degree. I participated in the musical productions and was dancing at a local ballet school to keep in shape.

I also saw Lee every day. By the end of our sophomore year, we started talking marriage. After that, everything moved along at a relatively rapid pace. Our parents would have preferred that we wait until after graduation, but we scheduled our wedding for the evening of May 20, 1972, immediately following our junior year.

One year later, after graduation from U of A, we moved back to Birmingham, which was our intention all along. In 1976, our son, Elliott, was born, followed by our daughter, Colley, in 1980. It all fell into place, just like we'd planned—four years, then a baby; four more years, and another baby. It seemed we were the perfect family, destined to live a happily-ever-after life.

The first sign that our lives might not be as perfect as we'd thought came in early 1981, when I began to experience persistent sinus pain and headaches. Over the next few months I went to various doctors and specialists, and eventually made several trips to hospital emergency rooms as my nose started hemorrhaging profusely. I also began losing weight—lots of it—and my headaches were increasing in frequency and severity.

Still I continued to deny the obvious, to hope for the best, and to pretend all was well—until I finally ended up in the hospital, waiting for the results of the biopsy. It was time to face reality—and make some serious decisions.

4

◇　　◇　　◇

DIFFERENT. THAT'S THE WORD THAT BEST DESCRIBED ME WHEN I awoke on Friday morning, still awaiting the biopsy results three days after checking myself into the hospital on that stormy Tuesday afternoon. My circumstances hadn't changed a bit since the previous night when I'd endured the painful procedure of having seventy-two inches of gauze ripped from my nostril, but I now understood what it meant to surrender my life to the Lord, and with surrender came peace. I hadn't *given up*; rather, I'd *given in* to His will.

It was still early morning when Dr. Poynor made his rounds. I'd seen him only once since the surgery, and when he walked in, ever the conservative, Southern gentleman in his starched shirt and bow tie, I felt badly about how I'd acted in his office the week before. He was the last of a long list of physicians I'd seen while trying to convince someone that something was wrong. After examining the inside of my nose and touching the so-called cyst with his metal instrument, his comment had been direct.

"This needs to come out *yesterday.*"

I retaliated with, "All you doctors want to do is operate!"

Undisturbed by my accusation, he called his partner in for another opinion. When Dr. Goldfarb concurred with Dr. Poynor's assessment, I said, "It can't be cancer, can it?"

"That's why we want to operate," Dr. Goldfarb said, "to see exactly what it is."

The next thing I knew I'd been escorted to Dr. Poynor's office, where I sat across from him, his desk between us covered with stacks of folders.

"Surgery on Monday?" he asked.

"Monday! Are you serious?" I was angry, but my anger was covering the fear that engulfed me. Someone had finally agreed with me that something was really wrong, but instead of feeling better, I was afraid. I was also rude, which was unlike me.

"I'm very serious," he answered.

I made some remark about calling later to let him know my decision, and then got up to leave. No "thank you so much for your time" or "nice to meet you"—nothing.

Now he stood at the end of my hospital bed, my discharge papers in hand as he peered at me over his tortoise-shell glasses, his nearly bald head shining slightly. "Good morning, Candy. Are you ready to go home?"

I was a bit taken aback by his question. "I guess so, but have you heard anything about the report? Is it back yet? Is the tumor malignant?"

"We've sent it to the Mayo Clinic for them to biopsy."

"So what do I do now?" I was much nicer than I'd been in our previous meeting, and I was also grateful that he'd been so insistent on my having this surgery immediately.

After I'd stormed out of his office that day, telling him I'd call and let him know what I decided about the surgery, he made a point to call me at home to say, "Candy, I don't care who does your surgery, but it needs to be done right away."

That nullified my accusation that all doctors wanted to do was operate, and it had convinced me to go ahead with the surgery. How glad I was that I'd listened to him! In spite of my gratitude to Dr. Poynor, however, there was still much I didn't understand. "Why is it taking such a long time to biopsy?"

"This is unusually difficult," Dr. Poynor explained, "because the tumor has all the characteristics of a cartilage bony-type tumor, but that type is rarely found in the head. It's like finding a turnip green in the ocean. It has all the characteristics of a turnip green, but turnip greens aren't found in the ocean.

"As to what you do now, if you were my wife, I'd take you to M.D. Anderson in Houston." Then he handed me my papers and a prescription for pain. "I'll want to see you in my office on Monday. I'll have some information by then. Come in around ten. Also, go by Medical Records and pick up a copy of your tomogram and pathology report."

Before leaving the hospital, I wanted to talk to Dr. Scofield, the head of the Pathology Department. Everything seemed so vague to me concerning the biopsy. I needed more specific information. While Momma and Daddy waited to take me home, one of the volunteer pink ladies at the information desk directed me to Dr. Scofield's office. I walked in to find a very distinguished-looking man behind the desk.

"Can I help you?" he asked, looking up from his work.

"Yes, sir. I'm Candy Wood. Dr. Poynor told me this morning that you were sending my biopsy off somewhere else."

"Yes. We're sending it to the Mayo Clinic."

I was confused. "Not Walter Reed Hospital?"

"No. We're sending it to Dr. David Dahlin at the Mayo Clinic. He's known worldwide for his research in this particular type of malignancy. In fact, he's the authority on bone cancer and has written several books on these types of tumors. We're sending it out this afternoon, so they may receive it by Monday."

I was encouraged. "Oh! Then I'll know by Monday?"

Dr. Scofield shook his head slightly. "No, I can't say that. Slides are sent to him from all over. It may take as long as two weeks before he gets to it."

"Two weeks!" *That's forever*, I thought.

"We'll get in touch with you as soon as we hear." Smiling, he added, "It's nice to meet you, Candy. It's not often we get to meet the patient."

◇　　　◇　　　◇

It seemed I'd gathered all the information I was going to get for now, so with two carloads of flowers, Momma driving one car and Daddy the other, we headed for home. Colley and Elliott met us at the door, bouncing and squealing with excitement, as Winky Tink, our gray peek-a-poo, who looked more like a mop than a dog, yapped and ran around the dining room table, sliding on the hardwood floors. Her barks echoed throughout the window-filled, high-ceilinged rooms.

Once home, everything *seemed* as it was before, but I knew it wasn't. I wanted to pretend the last four days had never happened, but I couldn't. There were the ordinary tasks of washing clothes, vacuuming, and doing the dishes that still had to be done, but they no longer seemed important. I didn't want to do anything, and yet I wanted to do *something*. I'd given God control of my life, but surely that didn't mean I should sit around and do nothing.

I didn't know anything about cancer, and I didn't know anyone who had it. But as soon as word got out, friends began to call with advice and recommendations. One name in particular came up more than once. He was one of the Southeast's most renowned head and neck cancer surgeons, so I made an appointment to see him Tuesday morning.

Later that evening, I called one of Birmingham's leading oncologists at home. "Hello, I'm Candy Wood," I announced after he answered the phone.

"You don't know me, but I think you go to my church. I've just found out I may have cancer...."

I can't remember what else I said, but he didn't seem to mind my calling.

"Candy," he said, speaking slowly, "let me give you some advice. Calm down. This doesn't need to be solved tonight. Nothing serious can happen if you take a few days to research your options."

After making and returning other phone calls and putting the children to bed, Lee and I had our first time to be alone and talk. We were aware of what the future might hold, and I wanted to talk about it. I felt guilty for not being the wife he'd expected. I didn't cook well, at least not like his mom. I also had a maid once a week for cleaning, like most of my friends. Lee didn't like the fact that I taught dancing two afternoons a week, not getting in until after he'd gotten home from work. He wouldn't have to be upset about that anymore, as I doubted I'd be teaching again or be involved in further musical theater performances. Lee also didn't like that at night I gave more attention to the children than to him.

Feeling very melancholy as we had this discussion, my face still very much swollen and my eyes black and bruised, I felt the need to say to him, "Lee, I know I haven't been the best wife to you these past ten years, and I'm sorry."

His cold, unemotional face said it all. "Well, you can start now by being better."

I promised him—and myself—that from that day on, for as long as I lived, I would be the best wife ever, totally devoted to him. I'd cook better; I'd watch television with him at night; I'd be interested in his work at a commercial roofing company. I have to admit, though, that at least some of my motives were selfish; I didn't want him to say after I died that I wasn't a good wife. I also wanted to ease my sense of guilt over not having been the wife I knew he hoped I'd be.

The weekend gave us an indication of what the following week would be like. As word spread about my cancer, friends and neighbors responded.

The telephone rang with offers of advice, comfort, and "whatever you need." Delivery boys came with flowers, fruit baskets, and plants. Neighbors arrived with casseroles, sweets, books, and other expressions of love. The postman brought stacks of beautiful cards and thoughtful notes.

In between phone calls, visitors, and looking after the children, I gathered information. I had three objectives: find out everything I could about cancer, figure out how God would get me through it, and see if there was any possible way to get the biopsy report back sooner. Resourceful and determined, two personality traits that would help me in my quest for answers, I called anybody and everybody I thought could help.

On Sunday morning I had an idea. A friend of mine from high school, Johnny Mears, had finished an anesthesiology residency program at the Mayo Clinic and had recently returned to Birmingham. Maybe I could reach him before he and his wife left for church. He might know Dr. Dahlin and could call to speed things up.

I called Johnny's house and filled him in on my situation. Then I asked, "Do you happen to know a Dr. Dahlin at the Mayo Clinic in the Pathology Department?"

"I know who he is, but I don't know him personally," he said, and then added, "You might call Raleigh Kent."

I'd forgotten we had another friend at the Mayo Clinic. Raleigh went to high school with Lee, and his wife, Dottie, went to college with Lee and me. I asked Johnny if he had Raleigh's number, and he said, "It just happens that he and Dottie have been in Florida all week and came through here yesterday on their way back to Rochester. Maybe they haven't left yet, and you can catch them at his parents' house."

I called Raleigh's parents' house, and Raleigh and Dottie were still there. Raleigh knew Dr. Dahlin, so I told him my story. "They sent my slides Friday and said they may get there by tomorrow. But they told me he may not get to them for two weeks."

A confident, "take charge" type of person, Raleigh said, "Listen, I'll go in first thing in the morning and pull your slides for him. Who's doing your surgery?"

"I'm not sure. Dr. Poynor wants to send me to M.D. Anderson in Houston."

"Before you do anything, Candy, we've just gotten a surgeon from Scotland who specializes in this type of surgery. His name is Ian Jackson, and he's incredible. From what you've told me, he's exactly who you need."

Raleigh was moving a little too fast for me, but he was so genuinely interested in my doing the right thing that I let him continue.

"Listen, Candy, I'm telling you, I've seen this man do things that have never been done before. If he has to take your head apart, at least he can put it back together again." Before I could respond, he continued. "I'll be glad to talk with him and make an appointment for you to see him. You and Lee can stay with us." Then he added, "I just wish you had a copy of your 'CAT' scan so I could take it back with me."

"I've never had a 'CAT' scan," I said. "I do have a copy of my tomogram, but I'm seeing a doctor here Tuesday, and I need to have it with me when I see him." But even as I was speaking, I picked up the big gold envelope containing my tomogram, which happened to be on the sofa beside me. I looked inside and blinked in surprise, stunned by what I saw.

"You're not going to believe this, but St. Vincent's gave me two copies of my tomogram. I *can* give you one! When do you want me to bring it to you?"

"We're supposed to eat with Dottie's parents at noon, in just a few minutes, and our flight leaves at three. Can you bring them right now?"

Raleigh's parents lived about two miles from our house. "I'm on my way."

Barely telling Lee where I was going, I rushed out the door. Dottie, mild-tempered and sweet as always, took one look at me when I arrived, my face swollen and blue, and hugged me. "Candy, I'm so sorry. You know if there's anything we can do…"

Raleigh, who was already convinced I needed to go to the Mayo Clinic for my surgery, interrupted Dottie, as her words trailed off. "I'll see Dr. Dahlin first thing in the morning and call you. I'll also take this tomogram to Dr. Jackson and check his surgery schedule." Things seemed to be moving along amazingly fast.

The rest of Sunday was spent anxiously awaiting Monday morning. When it finally arrived and no one called, I couldn't wait any longer. At eight I called the Mayo Clinic's main number. "I need to speak with Dr. Dahlin in pathology, please."

My call was transferred, and a man answered, "Pathology Department."

"I need to speak with a Dr. Dahlin. I know he's probably very busy, but if you could have him call me back as soon as possible, that would be great."

"This is Dr. Dahlin."

Astounded, I paused before continuing. "No, I need to speak to the real famous Dr. Dahlin, the one who writes books on bone cancer. Is that you?"

"Well, put it this way: I'm the only Dahlin in the department."

More amazed than embarrassed, I explained, "My name is Candy Wood. You don't know me, but I'm from Birmingham, Alabama, and—"

"Yes, Mrs. Wood," he interrupted, "I do know who you are. I've been discussing the results of your biopsy with Dr. Kent. I was planning on calling you shortly."

My heart pounded with dreaded anticipation. "So what is it?" I managed to ask.

He began to tell me everything I did not want to hear. "It's malignant," he said. "You have a grade-three osteosarcoma. It's extremely rare to find that particular type of tumor located in the head. They suspected correctly in Birmingham. Unfortunately, it doesn't respond to standard chemotherapy and radiation and typically has to be removed surgically. So it's most important that you find a capable surgeon."

At last I knew. The wait was over. It was a relief to finally be sure. A myriad of feelings engulfed me—sad, empty, discouraged, yet also a bold determination for whatever lay ahead. I sat quietly on the sofa—no tears, no hysterics—staring at the vase of spring flowers on my dining room table. *Now what do I do?* Surprisingly, I felt a sense of peace. I'd received more answers to questions in the last three days than I had in the entire year. Could this be what it meant for God to take charge? I didn't know for sure, but I suspected it just might be.

◇   ◇   ◇

As word of my situation continued to spread through our close-knit neighborhood, our little gray cottage became the center of activity. Each time the doorbell rang, Winky Tink ran yelping through the house.

"Mom! Someone's at the door!" Elliott would call from his room.

"I know, honey," I'd call back, knowing it was probably someone bringing dinner, "but I'm on the phone. Can you get it? Just tell them to come on in."

Momma did her best to try to watch after Colley, who was confused by the chaos in our house and needed a little extra attention, and Lee wasn't too happy about that.

"Does your mother always have to be over here when I come home from work?" he asked one night. "Do your parents think they should be around all the time? And can't people bring dinner before it gets this late?"

"Lee, people are just being nice. They're trying to bring it hot and ready to eat. And, yes, Momma does need to be here. But, no, my parents don't think they should be around all the time. It's me that wants them here. I need their help. I can't do it all. Besides, why does it matter to you if Momma's here all day? She helps with the children and leaves when you get home. She isn't bothering you."

Lee didn't say anymore, but the look on his face was answer enough, and it added to the tension I already felt.

◇   ◇   ◇

Then it was Tuesday. My appointment with the surgeon was at ten, and Momma took me. After filling out another patient information form, I was escorted to an examining room to meet a rather short, dark-haired man who was about my parents' age. There was no friendly small talk. In fact, he was rather cold and impersonal.

Still swollen from the biopsy surgery, I was also emotionally fragile and frightened. The doctor had me sit in an examining chair with a large light over it, similar to those in a dentist's office. "Open wide" was all he said, as he adjusted the light and stuck a metal instrument all the way to the back of my mouth, then somehow began pushing it up the back of my throat into the nasal cavity.

I didn't move a muscle, but I couldn't control my tears. I tried to say, "That hurts," thinking there might be something he could do to ease my discomfort.

His only reply was, "Don't talk, and don't cry."

I felt like a child being scolded, and it hurt my feelings. Staring over his head at the light and trying to blink back the tears that were by then trickling in a steady stream down my cheeks, I tried not to whimper, but I couldn't help it.

When he finished, he led me to his office and took a seat behind his desk. I sat across from him. He said something about this being a difficult situation and that he would cut down the side of my nose to get into the sinus area. I really didn't hear much of what he said because, regardless of his reputation as a fine surgeon, he'd hurt my feelings and I didn't like him. In all my thirty years, the only other doctor I hadn't liked was one I had to see when I was seven years old.

As tactfully as I could, I said, "A friend told me about a doctor at the Mayo Clinic, Dr. Ian Jackson. Do you know anything about him?"

He eyed me over the rim of his reading glasses and answered, "No, and I certainly wouldn't send a loved one of mine to the Mayo Clinic." And that was that.

◇　　　◇　　　◇

Later that day, after dinner, Lee suggested we all go on a bike ride. I really didn't feel up to it, but with the ever-present thought that I might never get to do something like this again, I agreed. Elliott followed on his own bike behind Lee, while Colley, dressed in a light cotton gown, rode in her bike seat in back of me. Passersby would have thought we were the perfect little family without a care in the world.

As we slowly made our way along the three blocks to the village, Lee cut through an alley behind our house, across the main street, and through the parking lot of the Steeple Arts Academy of Dance, where I worked as an instructor. The Williamsburg red wooden church-turned-dance-studio was a historic site, with its tall white steeple standing majestically against the evening sky. My mind drifted back to the students' performance two weeks before, when I'd been grappling with the idea of surgery.

I can't think about surgery today, I'd reminded myself when I arrived at the dance studio that night. Like Scarlett O'Hara in *Gone with the Wind,* I'd think about it tomorrow. The director of the studio had taught us to leave our personal problems at home before we came to work. We were to concentrate on the children and make them feel special.

No one suspected anything was wrong with me that night, as I'd learned to cover up how badly I felt. When the show was over, I stood at the double doors of the foyer, hugging the girls and telling their parents goodbye.

Finally, after everyone else had gone, I stood alone in the huge room that had once been a sanctuary, with the cool night breeze blowing through the open windows. Comforted by the quiet and not ready to go home, I sat on a bench and looked around. The grand piano sat silently on what was once the pulpit. The large oil painting of the studio director hung on the wall adjacent to the piano. The hardwood floors shone, even after all the feet that had scuffed their way across them through the years, during times of worship and times of dance. There were a lot of memories in that room. I'd taken dance lessons there myself in high school.

My mind sprang back to the present, as we biked our way past some of the larger old estate homes that faced Birmingham Country Club's golf course. The old prestigious English Tudor clubhouse stood out against the pale blue-gray sky. Though it was seven-thirty, daylight savings time provided us with light. The golfers had already gone home, so we crossed over the grass toward the golf cart trail. Away from traffic, we peddled up and down the small hills and through the old trees on the course.

By the time we finally left for home, darkness had fallen. The soft night air put Colley to sleep, her little blonde head drooping and then perking back up again. Sucking her thumb and clutching her blanket, she barely woke up when we got home and I laid her in her baby bed.

5

◇　　◇　　◇

THE RED FRONT DOOR TO OUR HOME HAD TWELVE WINDOW PANES. I didn't have any sort of window treatment on them, so I always knew who was at the door. Among the steady flow of visitors were two of my friends from high school, Lynn and Synthia, who wasted no time telling me why they'd come. They heard I was seriously ill and wanted to make sure I knew where I'd spend eternity should I die. It was very bold on their part, seeing as my prognosis wasn't good and dying was truly a possibility.

I greeted them at the door, and without even coming inside, Lynn opened a little yellow booklet called *The Four Spiritual Laws*, put out by Campus Crusade for Christ.

I'd seen one of those booklets years before at the University of Alabama. A girl had approached me on my way to class one day and asked, "If you died today, do you know where you'd spend eternity?"

I was irritated that she asked me that question. "Yes," I told her, "and I'm just as much a Christian as you are!" What made her think I might not be a Christian, or that she was a better one than I was?

This day, however, as I stood at my front door, listening to my two high school friends talk to me about the four spiritual laws, everything was different. I looked down at the booklet Lynn was holding, listening as she gave her explanation.

"See this throne, Candy?" She pointed to a picture of a throne with the letter "S" on it, standing for "Self." There was another picture of a throne next to it with a cross on it, standing for "Christ." I wasn't quite sure how to answer her next question: "Which one of these represents your life? Is 'self' on the throne of your life—or is Christ?"

> *The Bible is God's Word to you. How are you going to know what He says to you if you never read it?*

I didn't know all the "in" Christian lingo, but I told her very simply and honestly that God was now in control of my life. I told her that I knew where I would spend eternity, but right then I wanted to know how I was going to deal with all of this now.

She and Synthia were glad to talk with me, and I invited them inside. They sat down on the sofa across from me, with their Bibles in their laps. "Let's just read some scripture," Synthia suggested.

As she began to read from her Bible, I noticed it was underlined, marked, and starred. Without wanting to appear stupid, I asked, "Am I supposed to be reading my Bible?" I'd always wanted to please God, and if that meant reading the Bible, then I wanted to do that.

"Candy, the Bible is God's Word to you," Lynn explained. "How are you going to know what He says to you if you never read it?" Her answer was non-judgmental and non-condemning, and I heard with my heart as well as my ears what she was saying. Before they left, they prayed for me, and I was so glad they came.

Later that day Anne, my freshman college roommate from Huntingdon, came by. Anne's mother died of cancer when Anne was five. Being one who always wanted to cover my bases and figure things out ahead of time, I had some questions for her. We sat on my front porch in the afternoon sun, and I thought of Elliott, who was already six, and Colley, who wasn't even two. I so wanted my children to remember me.

"Anne," I asked, "do you remember your mother?"

"I don't remember much about her," she admitted, but then, being the positive person she was, she added, "but I have pictures of her."

My heart dropped. "Oh."

Obviously trying to encourage me, she said, "She did make a tape of her voice so I'd always know what she sounded like. I still listen to it from time to time."

"Umm…" I paused. "I guess I need to do that, too."

Anne had done alright without her real mom, and though I was glad to know that, it made me sad. I didn't want my children to be without me as their mom. Lee would remarry, and they'd have a stepmother like Anne did. That was good, but I didn't want someone else to raise my children.

Then Anne handed me a book about a woman missionary in Africa. I didn't know much about missionaries, and I wasn't a big reader. I hadn't even known there were people who read Christian books about missionaries. But Anne and her husband, along with several other couples, had recently left our church to join a new congregation in the area, which they felt was more evangelical and better served their needs. I didn't think they were weird or anything; in fact, I didn't think about it much at all. Now, as I gazed down at Anne's book, I was intrigued with all the messages God seemed to be sending my way.

◇   ◇   ◇

One of the tasks that took priority on my list of things to do before my surgery was to see my two grandmothers in Wetumpka (the Indians called it "rumbling waters"), Alabama. To the east of Montgomery, the state's capital, it was a short two-hour drive to Wetumpka. Both MaMaw and Bubba lived three blocks from the arched stone "river bridge" that crossed the nearby Coosa River.

Momma drove, and Colley and I rode along, passing all the familiar landmarks we'd seen countless times over the past twenty-two years. *What if this is the last time I see these places? What if this is the last time I see my grandmothers?* After turning off the interstate, we took the back roads. Not much had changed since I was a little girl, and the directions were as simple as ever: Turn left at the fork in the road where the gas station burned down; then go several miles through the cotton fields and past the little white country church on the left, the one that sat all by itself in the middle of a grassy field at the end of a long dirt road, the one that looked like the church in the movie *Hello Dolly* with Barbra Streisand. Beyond the church, we turned left at Cherry's country store and gas station, which amounted to two pumps and a few folks passing the day in rocking chairs out front. From there it was another twenty miles or so to Wetumpka.

Bubba and Pap, my mother's parents, lived in the country when I was growing up, and I always thought their house was fun to visit. There were chickens to feed and eggs to gather, and early in the morning I'd help Bubba with the chores. I'd stick my hand under one of the fat hens to see if she'd laid her eggs. Sometimes I'd make one of the hens mad and her wings would flutter, stirring up the hay and causing the other hens to get in a flutter as well. Bubba had banty hens, and fried banty eggs were my favorite breakfast.

Pap was the town dentist, but early in the morning before work he'd put on his rubber boots, and I'd put on a pair, too. With his milk bucket in hand, he'd go out to the barn, with me right behind him, to milk Bess, the yellow milk cow. Sitting on an upside-down bucket, Pap would take Bess's udders in his hands and pull one, then the other, one, then the other. Each squirt helped fill the bucket with fresh warm milk.

Pap's hobby was raising homing pigeons, and there was a separate coop for them. He named one Candy, and she rode on Pap's shoulder everywhere, even into town.

After Pap died when I was fifteen, Bubba sold the country home and moved into town. The quaint little brick house in the old section of Wetumpka was easier for her to keep up, but visiting there was never quite the same.

In her seventies and no taller than five feet, Bubba didn't have one gray hair and had already outlived all but two of her ten brothers and sisters. I was the only one of five grandchildren who lived close enough to see her often.

"Bubba, we're here!" I announced, knocking on the locked screened door.

"Well, I'll just declare!" she exclaimed, leaning down to give Colley a kiss. "And who is this you have with you?"

And then we followed her to the breakfast nook. "Looka here," she said, handing me a tin box. I knew what was inside without having to open it.

"Teacakes!" I smiled. "Oh, Bubba, thank you. They're my favorite!"

We sat down at the kitchen table, the sun shining through the window on the shelves of her pampered purple violets.

"I can't stay long, Bubba," I told her. "We have to be back in Birmingham to pick Elliott up after school. I just wanted to come by and see you before I have surgery next week. I don't know when I'll be well enough to come back down after that."

We didn't discuss my pending surgery much, but I'm sure Bubba knew more than she let on.

My other grandmother lived a short five blocks away in a little five-room apartment behind the First Baptist Church. As in most Southern towns, the Baptist church is usually the largest in town, and Wetumpka was no exception. MaMaw had moved there from Tuskegee several years after my grandfather died, and it was obvious she was expecting us.

"Candy..." She hugged me, not needing to say anything else.

"I'll be alright, MaMaw," I assured her. "Really I will." I wasn't sure how much Daddy had told her, but he was her only child, and I was her only grandchild.

The drive had worn me out, and I loved MaMaw's bed, with its soft mattress and the old cotton spread, worn smooth over the years. "I've just taken a Tylenol," I told her, "so I'm going to lie down a minute."

Before I knew it Momma was calling from the next room. "If you're wanting to go to the farm, Candy, you need to get up."

"Next time I won't sleep through my visit, MaMaw," I apologized with a laugh, and then added, "I'll let you know where I'll be going next week." I still didn't know where I'd be having the surgery; I just knew it would be one day the next week.

◇   ◇   ◇

While I was there, I decided to take a trip to the old farmhouse. It was a quick twenty minutes "up the road," as we say in the South. Up the road in that case meant way out in the country in a community called Fleahop. The story goes that one spring, a long time ago, the area schoolhouse was hopping with fleas, and that's how this little community got its name.

Now some might not be so proud to say they were from a small country town with a name like Fleahop. But that's not how I saw it. My daddy's family, the Williams clan, was from around there, and I considered it one of the most glorious places on earth. MaMaw and Granddaddy Williams's house sat on twenty-five acres of land that stretched alongside a dirt road. Their toppled, weathered mailbox was still standing, and though no one had lived there in seventeen years, not much had changed.

"Momma, just drop me off and let me be alone awhile," I said. "Not long, just fifteen or twenty minutes. You and Colley can ride around somewhere, can't you?"

Momma understood my need to be alone at the old homestead. She turned onto the red dirt driveway lined with pecan trees that led up to and circled the house that my great granddaddy had built in 1904. The tires crunched on the rocks, taking me back to a time when there were no thoughts of cancer and surgery and death. Some passersby might think the farmhouse was a shack where poor people lived, but I knew it was a house so rich with love and memories that all the money in the world couldn't buy it.

Momma dropped me off, and the sight and sound of her car faded into the distance as she topped the hill on the little county road. There at last, without a single distraction, I stood alone. *Okay, God, it's quiet now. I need this time—just You and me.*

In the quiet stillness of the day, I stepped out into a clearing in the backyard. Then, in helpless desperation, I screamed to the cloudless blue heavens.

"God!" My voice echoed ominously.

"God!" I screamed louder.

"Are you there? Can you hear me?" I kept raising my voice, as if trying to reach someone in the far distance. I knew God could hear and that He was listening, so I continued.

"What am I supposed to do? Tell me! What am I supposed to do? Don't you see? Just *tell* me!"

My pleadings sounded so dramatic. Was that all it was, just more drama on my part? No, they were earnest cries for direction. No tears, just an inner expectation of some sort of answer I knew would come. His Presence at that moment was so real I wouldn't have been surprised if I'd heard an audible voice from above.

Making my way around to the front of the house, I sat down on the top step of the porch, where the rocking chairs sat unused and propped up against the wall. The small front yard was the stage on which I'd perform for our Sunday visitors, showing off my backbends and cartwheels to their overwhelming applause. Sometimes I complained about going to the farm every week; I wanted to go to Sunday school with my friends.

Now, twenty years later, I sat on the top step with only the memories of a childhood full of unconditional love. The lessons I learned from those fine country folks on those Sunday afternoons had more of an impact than any Sunday school class could ever have given me. No, I didn't know even the simplest, most-read Bible stories, but I knew a lot about God's love. And I knew clearly that He was present that day.

I left the farm with no clear answers, but I'd had some much needed alone time—though, of course, I hadn't really been alone.

◇　　　◇　　　◇

The next day, with our bags packed, Lee and I and the children pulled out of the driveway to escape the deluge of calls, visitors, and doctors' appointments. The destination was the home of my best friend, Tricia, from high school. Tricia lived in Mobile with her husband, Johnny, who was Lee's ATO fraternity little brother. Tricia and Johnny didn't have children and didn't have plans for the weekend, so I was free to enjoy uninterrupted quality time with my family. I truly looked forward to our trip.

We weren't out of Birmingham long, however, when I panicked. Away from the diversions of home, I could think. I looked in the backseat at my children and realized again that I might not see them grow up. I had that sick knot-in-the-stomach, lump-in-the-throat feeling, a paralyzing fear that swept through me like an icy wind. I couldn't seem to get rid of the lightheaded, faint sensation that left me weak. Lee was talking, but I wasn't hearing. I wanted to tell him what I was feeling, but I couldn't because Elliott would hear, and he was smart enough to understand.

By the time we pulled into their drive, my brain was exhausted and so was I. The table was set with Tricia's best china, sterling silver, and fresh flowers. A gourmet meal followed that I couldn't seem to swallow.

After dinner I excused myself and went to Tricia's room to be alone. Sitting Indian-style on her floor, I held a little olive-wood Bible in my lap that my mother had brought back from her trip to Israel. Sadly, it had never been read.

"Lord," I asked aloud, "what am I going to do? Where am I going to go? Here it is Friday, and I have surgery scheduled for two places next week. You're the only one who knows what exactly is going on with me and where I need to go. I'm waiting on You."

It was true. I'd been waiting on Him for direction. I honestly believed He'd give me a clear answer, but time was running out.

"God, I've got to know. I promise if You make it clear where I'm to go, that's where I'll go. I know You aren't going to drop me a note or write it in the sky, but if You'll just make it clear…"

Raleigh had told me that Dr. Jackson had been out of the country in Spain for three weeks, and though Raleigh hadn't actually spoken with him personally, the doctor was expected to return late that Friday afternoon. The surgeon from Birmingham said his surgery schedule was open should I decide to have the surgery done there. Plans had already been made for Houston, but something inside told me I wouldn't be going to M.D. Anderson.

I had to think about it. Dr. Jackson was head of the Plastic Surgery Department at the Mayo Clinic. He was a craniofacial surgeon, though I didn't quite understand what that was. It didn't make sense that I'd have a plastic surgeon/craniofacial surgeon operate on a tumor in the center of my head. Logically it seemed I needed a neurosurgeon. The doctor in Birmingham was a well-known head and neck surgeon, but he'd hurt my feelings, and I didn't like him.

I was back where I started. None of my choices seemed right at that point.

"Okay, God, I'm going to call Dr. Jackson. He should be home by now."

I got his home number from directory assistance, and his wife answered. I asked to speak to him and apologized for calling on a Friday night at home.

"Oh, no problem," she answered with her lovely Scottish accent. "Just one moment."

As soon as her husband picked up the phone and greeted me, I said, "Dr. Jackson, I know you just got in from Spain, and I'm sorry to call you at home, but my name is Candy Wood and I'm calling from Birmingham, Alabama. You don't know me, but I'm scheduled for surgery with you next week, and I have some questions to ask you."

"Actually I do know who you are," he said. "I stopped by the clinic on my way home from the airport this afternoon and ran into your friend Dr. Kent in the hall. He had your films, and I've taken a look at them. What can I answer for you?"

He didn't seem disturbed at all, and I was encouraged, so I jumped right in with my questions. "First, I'd like to know what you think and how you'd do this surgery. I've seen someone here who told me he'd make an incision down the side of my nose and through the lip, cutting across the top of the teeth. Is that what you'd do?"

"Of course, I need to take a look at you. But judging from your scan, I'd enter across the top of the head, making an incision from ear to ear, which will enable me to cut across the top of the skull. Then we'll have to see once we get in there."

"How do you cut across the skull?"

"We use a little saw."

Horrified, I envisioned a small handsaw cutting back and forth across my skull. Too preoccupied with what he'd just told me, I didn't hear much else. I'd never heard of such a thing, since craniofacial surgery was a relatively new specialty.

"Candy, if there's anything else you need to talk to me about, feel free to call." He was genuinely warm and kind, and his accent was charming. But...I didn't like the sound of the surgery.

After I hung up, knowing I'd promised God I'd go where He led, I looked up and prayed aloud, "God, please don't pick him."

Now what do I do? I thought. *I guess I'll call the surgeon in Birmingham too. Okay, God, I'll do my part. Now You do Yours.* A decision had to be made, and my family knew I was the only one who could make it.

When the doctor answered the phone, I apologized for calling him at home. Then, as tactfully as possible, I told him I'd just spoken with Dr. Jackson. "I know if you thought there was anyone who's had more experience with this type of surgery than you that you'd be the first to tell me. So what do you think?"

His response was harsh, and his tone cold. "If you want to go to the Mayo Clinic, then go. It seems like you've already made up your mind anyway. I really don't have time to discuss this with you."

I began to cry. "I'm thirty years old and I'm scared to death. I just wanted your opinion."

"You can talk with my secretary Monday morning."

That was the end of the conversation.

At first my feelings were hurt, which made me cry all the more. Then it dawned on me that I could never go through what I was about to endure with someone that unfeeling and unsympathetic, no matter how good a surgeon he was.

Oh, no, that means I have to go to the Mayo Clinic! I don't want to go there. But I can't stay here, and Houston just doesn't feel right.

"So, God, do I go to the Mayo Clinic?" I asked out loud. Everything in me knew the answer. It was so overwhelmingly clear at that point that I'd have jumped off a cliff before I considered going anywhere else. Then I thought about that saw and my conversation with Dr. Jackson, and I got mad at God.

"Okay, God, I'll go because I said I'd go wherever You led. But this is crazy!" I continued speaking as if He were sitting right there with me. "I'll probably die, and it will be all Your fault! But I don't want to die. Please, God, I don't want to die!"

I burst into tears, as sadness engulfed me. I wiped my runny nose and my tear-streaked face and continued to cry out to the Lord. "God, can't You give me some comfort? Can't You do something to make me feel better? I just want comfort."

I looked down at the small, unopened Bible in my lap. Picking it up, I remembered Barbara, the girl on the ski trip, and how she read her Bible every day. Then I remembered what Lynn and Synthia said about the Bible being God's Word to us. "How are you going to know what He says to you if you never read it?" they'd asked.

"God," I said, as I picked up the little book and stared at it, my bottom lip trembling, "I know there has to be something about comfort in here, but I don't know where to find it. I know You probably don't like to do things this way, but since I don't know where to find it, I'm going to close my eyes, open the Bible, and point on the page. Then I'll assume that it's a word from You—kind of like what Lynn and Synthia said."

I closed my eyes, opened the Bible, separating the crisp pages, and pointed my forefinger onto a page. In the center of the Bible, in the book of Psalms, my finger pointed to 118:17: "I shall not die, but live and declare the works of the Lord."

Could there be a mistake? I looked at the words again. *Does God work this way?* I'd been prepared to take the best verse out of three, but I decided to stay with the first one. Still, it was perplexing. Of all the verses in the Bible, my finger pointed to one that addressed the subject I'd asked about—death. It was also a comforting, encouraging verse. In my immature, childlike faith, I'd cried out to the Lord, and He heard and answered. I was His frightened child, and He met me right where I was in my faith.

6

◇   ◇   ◇

It was Monday morning, May 31, 1982, the day before I was to leave for the Mayo Clinic. I was completely caught up in the chaos and preparations—getting packed, making sure I had all the necessary medical records, confirming arrangements for the children for the next four weeks, tying up loose ends around town at the bank and post office, and answering the phone as friends called to wish me well.

During the course of that busy preparation day, I received a phone call from my friend Ginny, who lived about an hour away in Tuscaloosa. She and her husband were friends with two of Lee's fraternity brothers from the University of Alabama, and the three men, along with the two married men's wives, had recently become involved in a strong church.

If I'd described them at the time, I'd have said they were very religious, more so than Lee or I. They seemed to have something we didn't, and I knew they'd been praying for me over the recent weeks, as we'd talked several times on the phone. I'd even found myself thinking how we tend to call on people like that when things get difficult.

That particular day, Ginny called to tell me God had spoken to her during the night and said the five of them—the single man plus the two married men and their wives—were to come to Birmingham and anoint me with oil, lay hands on me, and pray for my healing. I didn't quite know what she meant about God speaking to her, whether it was out-loud or not, and I didn't know anything about being anointed with oil. But at that point I was seeking, searching, and open to anything, so we quickly agreed they'd come that evening after they got off work.

True to their word and despite the thunderstorm moving east from Tuscaloosa to Birmingham, they piled into the car and drove to our home, arriving just after dinner. Momma and Daddy took Colley and Elliott for a ride so the rest of us could be alone without interruption.

This typically high-spirited group had arrived in a somber mood and explained they were "on a mission." I didn't quite understand what that meant, but when they said they were obeying God's direction, I could relate, as I felt led to go to the Mayo Clinic.

Was that the same thing? This personal interaction with the Lord about decisions and guidance was very new to me, but He'd made His presence known in very tangible ways. Each time something happened that couldn't easily be explained away in natural, human logic, I found myself wondering, *Does God work this way?* I was coming to the conclusion that He did, and the key was to be open to however He chose to do things.

Somewhere inside, something supernatural was going on. True, there was some dread involved with the entire situation, but there was also an indescribable, underlying peace that filled my soul. It was, as the Bible says, a peace that isn't easily understood, and I certainly didn't understand why I was experiencing it in the midst of such a difficult time. But it was real; I couldn't deny that.

As Lee and I and our guests sat down in our cozy, brightly decorated living room, my demeanor didn't match the décor. I may not have had a lot of understanding about what was going on, but I knew it was serious, and I knew God had orchestrated it.

We talked awhile, and then everyone gathered around me while I sat on the sofa. As they prepared to pray for me, my mind flashed back to when I'd first met Ginny at summer school twelve years earlier. Ginny had changed since then. Though she still had a fun-loving spark, she was also quite serious about her life and her faith in Christ. She'd since married, and both she and her husband were actively involved in their church in Tuscaloosa.

Bob, a friend of ours, was there with his wife, Becka. Bob was Lee's big brother in their college fraternity, and during Bob's senior year he'd become involved with his church and a small group that met regularly to study the Bible and pray. Lee and I hadn't understood Bob's level of commitment, though we once attended church with him. The congregation met in a bicycle shop, which I thought was odd. I also thought it odd that everyone in that little church was so excited about their faith. When we attended that one service with Bob, I told him I taught seventh grade Sunday school and was involved in the women's organization at my church. I thought that would convince him I was just as big a Christian as any one of those excited people at his church. But that Monday evening, as they gathered around me to pray, I realized I'd really been trying to convince myself.

Bob and Becka, Ginny and John, and their single friend John, stood around me to pray. Single John was also one of Lee's fraternity brothers, so I knew who he was but, until that evening, I'd never met him.

As each of the five laid a hand on my shoulder or head, Ginny pulled out a small bottle of oil and touched a drop to my forehead. Then they began to pray individually. It was a new experience for me, though no heat rushed from my head to my toes, nor did I experience any thunder or lightning. But something incomprehensible happened.

With my eyes shut, I saw a vision. I wouldn't have called it that at the time, but it was as real and familiar as if I'd seen it before. I saw Jesus, standing in the corner of the room. He looked similar to what I'd seen in pictures: kind and gentle with a slight smile, wearing a white robe. What struck me most was the way He stood, not with His hands outstretched, as if beckoning me to come, but with His hands behind Him, appearing to stand "at ease," like a watching soldier or sentry.

As the vision faded, I began to question if I'd actually seen it or just imagined it. Then I realized that if I'd imagined it, His hands would have been outstretched, as I was accustomed to seeing in Bible story books. Instead, He'd stood in such a way that seemed to say He was watching over me, overseeing the care that would be given to me, controlling the final outcome. It wouldn't be the last time I'd see that vision.

I also experienced for the first time the feeling of powerful prayer, which words can't adequately describe. I wasn't healed and my head still hurt, but something real took place, and a sense of peace filled my soul.

Momma and Daddy were putting the children to bed when our guests left. Taking Colley from my mother, I held her close and rocked her, staring down at her sweet little face. She was sound asleep and had no idea that what was going on in our family would forever affect the rest of her life. But Elliott did.

I laid Colley in her bed and tiptoed into my son's room. He was still awake in the top bunk. I climbed up and sat next to him.

"Elliott, you know I'm going away tomorrow to have surgery," I said, trying to figure out how to word what I wanted to say. I'd seen a movie once where a little girl's mother died, and the little girl was mad at God for taking her away. I didn't want Elliott to be mad at God.

"You know, Elliott, this is very serious surgery I'll be having."

"Yes, ma'am." His dark brown, nearly black eyes locked into mine. He'd been such a trooper for the past year, coming home after school and quietly watching TV so he wouldn't disturb me while I rested. He'd seen me hemorrhage, and I was sure he'd overheard telephone conversations and visitors' remarks. If he was frightened I didn't know it, which concerned me more than if I had. My face was still swollen and a little blue from the biopsy. He'd witnessed a lot and had been so brave.

"Elliott," I said and then paused, searching for the right words. "It's possible I may not be able to come home. God may choose to take me home to heaven." He didn't say anything, so I continued. "If He does, I don't want you to be mad at Him. He loves me, and He loves you." I paused again. "I'll be in Heaven with Him, and I'll wait there for you when you come in a long time. Do you understand what I'm saying?"

"Yes, ma'am."

I hugged him, then reminded him how much I loved him and what a good boy he'd always been and how proud I was of him and that I was going to miss him while I was away. "I'll call, though, every night. Okay?"

"Yes, ma'am." He didn't ask any questions, so I said our prayers and climbed down the ladder. It was hard to leave him, not knowing what he was thinking.

◇   ◇   ◇

On Tuesday I waved goodbye to Colley and Elliott, who were staying with Lee's parents. I remember thinking how glad I was that the children were in a safe and loving environment, even as my own parents drove us to the airport. As Lee and I sat together on the last leg of the short, thirty-minute flight from Minneapolis to Rochester, I looked down and saw waves of tall green cornstalks, growing in what looked like perfect squares.

"They were serious," Lee remarked, peering over my shoulder at the ground below. "The airport really is in the middle of a cornfield." Lee was referring to his high school friend and our Mayo Clinic contact, Raleigh Kent, and his wife, Dottie, who were waiting for us at the top of the steps in the small three-gate airport. Dottie welcomed us with her ever-present smile, while Raleigh offered to help us with our carry-on luggage.

How can this be? It's all happened so fast! We were 1,000 miles from home, staying with a couple we didn't know well but grateful they'd insisted we do so.

Now I was glad they had. It was so much more comfortable being in their home than in a motel room. The Kents' small apartment was decorated with warm antiques, and Dottie's feminine touch was evident as we followed our hosts to the master bedroom.

"Oh, no," I told Raleigh, spotting the second bedroom with its single antique sleigh bed, "we don't need to take your bedroom."

But again they insisted, and I immediately felt at home and at peace— as much as I could under the circumstances.

It didn't take but a few minutes to settle into their charming bedroom because there wasn't much unpacking to do. I figured all I needed was something to wear to the clinic visits and nightgowns for the hospital. I hadn't let myself think I might need clothes for the few weeks after I got out of the hospital. Who knew what might happen during the surgery? So I packed one pair of slacks and two sweaters. That was it.

Raleigh and Dottie knew we'd had a long day and were tired, but Dottie had made brownies before we arrived. "They're really good with a glass of milk," she said. "And Raleigh just loves chocolate." It didn't take much to persuade us to join them.

As we munched on the delicious treat, I plied Raleigh with medical questions, hoping for some encouragement. At other times, we discussed everyday events and reminisced about high school days, and I actually found myself laughing and having a good time. My mind was like a smorgasbord, full of different thoughts and ideas, jumping from happy moments to serious considerations. One minute I'd be optimistic, the next morbid—yet I was glad to be in their home with them, rather than stuck in a motel room with Lee. Everything seemed so much sadder when it was just the two of us.

◇   ◇   ◇

The next morning, Raleigh escorted us to the clinic for my pre-op tests. Like obedient puppies, Lee and I followed as we entered the gray, twenty-story building. We had to hustle, as Raleigh pressed ahead, turning occasionally to give us bits and pieces of the clinic's history. He told us about the Mayo brothers, William and Charles, the two physicians who had come to this tiny Midwestern town back in the early 1900s and set up a new, nonprofit form of medical care.

"Let me see your packet," Raleigh said as we arrived at Desk C in the Hilton Building. I handed it to him, and he passed it to the nurse, who politely indicated two chairs in the waiting area. As I looked at the approximately 100 chairs, nearly all of them occupied, I thought, *If all these people are here for blood work, it's going to take forever!*

I was wrong. Within fifteen minutes I was called into a smaller waiting room, this one with only about ten chairs. Almost immediately I was then brought into a small cubicle, where a nurse looked at me and said, "Candace Wood?" When I confirmed my name, she smiled, put a label on the blood tube, and handed it to me. "Check the name and make sure it's correct," she instructed. I did, it was, and I handed it back to her.

Gently she inserted the needle into a vein in my arm, and the tube filled with the deep red liquid. She handed the tube back to me and asked me to check the name again. *Wow. They must want to be really sure there aren't any mistakes with my blood sample.*

The next card in my packet was for radiology, where I was scheduled for a lung x-ray and a CT scan of my head. I'd never had a CT scan and didn't know what to expect.

Raleigh left us there, knowing the procedures would take awhile. The people who handled these tests were every bit as careful as the lab technicians to check, double-check, and triple-check my identity throughout the procedure.

The attendant led me to an examining room that contained a long table with some sort of covering over it. He positioned me on the table and securely strapped down my head. Then he joined another technician behind a glass window, having instructed me not to move. I didn't, but I couldn't help glancing at them out of the corner of my eye—until the covering over the table moved and stationed itself above my head and I could no longer see anything except the inside of the tunnel. I soon heard clicking sounds, and then the tunnel moved ever so slightly before the clicking sounds resumed. This continued for about forty-five minutes, while I wondered if the technicians could see anything—and if they'd tell me if they did.

Lord, what do they see? When the covering finally moved back from over my head, my heart raced with anticipation.

"Mrs. Wood, are you all right?" the technician inquired.

I assured him I was, fully expecting him to undo the straps that held my head in place, but he didn't. Instead he said, "I need to insert some dye into your vein. Have you had anything to eat or drink this morning?"

When I told him I hadn't, he nodded. "Good. Sometimes the dye makes patients nauseated. You'll feel a little heat as the dye runs through the vein. It shouldn't be too uncomfortable."

I didn't like any of this. "What's the dye for?"

"For contrast. It gives us a contrast from the scan without the dye and enables the radiologist to read the scan."

"What did you see?" I asked, wanting to know but afraid of what he might say.

He smiled. "I'm not a radiologist."

I knew that, but I was sure he knew something. He just couldn't—or wouldn't—tell me. But it was on the screen in that room behind the window where he'd stood with the other technician, and I was sure they could see it.

It. The tumor. The thing that had invaded and completely changed my life and now threatened my very existence.

The heat from the dye rushed through my body—warm, as the technician said. It was a strange sensation, not really painful, and my breathing became short and quick, even as my heart raced at the thought of the unknown.

"Let me know if you feel any pain in your shoulder," the technician said. "Sometimes the dye does something there."

There was no pain, and I was grateful. Then the machine was inching back over my head—more clicking and more rotating of the tunnel. Finally it was over.

The technician unstrapped my head and helped me sit up. "That feel better? Do you need to sit a minute?"

I shook my head. "No, but thank you. I think I'm okay."

◇   ◇   ◇

With the tests behind me, Raleigh, Dottie, Lee, and I went off to enjoy what was left of the day. I was tired, but I wanted to experience every moment of the time left before going to the hospital. We rode bikes around Rochester, and then had dinner before returning to the Kents' apartment.

My parents got into town later that evening, having opted to drive all day Tuesday and Wednesday so they'd have a car once they got there. They stayed in a motel, stopping by to see us before turning in for the night. Raleigh and Dottie welcomed them and did their best at keeping things hopeful and upbeat, with Raleigh fielding our multitude of medical questions, while Dottie offered love and support.

◇   ◇   ◇

Throughout the night, I was awakened every hour by the music from the nearby monastery and the ringing of bells in the distance. Two more hours, one more hour... Between the hourly serenades of music and chimes, interspersed with thoughts of cancer, surgery, and dying, my rest was sporadic at best.

My appointment at the clinic was for nine-thirty, and though I was awake, I didn't want to get up. I wanted to stay safely tucked between crisp blue and white cotton sheets. Quietly I surveyed Raleigh and Dottie's room, thinking how light and bright and airy it was. The antique white wicker pieces gave the room an added charm.

The first rays of sun peeked through the window, as if trying to awaken the bright red geraniums in the wicker stand under the window. Surprisingly, I found myself humming a song, one I wasn't familiar with but seemed appropriate—and optimistic—for my circumstances. The only words I knew were, "I've got a lot of living to do," and I was relatively sure it was from a musical, though I didn't know which one. Had God put that song into my head? Was it His way of encouraging me? *Does God work that way?*

◇   ◇   ◇

I began the day by returning to the clinic to meet Dr. Jackson. Lee and I and my parents rode the elevator to the sixth floor and stepped out into one huge room. Five rows of about ten chairs each faced the east side of the brightly lit room, with the same number facing the west. The words "Plastic Surgery—East" were clearly visible over the nurses' station. A blackboard on an easel contained a list of the plastic surgeons' names, including the words "Dr. Ian Jackson, Department Head." I was in the right place.

With my blood work, scans, and other tests done, I'd finally hear the verdict. I signed in with the nurse, and then we found seats in the chairs lining the wall. Too nervous to talk, I took in my surroundings. The waiting room was nearly empty, though it was nicely decorated with large, live, green potted plants and mosaic tile walls. The room seemed to demand a sort of respectful silence, and its few occupants complied. Everyone seemed "dressed" for the occasion, with Daddy and Lee in coats and ties. Even the nurses, sitting quietly behind their stations, wore immaculately starched white uniforms, lending a dignified atmosphere to the scene.

My eyes fell on one young girl, sitting alone and reading a book. I noticed she held the book right up to her face, and I wondered if she had problems with her eyesight. Later, when she lowered the book, I realized what was wrong. Her face was disfigured, and it startled me. It was the first time I'd seen anyone with a facial disfigurement, and it occurred to me that the girl might be Dr. Jackson's patient.

. *Is that what I'm going to look like after my surgery?* The reality of Dr. Goldfarb's words hit hard: "You could lose the right side of your face." A cold, sick feeling swept through me, distracting me and preventing me from hearing my name being called.

The nurse repeated my name, and this time she got my attention. The time had come for me to hear the words I'd anxiously awaited and yet dreaded....

7

◇   ◇   ◇

I picked up my purse and yellow spiral notebook. None of us said a word, though our thoughts were evident on our faces. My parents' only child was facing the trial of her life, and there was nothing they could do to fix it. After seeing fourteen specialists in the previous year, we were finally going to get some concrete answers—at least we hoped so. With Lee following, I made my way toward the nurse.

"Candace Wood?" she asked as I stepped through the door from the waiting room, noticing as I did that she didn't have as strong a Minnesota accent as most of the people I'd met there.

"Yes," I said, nodding.

"Could you verify your birth date?"

"August 29, 1951." I was only thirty years old.

"How are you?" she asked, as she led us down a short hall and opened the door to one of the examining rooms.

"Okay, I guess." I tried to smile, but my voice was weak and I was scared.

"I'm Connie, Dr. Jackson's nurse. You two can have a seat here."

Though she was about my age, she seemed older. Her smile was warm and her voice comforting. Sensing my apprehension, she stood in the door and asked questions about our home and children, keeping me distracted for a moment or two. Then she announced, "Dr. Jackson will be in to see you in a minute." Then she closed the door behind her.

"She was nice," I told Lee.

He nodded, his lips pursed.

"This is nice, too," I said, referring to the examining room. "It's so clean." The golden colored cork tile floors were waxed and shiny, giving the room a warm glow, not at all stark and cold like so many I'd seen.

Lee nodded again.

I heard male voices in the hall outside the door. That must be him.

Two men entered, but neither identified with my preconceived idea of someone from Scotland, with fair skin and blue eyes. The shorter of the two was the first to speak.

"Hello, Candy. I'm Dr. Jackson, and this is Dr. Laws. It's nice to meet you. Did you have a good flight from Alabama?"

"Yes sir," I lied, not wanting to admit it was awful. The last time I'd flown was two months before, and I'd begun to hemorrhage from the nose. Throughout this last flight, I was afraid it would happen again, so I was tense and anxious, though nothing happened.

Dr. Jackson's Scottish accent was charming, and he was very handsome, with his dark hair and tanned face making his smile appear even whiter. Dressed in a navy double-breasted blazer, he held my chart in his left hand and greeted Lee with his right.

"Dr. Laws is from the neurosurgery department," he said. "He's here to take a look as well. It's necessary to have a neurosurgeon present in surgeries such as these." Dr. Laws stood, while Dr. Jackson sat on a stool in front of me and opened my chart. "Well, now, let's take a look."

I interrupted him before he could speak, handing him my open spiral notebook. "I thought you might want this. I've written down my medical history for the past year."

He glanced at the first page and politely handed it back. "I don't need it. I have all I need right here."

"You don't need to know my medications or symptoms?"

"No, no." His voice was calm. "This shows us what we need to know." He placed the CT scan on the lighted screen on the wall and pointed his pen to a clearly solid white area on the CT scan. "This large mass is a tumor." He traced it with his pen. "We have a very difficult situation here. As you can see, it's a very large—"

I interrupted him again. "How large?"

He thought a second and then answered, "Eh, probably about the size of a baseball, I'd say."

"A baseball? They said in Birmingham a golf ball!"

"They were looking at a tomogram when they told you that. These were the CT scans that were taken yesterday. The *problem* is not so much the size as it is the type and location," he said, emphasizing the word *problem.*

He then reminded me that the tumor was already a grade-three osteosarcoma, which was rarely found in the head and typically didn't respond to radiation or chemotherapy. He laid all the information out on the table, no sugar-coating. I liked that approach—upfront, honest, no surprises.

"We'll make an incision across the top of your head from ear to ear and then down the middle of your face around the nose." He illustrated with his finger on my head and face. "We'll then cut through the middle of your upper lip and across the top of your teeth, the same place they cut for your biopsy in Birmingham. This will enable us to peel both sides of the face back."

Somehow I remained calm. "Last week on the phone you said you'd only have to cut across the top of the head. Now you're telling me you have to cut down the middle of the face, too?"

"Yes. I thought I could access the tumor from the top, but after seeing these scans today…" His tone went from explanatory to apologetic. "I know it's a lot to think about."

I dreaded his answer to my next question, but I had to ask. "How do you get to the tumor this way?"

"We cut across the top of the skull and down the middle of the face. Then we remove the front portion of the face, including the orbit of the right eye and the nose." He paused. "Candy, eh…the CT also shows that the tumor has invaded the main vessel to the brain, as well as your optic nerve. You'll lose the right eye and possibly the left."

I heard and understood everything he said. I wasn't in shock, but neither could I fathom someone having that kind of surgery and actually living through it. I couldn't imagine having that kind of surgery at all, or even that it could be done. But I knew he wasn't making it up.

I didn't say anything; I had to think. This was so much more involved than anything I had imagined. Finally I asked, "How much of the tumor can you get?"

"We won't know until we get in there. Part of it is in an inoperable area of the head, but we'll just have to see."

Nothing sounded hopeful, especially for a cure. I started voicing my thoughts as I considered my options, wondering why I wasn't hysterical. As if conducting a business meeting, I asked, "If I don't do anything, how long will I live?"

"Eh, it's hard to say. Six months, maybe longer."

"If I do have the surgery, how long will I live?"

"Eh, well, I operated on a girl two years ago that had a tumor similar to yours. She's just finished her freshman year of college."

"Do you really think I'll live through this surgery?"

"I certainly hope so." He smiled. "I hope you're eating a Popsicle Saturday night!"

He seemed so certain, but I had to ask. "How many times have you cut into someone's skull?"

"About 2,000."

"How many died?"

"Only two, and they were both very sick babies."

I knew the majority of his patients were disfigured children. He was one of only a handful of craniofacial surgeons in America, and because of his vast experience in a new kind of entry into the head, he was seeing patients like me with difficult, life-threatening tumors.

He smiled again. "If you don't have any other questions, why don't you and Lee go and talk about what you want to do and come back later this afternoon?"

As the two doctors started to leave, Dr. Laws turned around and said gently but emphatically, "By the way, Candy, we won't be replacing the bones to your face. You will wake up severely deformed."

As I sat there trying to understand all that I'd heard, I began to realize we were no longer talking about the possibility of my waking up from surgery with a deformed face or blind. We were talking about disassembling my head and face in order to save my life, or at least extend my life, even if just for a few months. I had some big decisions to make.

By now it was nearly lunchtime. We walked out of the clinic into the warm Rochester sunshine. Momma and Daddy went to their car, while Lee and I walked to a little sandwich shop to eat.

"Candy," he said, "do you want to go to M.D. Anderson for a second opinion?"

"No. I've done everything humanly possible, and I know this is where God sent me. My life is in His hands, and it's a good place to be." I meant every word, and I was actually relieved that there was nothing more I could do.

After lunch, I was scheduled for some pre-op tests and another visit with Dr. Jackson. When that was finished, Lee and I went back to the Kents' apartment for an early dinner. Dottie, knowing I'd have to fast after midnight, went to a lot of trouble to make me a special meal. Three glass vases filled with fresh flowers graced the middle of their table.

"I thought your momma and daddy might like a home-cooked meal after their long drive this week," Dottie commented. I appreciated her thoughtfulness and wonderful cooking, but I didn't have much of an appetite, despite a menu that included Southern green beans, new potatoes, and chicken breasts cooked in what everyone else said was a delicious sauce. I did manage to eat the homemade lemon icebox pie, one of my favorites.

When the meal was finished, Raleigh suggested we go to the hospital and get checked in. It was after six, and we'd put off the inevitable until the very last minute.

8

◇   ◇   ◇

LEE AND I, ACCOMPANIED BY MOMMA AND DADDY, RALEIGH AND Dottie, went straight to admissions at St. Mary's Hospital, a beautiful old brick building several blocks from the Mayo Clinic. Spanning two city blocks, St. Mary's was the older of the two hospitals used by the clinic, the other being the Methodist Hospital adjacent to the clinic's buildings.

After answering all the preliminary admissions questions, I was taken by wheelchair to my room on Second Francis, the second floor of the Francis building, which was the plastic surgery floor and burn unit.

There's no turning back now, I thought, as the orderly wheeled me into my room, with everyone else trailing along behind.

The immaculately clean room wasn't plush or elaborate, and I felt a spark of concern when I spotted the half-bath connecting my room with the room next door. I'd never shared a bathroom with another patient before, and the tubs and showers were all down the hall, rather than in individual rooms.

Brown-and-gold geometric-print curtains covered the window overlooking a grassy courtyard. It was early evening, but because of the time of year it was still light and wouldn't get dark until nearly nine. The warm weather enticed people to stay outside as long as possible, and I could see patients, visitors, and medical personnel strolling through the courtyard, as I sensed I'd come to a friendly hospital.

I soon learned that, like me, most of the patients had come from out of town, so with few exceptions, family members were the only visitors. I also learned there was a sunroom about three doors down from my room where patients and visitors gathered to play cards, checkers, or other games.

Momma and Daddy had already met the parents of Brenda, the young girl I'd seen in the waiting room. As it turned out, Brenda's room was only two doors down from mine. She was thirteen, and she and her family lived out West. Brenda had been born with a condition in which the cartilage in her face didn't form. She was also almost legally blind and had been undergoing reconstructive surgeries all her life. In this particular surgery, Dr. Jackson was going to shape or build her a nose.

I never saw the lady in my adjoining room, and the man across the hall coughed almost constantly. "I hope that guy doesn't have tuberculosis," Daddy commented soon after we arrived in my room. We always referred to Daddy as the "optimistic pessimist" or the "pessimistic optimist" because he either cheerfully told bad news or skeptically announced good news. Good, bad, or indifferent, Daddy approached the telling of any news with his sharp wit and passion for life. As the man across the hall continued to hack, Daddy said, "I wish he'd close his door." I knew his concern for me, and the frustration at his inability to fix my situation was weighing heavily upon him, allowing a somber tone to creep into his words, which was so unlike him.

As the evening hours waned, I met my evening nurse, Sherri, who'd come on for the seven-to-three shift. Each nurse was assigned three or four patients so the patient had the same nurse throughout the entire shift. I liked that. I also liked the fact that my records were hung on the wall right outside my door so there was no chance of their getting lost.

Mine was a busy room that night. Besides my own family and Raleigh and Dottie, others visitors kept appearing. First the chaplain of St. Mary's came to introduce himself. He tried to be comforting, but I was pre-occupied with my thoughts. A little while later there was a knock on my door, and a young man in casual street clothes introduced himself.

"I'm Doug Mitchell. I went to seminary with a friend of yours from Birmingham—Jim Robey. He called to tell me you were here."

I welcomed him, and then he explained, "I'm the chaplain at another hospital here in Rochester. I wanted you to know that my wife and I are here for you. In fact," he said, turning toward my family, "I'd be happy to sit with you tomorrow while Candy's in surgery."

We were impressed by Doug's kindness and immediately accepted his offer. Soon after he left, another visitor took his place, this time a man about my age, dressed in a coat and tie.

"I wanted to stop by and say hello," said Guy Fogle. "I went to medical school with George Joe, a friend of yours from Birmingham, and since I'm doing my residency program here, he asked me to check on you."

Then there was another tap on the door. A nice-looking man, also about my age, walked in, carrying my chart. He was tall—well over six feet—with a tanned face and a nice smile. He wore a khaki suit, and he quickly intro-duced himself as Dr. Michael See, explaining he was on his last day with Dr. Jackson's service, as medical school residents rotate different specialties.

With my chart in hand, he sat down on the edge of my bed and briefed me on the surgical procedure scheduled for the next day. I'd heard it already, but I listened intently. When he was finished, he patted my knee and asked if I had any questions.

"Do you know what time I go down in the morning?"

Though he was unable to answer that particular question, he didn't seem anxious to leave and stayed to chat with us, so I decided to ask him another question.

"Dr. See, do you believe in miracles?" The more I heard about the surgical procedure I was to undergo the next day, as well as the risks involved, the more I knew I needed a miracle.

Dr. See smiled. "Candy, I played on the Missouri football team that *beat* Alabama several years ago," he said, emphasizing the word *beat*. "Miracles happen every day."

Once again I caught myself wondering, *Does God work this way?* I knew exactly what he was referring to, for I'd attended the University of Alabama, where the famous Bear Bryant was head coach of the Crimson Tide's football team. We'd won many SEC championships, always played in the big bowl games and national championships, and Coach Bryant was on his way to becoming the winningest college football coach in sports history. I knew how miraculous it had been for Missouri to beat U of A and had even attended that game. It seemed Dr. See had spoken the words I needed to hear.

As the evening progressed, my night nurse handed me a pair of heavy white tights. "I have a gift for you," Sherri announced. "They help prevent blood clots."

I didn't like the sound of that, but I put them on anyway. Then, acting silly, I asked Momma to get out her camera.

"Take a picture for Blue Cross to prove these were surgical stockings," I teased. "Then maybe they'll pay for them!" I posed, pulling my long pink and white striped seersucker robe up to my knees to show off my white-stockinged legs.

As Sherri left my room, she took Momma down the hall to show her the patient refrigerator and beverages. Momma knew I liked grape juice and crushed ice, and now she'd know where to find them. Then everyone except Lee left, and the two of us were alone. The familiar sadness settled upon us, accompanied by dread of what was to come. I had to take care of business.

"Lee, let's talk about my funeral…just in case."

He didn't want to, but I insisted. I wasn't in charge of anything else in my life, so I should at least be able to have a say in my funeral.

"I definitely want 'Fairest Lord Jesus' sung." I'd been raised with the good old Baptist hymns, and "Fairest Lord Jesus" had long been one of my favorites. By the time I finished giving Lee my specific requests, I realized I didn't know what scriptures to suggest. I wanted people to know I'd surrendered my life to the Lord and knew I belonged to Him.

Next I wanted to write to my children. I'd bought brightly-colored stationery for that purpose, to be opened when they turned eighteen— another "just in case." I wrote how much I loved them and was proud of them, and I listed the many things I appreciated in each of them. I also reminded them how much God loved them. Then I sealed each note with a cute jelly-bean sticker and put their names on the front of the envelopes.

Finally, I gave the notes to Lee for safekeeping. I also wanted to record a message to my children like my friend Anne had told me her deceased mom did for her. I'd have to do that in the morning, though, because the tape recorder was in my parents' motel room. Momma had promised to bring it the next day.

I no sooner finished writing my notes than Sherri came in and brought me a pill. "This will help you sleep."

I didn't want to sleep and politely declined the pill. If I didn't make it through surgery the next day, I certainly didn't want to sleep away the last night of my life. I wasn't being morbid, just practical.

You are the Potter, and I am the clay. The words floated through my mind, and I tried to place them. Then I remembered. We sang them at the Baptist church I attended in junior high, fifteen years ago. I tried to recall how the song went, getting stuck on one word in particular. *While I am waiting,* something *and still.* What was that word after waiting? And then it came to me. *Yielded!* It was a song about the Potter molding me for His purposes, and yielding was my part in the process.

Dutifully and stoically, Lee stayed in the room with me, dozing in a chair and occasionally sitting on the bed beside me. His face was sad, and it was a bittersweet time together. We didn't talk much, with both of us lost in our own private thoughts. I may have slipped off to sleep periodically, but each time I awoke I noticed the clock was that much closer to Friday morning.

That same night, back in Birmingham, about fifty people were gathered for a prayer service at our church. Lee and I had been members of that church for nine years, and our children had been baptized there. I'd called Molly, who once puzzled me with her statement that she'd backslidden by not reading her Bible daily, to ask her to organize the prayer meeting. One of our ministers led it, and each person in attendance signed a small daily devotional book titled *Streams in the Desert,* which they later presented to me. It was the first devotional book I'd ever owned.

The morning nurse's name was Patti, and she came on at three. She was fair-skinned with short blonde hair, which wasn't unusual, as most of the nurses at the clinic were of similar heritage, with fair skin, rosy cheeks, very little makeup, neat and clean and very professional.

"How are you doing this morning?" she asked, as she took my vital signs.

"Scared. Do you know when they're taking me down? I want to make sure my parents get here before I go."

She hadn't received the surgery list for the day, so she couldn't answer my question. I was thirsty, but I wasn't allowed anything to drink. I decided that being thirsty was okay, so long as it meant my surgery could be put off a bit. I needed more time to call my children and to record a tape for them.

"When will they shave my head?" I asked—not that it mattered, but I was curious.

"They don't do that until you're in surgery. You'll already be asleep."

My parents arrived just in time to hear Dr. Paul Heath, one of Dr. Jackson's residents, updating me on my situation. Dr. Heath was close to my age and planning a career in plastic surgery. He'd stopped by before going down to the operating room.

"Candy, Dr. Jackson postponed your surgery until he's finished some of his less complicated procedures. He has about four or five ahead of you."

"So what time does that mean?"

Dr. Heath didn't know but explained Dr. Jackson's reasoning. "This way he'll be able to take as long as he needs because you'll be his last patient."

I guess that's good, I thought, though I was ready to tape the messages to my children and get on with it. The waiting was becoming agonizing.

Shirley, the afternoon nurse, came in at 2:30, wheeling an IV pole. I'd been wondering if it would get too late for Dr. Jackson to operate.

Shirley answered my question without my even having to ask. "Candy, they're almost ready for you."

Suddenly my impatience disappeared, and I thought, *Already? Oh, no! This is it.*

"This is your pre-op medication," Shirley explained. "You'll feel a little drowsy." She inserted the needle in my arm and taped it in place. Everyone was there, including Raleigh and Dottie.

Then, despite the Demerol that was starting to kick in, I realized I hadn't made the tape for my children. "Momma, get the tape recorder back out. Is there a fresh tape in it?"

Momma assured me there was, and with the microphone up to my mouth, I began a slurred message to my children. When I finished, I knew I'd taken care of everything—the notes, the messages, the funeral arrangements, even thank-you cards. I'd visited my grandparents, spent quality time with my parents and expressed my gratitude to them. I'd squared things with Lee, sorry that our marriage, though committed, hadn't been what we'd hoped. I'd called my friend Judith to tell her the surgery time had been delayed so she could relay the message to others. In other words, I'd checked everything off my to-do list before…well, just *before.*

If I die today, at least I'll feel loved. I wish everyone could feel this loved and cared for!

By the time the orderly transferred me to the gurney, I was sedated but not so much that I wasn't aware of my surroundings. My family was able to accompany me down the hall to the elevator before we said goodbye.

"I love you," I told them one last time, hoping and praying they knew how much. Then the elevator doors closed, and they were gone. The next thing I knew I was in a room about nine by twelve feet in size. The walls were tiled like a large shower, and someone was hosing off the legs of the gurney.

"What are you doing?" I asked.

"We do this before you go into the surgical unit," the attendant explained. "Just a precaution."

I was impressed. I knew my daddy would be too.

The Demerol dulled my anxiety as I was wheeled into the holding area, a large room where patients waited to be taken into the operating room.

"Candy."

I looked up and saw a man standing beside me. "My name is Jesse Muir. I'm an anesthesiologist. I won't be yours, but I went to medical school with Johnny Mears, a friend of yours from Birmingham. He asked if I'd stay with you in the holding area."

I smiled sleepily. I appreciated the gesture, and it helped the time pass.

Demerol or not, I was suddenly wide awake when they arrived to roll me into the operating room and then shifted me from the gurney to the operating table. The cold metal was a shock to my bare skin where my hospital gown had come open in the back, making me even more alert. I looked around the room, surprised it wasn't larger. The lights seemed extremely bright, probably because of the white, sterile walls. And it was very cold. I was shivering when the nurse came and tucked a warm blanket around me. I thanked her, feeling a bit like a frightened child being tucked in by my momma, yet grateful for every kind word or gesture.

I continued to watch the nurses and technicians in their green surgical scrubs and hats, their faces covered with masks and only their eyes showing, as they focused on their jobs. I wondered if they were the last people I'd see on this earth. I knew Dr. Jackson wasn't anticipating that, but I had to consider the possibility. The clock on the wall told me it was three o'clock. It was then I heard Dr. Jackson's voice.

"Eh, Candy," he said, using the common Scottish expression *eh* that I'd learned was the equivalent of *well*. He smiled as he looked down at me and asked, "How are you doing?" His Scottish accent seemed to brighten the room, as he stood beside the operating table, his mask hanging around his neck and his hand on my arm.

I don't remember what I said, but I heard the anesthesiologist speaking to me, and I knew it was time. Dr. Jackson turned to wash his hands in the sink a few feet away.

"Wait," I said, looking at the anesthesiologist. I knew the minute he started the IV I'd be out. "May I pray first?"

I was surrounded by four or five attendants, and the shiny silver stand with a sterile green cloth and surgical instruments neatly arranged on it was placed beside me. Everyone waited.

"Oh, Lord, You know what I want. I want to live and see my children grow up. But whatever You want is okay."

Then I saw it—the same vision I'd seen the night my Tuscaloosa friends came to pray for me. Jesus stood in the corner of the room, dressed in a white robe. His hands weren't outstretched, as if He'd come to take me home to heaven, but they were behind His back, as if He'd come to watch over me and all that would take place that day.

I smiled. "I'm ready."

"Count to ten for me," the anesthesiologist said. "Your arm may feel warm."

I'd done that before and knew I'd be asleep before I got to ten, but that was okay. I had peace now—peace with the Lord, peace that no shot of Demerol could give me.

"One, two, three…four…fi…"

9

◇ ◇ ◇

IT WAS NEARLY MIDNIGHT WHEN I WOKE MYSELF UP, YANKING ON THE tube that ran down my mouth and throat.

"It's taped down," I heard a woman's voice say. "It has to stay there." Then the owner of that voice gently but firmly moved my hand away from my mouth.

As if trying to see my way through a thick fog, I looked around the room, seeking something familiar and trying to figure out where I was.

"Candy, did you hear me?" This time I recognized Lee's voice. "They got it all."

Somehow, even in my confused state, I understood what he said, and I breathed a half-conscious sigh of relief. I didn't think to ask about my face—how much of it was gone and how much remained. Nor did it register that because I could see the woman who'd spoken to me I'd obviously not lost my eyesight. The only conscious thought I had, beyond relief at Lee's assurance that the surgeons had been successful in removing the entire tumor, was that I wanted the tube out of my mouth and throat. I tried again to jerk it out, but again the attendant pushed my hand away from my mouth.

◇　　　◇　　　◇

In a cathedral-ceilinged room, with high beams and long, old-fashioned windows, my parents, along with Lee and Dottie, sat in comfortable stuffed leather chairs, waiting for news. Dr. Jackson had unexpectedly and miraculously replaced the bones in my face. When he finally entered the waiting room and announced the good news, everyone was elated. They then went to the recovery room for one quick look, relieved that I was alright and overwhelmed that Dr. Jackson had put my face back together again.

Later, as Dottie stood beside my bed, she took my hand and whispered, "Candy."

I immediately recognized her voice.

"You…look…beautiful," she said, taking time to emphasize each word.

I lifted the corner of my lip in an effort to smile.

◇　　　◇　　　◇

Dr. Jackson had been right. He'd said I'd be feeling better the next day, and I was! In fact, I was sucking on a Popsicle by Saturday night and had even spent much of the day on the phone, talking with friends and assuring them I was alright—even though I was still groggy from pain medication and didn't remember the conversations afterward. But it was those phone calls that convinced my daddy I was going to make it.

"She must be okay," he commented to my momma when they walked into my room on Saturday evening and saw me with the receiver to my ear. "Look, she's already on the phone!"

When my parents arrived, I hung up and announced to Shirley, the head nurse, that Momma would be staying there with me that night.

"You won't need that," Shirley said, explaining that everyone needed to go home and get some sleep and that I'd be fine on my own. "If you need anything, just push the button, and we'll take care of you."

Based on previous experiences, I had a hard time believing her. "I want Momma to stay. I feel more comfortable with her here at night."

While I continued to try to convince Shirley to let Momma stay, Dr. Jackson and his entourage of residents, interns, and fellows poured into my room, spouting medical jargon and terms I'd never heard before and that sounded more than a bit ominous. When Dr. Jackson leaned down to smell my nose, I was really confused.

"Why are you doing that?" Momma asked.

"To see if I can smell any infection."

"What would it smell like if there was an infection?" Momma pressed.

"Rotten bananas. But it doesn't. It seems to be doing okay."

Infection? The very word terrified me. What would happen if I got an infection? I'd heard of people who died from infections.

Then Dr. Turkula, the only female doctor on Dr. Jackson's service, asked, "Does the light still hurt your eyes?"

I said it did and closed my eyes as she turned on the light behind my bed.

"It's normal for them to still be sensitive," she assured me in her soft, gentle voice. Then, using her penlight, she checked the incision across the top of my head.

Was it alright, I wondered. *Why did my head hurt so much? It hurt above my teeth too. Was that normal?*

"Do I have fluid in my sinuses?" I asked. "Do I have a sinus infection?"

"You don't have sinuses anymore," she explained.

"No sinuses? What's there now? And why can't I breathe out of my nose?" It seemed all sorts of quirky things were going on, and I had so many questions. Even when I got the answers, they didn't always make sense.

"Dr. Jackson sewed your nostrils closed," she said.

I vaguely remember hearing Dr. Jackson say the nostrils were sewn up, but I didn't remember why. "Why'd he do that?"

"To keep germs from getting into that open cavity. It's real important that you not get an infection in there."

All I could think of was that I had an "open cavity" in my head. What did that mean? And why did all the doctors seem so thrilled with the outcome of the surgery when I now had an open cavity somewhere in my head, I was in a lot of pain, and I couldn't tolerate light?

As soon as Dr. Jackson and his entourage were gone, I decided to try again to convince my night nurse that Momma should be allowed to stay with me. I took a deep breath and presented my case as convincingly as I could, and then turned my eyes to Momma, my heart racing as panic gripped me. Momma quickly voiced her agreement to the plan, confirming her willingness to stay as long as I needed her.

"You need to talk to Martha down the hall," Shirley said. "She has a good attitude."

What was that supposed to mean? I thought I had a pretty good attitude. I was always nice to the nurses. I was always appreciative. Sure, I was scared. Why wouldn't I be? And why couldn't my momma stay with me?

Lee was no help, immediately siding with the nurse. "You'll be fine, Candy. We'll be here in the morning." His words were meant to reassure me, but they didn't.

Shirley continued to encourage my family to go home, as her comment about Martha and her "good" attitude continued to replay in my mind. "There's one nurse assigned to Candy and three other patients on the hall," she explained. "The best thing for you to do is go back to the hotel and get some rest. Let us take care of Candy. All she has to do is push the button, and the red light goes on outside over her door."

Despite my concerns and protests, Shirley succeeded in convincing everyone that it was in their best interests—and mine—for them to leave. Before doing so, Daddy wrote down the hotel number for me. "Call us anytime," he said.

I checked the number. "Daddy, you wrote 3314. Today you told me the number was 3324."

Their surprise registered on their faces, as Momma said, "Bill, she's right. It is 3324."

Daddy looked relieved. If I could remember numbers, I really must be alright.

◇   ◇   ◇

Raleigh and Dottie came to see me every evening, with Raleigh doing his best to explain things to me.

"Candy, you're not seeing the big picture. Dr. Jackson was able to remove the entire tumor. He also put your face back together again. You're focusing on minor things."

Open cavities, severe pain, and light sensitivity seemed pretty major to me, yet everyone agreed that the outcome of my surgery was miraculous. The tumor was gone, the bones in my face had been replaced, and there was no need to be concerned about other issues that would work themselves out in time. I knew they were probably right, but it was hard to stay focused on that fact.

◇   ◇   ◇

Within days the nurses were encouraging me to walk, just a little at first, but more each time. I didn't resist because I didn't want to stay in bed and risk getting pneumonia, but I also wanted to go down the hall and meet Martha, the one with the good attitude.

Martha had been traveling from Rockford, Illinois, with her fiancé when his small company plane crashed. The plane burst into flames, with

Bill, Martha, and the pilot inside. The pilot and Bill sustained only minor burns, but Martha was seriously injured and had to begin the long and painful recovery process, which included frequent visits to the Mayo Clinic for skin grafts to replace the burned tissue. This was one of those visits.

Shirley walked me down to Martha's room one day, and I stuck my head in the door and introduced myself. "Hi, I'm Candy. I've heard so much about you, so I wanted to come down and meet you."

Her reply was terse and to the point. "Can you come back another time? I've had a bad day."

What was so good about that attitude? Even at my sickest, I was nice to my visitors.

I shuffled back to my room, determined to be a better patient. I'd have to wait to get to know Martha and witness her good attitude some other day.

◇   ◇   ◇

One night during that first week after my surgery, I awoke to a lot of commotion. What could be happening in the middle of the night?

Something with wheels clattered past my closed door. I heard several nurses' hushed voices, and it was obvious they were in a hurry. I'd been in enough hospitals to know that something big was going on.

If only my momma were here! But Shirley and the other nurses had convinced everyone to leave me alone in my room, and now I was terrified. Balled up in a fetal position, I listened as hard as I could, my heart pounding in my ears.

The silence was the worst—no paging of physicians or nurses over the intercom, no noise from the nurses' station. What could it be? Had someone died? Would I be next?

I pushed my nurse's call button and knew the light was on outside my door. Thankfully a nurse arrived quickly.

"Everything is alright now," she assured me. "A patient down the hall aspirated."

"Who was it?" I asked, wondering if it might be Martha or Brenda, the only patients I'd met so far. "And what does aspirate mean?"

As it turned out, it was indeed Brenda, the girl I'd seen in the waiting room that first day at the clinic.

"She's alright, Candy. She just needed to cough up some stuff, but her mouth was wired shut. They had to cut the wires. She's alright now."

Brenda was a teenager, but she'd been having surgeries since she was born. Now she was dealing with aspirating and having her mouth wired shut. No matter how hard I tried, I couldn't get her off my mind the rest of the night; I decided to go talk with her the next day.

I waited until Momma came in the morning, and then she went with me to Brenda's room. Brenda's momma was there too, and as the mothers visited, Brenda and I bonded. I felt like the older professional surgical encourager, but in truth, Brenda was the brave veteran.

"Let's take a picture," I suggested, sitting down on the edge of her bed.

"Your fingernails are painted," she observed, smiling as best she could.

I nodded. "My momma thought it would make me feel better if she painted my nails. She was right!" It also made me feel better to wear a little pink blush on my otherwise anesthesia-yellow face. Pink lip gloss helped, too. There was just something about making myself look healthier that affected the way others responded to me. They commented on how good I looked, and that made me believe I must be doing better. It was a way to "trick" my mind into not being as afraid.

"Say cheese," Momma instructed, as she took several shots of us together. We looked pretty rough, Brenda and I—except for my pretty red fingernails!

◇   ◇   ◇

Meanwhile, news had spread back in Birmingham that Dr. Jackson had not only removed the tumor in its entirety, but he'd also replaced the bones in my face. Letters, cards, flowers, gifts, telegrams, and phone calls flooded my Second Francis private room—not to mention visitors, primarily friends of Dottie and Raleigh.

As I read through the many cards and letters, I noticed something unusual—there were Bible verses on some of them. One in particular kept surfacing: Romans 8:28: "We know that in everything God works for good with those who love him, who are called according to his purpose." I wasn't familiar with it and didn't quite understand it, but I was determined to ask someone about it the first chance I got.

One of the emotions I wrestled with during these first days after surgery, even as I read the many cards and letters of congratulations and well wishes for my recovery, was guilt. A high school friend of mine named Diane had cancer. She was my age and lived in Birmingham with her husband and son, who was Colley's age. The cancer had spread to her liver, and she wasn't expected to live much longer. Dottie also knew her and told me that Diane and her husband had gone to Hawaii for one last trip.

The irony of the situation haunted me. Here I was in the hospital for surgery on what was supposed to have been an inoperable tumor, and it looked like I was going to make it, while Diane was on a farewell trip with her husband.

I knew I wasn't completely out of the woods, but it was obvious God had worked through the surgeons to give me a miraculous outcome, and for the time being, I was doing well. Diane, on the other hand, had been a very involved, outspoken Christian, even back in high school, going so far as to bring in an evangelist to speak to our high school sorority meeting. During his gospel presentation, I'd once again—as I had so many times throughout the years at church—asked Jesus Christ to come into my heart and to forgive me of my sins. Ironically, that was the same day I was elected chaplain of our sorority freshman class, probably because I was known for being very moral. But there in the hospital, beginning my recovery process, I wondered why God would let me, a brand new Christian, live, instead of Diane, who was such a strong Christian and had so much more to give.

"I don't understand, Doug," I said, speaking to my new minister friend who'd stopped by to see me. "Diane is obviously such a better Christian than I am. Why would God do it this way?"

"I can't answer that question," Doug admitted. "At the same time, God isn't looking at the two of you and saying, 'One has to die, and one will live.' He could allow both of you to live if He wanted to, or He could choose for neither of you to live. That's completely His choice."

I imagined he was right, but his answer didn't explain the seeming unfairness of it all.

◇   ◇   ◇

By the time I'd been in the hospital for twelve days, I'd learned I could trust the nurses. They really did come when I pressed the call button, and they really did do what they said they would. When Dr. Laws, my neuro-surgeon, told me it was time for me to be released, I panicked. I didn't think I was ready to be away from the hospital and the care I received there. What if something happened? My head felt so fragile that it seemed it might break. I also had double vision and was wearing a patch over one eye.

"Just one more day," I bargained. "Please, Dr. Laws, let me stay one more day."

He smiled that big smile of his. "Okay, Candy, one more day."

My twenty-four-hour reprieve passed far too quickly, with Raleigh and Dottie showing up bright and early to drive Lee and me to the hotel where we'd stay until I was well enough to go home.

We'd only been at the hotel a few days when I was brushing my teeth and noticed toothpaste coming out of one of my nostrils. *Maybe I just got toothpaste on my upper lip,* I reasoned. After all, my upper lip and the right side of my face were numb. I gargled with mouthwash and noticed green fluid dripping out of my nose. There was no mistake. Something was seriously wrong, as I'd sprung a leak! My heart pounded in overtime, as I realized the nostrils that were supposed to be sewn together inside were obviously not.

When I told Lee what was happening, he suggested I call the clinic. But I didn't want to call the clinic; I wanted to *go* to the clinic—right away.

Dr. Jackson was seeing other scheduled patients when we arrived, so his two residents came in to take a look. They, like everyone else, were so excited that I was doing so well that they didn't seem alarmed that my nose was leaking.

"That's no problem," one of them said. "One of the sutures must have come loose. When you swished the mouthwash around in your mouth, there must have been an opening where you were cut across the top of your teeth. The mouthwash got through and just came out an opening in the nostril. It's no big deal."

No big deal? Well, it certainly was a big deal to me! I was mad that they seemed so unconcerned. All I could imagine was mouthwash sloshing around in my head and coming out of a place in my nose that was supposed to be closed up so I wouldn't get an infection.

"Candy, think of this like a car," the resident said. "You've had a tune-up, but there's one little thing that needs to be fixed. It's not going to make any difference in the car."

"I'm not a car," I said, my anger and irritation evident. "I'm a person, and I'm scared."

The residents had tried their best to comfort me but weren't succeeding. I convinced them to let me see Dr. Jackson.

"So, Candy," he said with his Scottish lilt, "you have mouthwash coming out of your nose." He didn't seem worried either; in fact, he was nearly grinning when he spoke to me.

"And toothpaste!" I added.

"I guess that's better than spaghetti."

I didn't think he was funny.

"Everything looks quite good," he said, obviously pleased at my progress. I still wasn't convinced.

Finally, after seeing how anxious I was, he leaned back in his chair and told me, "Eh, well, I'm not usually good at being a counselor. Do you want a prescription for Valium? That helps with the anxiety. Or I could arrange for you to see a counselor if you'd like."

I declined on the counselor and opted for the Valium, though I was still dissatisfied when I left the clinic. I didn't understand the new anatomy of my head, and I was always anxious about things I didn't understand.

◇   ◇   ◇

After I'd spent two weeks in the hospital and a week with Lee at the hotel, Lee left for home, and Momma flew up to spend my last week in Rochester with me. It was so enjoyable having Momma with me again. She was more sympathetic than Lee, and a lot more fun. Each day we did something to get me outside. We shopped for scarves to cover my shaved head. We ate out, which gave me an incentive to eat, though I had little appetite. I sat at Dottie and Raleigh's apartment pool one day, but I was too weak to be in the heat for long. We also fed the geese at Silver Lake, not far from the clinic.

My last visit to the clinic was bittersweet. In some ways I was sad when Dr. Jackson told me I could go home. I liked the security of being in Rochester, in case something went wrong. I'd grown to like the people, too. Midwesterners are genuinely friendly and welcoming, and everyone at the clinic made a point to cater to the patients, most of whom were from out of town. The crisp, clean town of Rochester held a special spot in my heart because it was the first place I really experienced a relationship with the Lord and saw Him work in very tangible ways in my life. It was a bit like remembering the place you fell in love with someone. Besides, I was ready to see my children. It was time to go home.

10

◇　　　◇　　　◇

A LARGE, BRIGHT YELLOW BOW ON THE MAILBOX AND A "WELCOME home, Candy" banner hung across the porch, greeting me when I got home. Elliott couldn't wait to show me the surprise. "Look, Mom," he exclaimed, his face shining with excitement. "Look what's in your room!"

I stepped into the familiar room to see it decorated with signs of encouragement, written by my many friends, and my heart swelled with gratitude. But despite my pleasure at such a warm welcome, I was exhausted from the trip and couldn't wait to crawl into my own bed for a nap.

I did, but I decided it was the last day I would waste in bed. It was summertime, and I had small children who should be enjoying these long, warm daylight hours. Because of double vision and the fact that I was still taking pain medication, I couldn't drive yet, but I could receive visitors and answer phone calls. My friends, as well as people I didn't know, brought meals so I didn't have to cook. I also had a maid two days a week to help with the everyday household chores so I could conserve my energy for my children. More than ever, I cherished the time I spent before bedtime, reading to Elliott and tucking Colley into her baby bed.

"Thank You for this time, Lord" I whispered, as I rocked little Colleybug a bit longer than usual, her tiny body snuggled up against mine, her head cradled in my arm. In the quietness of her room, I listened to the soft sucking sound of her thumb in her mouth as she held her beloved blanket next to her face. I was enjoying the simple things of life more than I'd ever thought possible.

◇   ◇   ◇

On July 4, our supper club of eight couples and their children had planned a cookout at Judith's house. Still recovering and tiring easily, I decided to stay home and let Lee and the children go. Though I was feeling better, I hadn't yet been around that many people and that much excitement. But within an hour of their leaving, I wanted to be with them. It was two miles to Judith's house, and I was sure I could drive that far.

As I climbed into my car and backed out of the driveway, I found myself thinking, as I so often did those days, *This time last month I didn't even know if I'd live or die, and here I am, driving to a cookout to spend time with my friends and family.*

Of course, everyone was shocked, excited, and also concerned that I'd gotten into the car and driven by myself.

After eating the typical July Fourth grilled burgers and hot dogs, baked beans, and potato salad, we crossed the street to find a place on the country club golf course to sit and watch Birmingham's fireworks display from high atop Red Mountain. I sat on a blanket with Lee and the children, watching the big bursts of bright lights in the sky and thinking, *I can't believe this!* Life actually seemed normal again.

I'd never experienced a July Fourth like that before. I was with my group of girlfriends who'd been in my playgroup since the children were babies; the group later turned into a supper club. They'd been through a lot with me and taken care of my children as if they were their own. It was a very emotional night.

◇   ◇   ◇

After that first real outing on July Fourth, I made it a point to get out at least once a day. It exhausted me, but I felt so much better emotionally than when I stayed cooped up inside. Each day one of my friends picked me up to take me to lunch, which was really good for me because I needed to gain some weight. I'd lost my sense of taste and smell, and had been drinking Ensure for extra calories. People continued to bring dinner to our home each night throughout the remainder of the summer, and I spent as much time as possible with my children, even taking them to the pool for a couple of hours each day.

"Candy, you've got to slow down," Lee warned. "You're going to wear yourself out. Besides, you have time for everybody except me. You're always telling me how tired you are, but the minute the phone rings or someone comes over, your voice changes and all of a sudden you're fine."

He was right. Phone calls and visits from friends and neighbors did revitalize me, but Lee didn't like having our life and household disrupted. He also didn't appreciate all the attention I received when we were out somewhere, though I thrived on it. Still, I'd promised myself that if I survived the surgery, I'd be a better wife to Lee, and I was determined to keep that promise.

What Lee didn't understand and I didn't want to admit, even to myself, was that visiting with friends kept my mind off the negative aspects of cancer. I wanted to do whatever I could to remain hopeful. It seemed a selfish way to think and live, but I knew if I didn't do well emotionally, I probably wouldn't do well physically either.

Besides, I didn't want people to think God wasn't doing His job. As ridiculous as it might sound, I was protecting God, although it wasn't my responsibility to do that, since He was perfectly able to take care of

Himself. And then there were my children. I'd missed them so much while I was in the hospital, and they needed my time. I wasn't quite sure how everything I was going through was affecting them, so I tried to keep things as normal as possible, but by the end of the day, I was exhausted and wanted to sleep.

Lee was right. I was worn out, but I didn't seem able to stop myself. I didn't want to waste one single minute of life. I'd seen how fragile life was, and I didn't want to take it for granted. What if the tumor came back and I'd wasted my time sleeping?

◇   ◇   ◇

Not long after our July Fourth outing, Lee played in a golf tournament, and the awards dance was Saturday night. It was the first big event of the summer that I'd seriously considered attending, and I wanted to look my best.

"If I go, I'm going to look cute," I announced. "I don't want anybody feeling sorry for me. I have to figure out what to wear."

I finally chose a red and white blouse and white pants, accented by a red bandana on my head. Since only the top of my head was shaved, the bandana would completely cover the bald area. My remaining hair was cut below my ears and turned under, so the bandana was a perfect solution.

I felt like a celebrity when I walked into the ballroom. Everyone was so amazed and excited to see Lee and me and to know I was doing so well. Despite the scar down the middle of my face, a crooked eye, and a lumpy forehead bone, makeup had made the difference, and I knew I looked good—even if I was still too thin.

The band was loud, playing Motown hits, and it felt good to dance again. I knew I'd be wiped out the next day, but I was having so much fun that I didn't care.

As we headed for home that night, Lee said, "You like all this attention, don't you?"

Despite my vow to be a better wife, I didn't like his resentful tone. "What do you mean?" I asked, trying not to let my own resentful tone show through.

"I mean, you like it." His voice had moved from resentful to cold and hard. "Don't say you don't."

And so I said nothing.

◇   ◇   ◇

Each month the Christian Women's Organization held a luncheon at a well-known private dining facility called The Club, which sat atop the highest point of Red Mountain, overlooking the city of Birmingham and the surrounding area. Glass windows encircled the 1950s-type structure, and the program always included some girly things, such as a fashion show or flower decorating or how to spruce up your home. Then someone would share a brief testimony about how God had worked in her life. The luncheon was a way for members to bring their non-churched friends to a non-church location.

I'd never been to one of those luncheons until my mom and I were invited to this non-denominational gathering of mostly middle-age-plus women. When we arrived, I was overwhelmed at the number of people who wanted to encourage me.

"My Bible study has been praying for you."

"You're on our Sunday school prayer list."

"Oh, my goodness, are you Candy Wood? Our church has been praying for you."

As I passed behind one table, a lady named Barbara Barker saw me and her face lit up. She reached up and laid her hand on my arm and exclaimed, "Candy, what a surprise! We've all been praying for you, and the girls in my Bible study have kept me informed on how you're doing, but I surely didn't expect to see you out so soon."

I smiled, pleased to see a familiar face. Barbara taught ballet at the same studio as I, and her husband was the minister at Briarwood Presbyterian

Church, where I'd once visited with my boyfriend when I was in the eleventh grade. The unusual thing I remember about that church was that everyone carried a Bible. When the minister mentioned a verse, there was a rustling of pages while everyone found the reference.

Barbara and I didn't know one another well, but I'd often seen her in the studio office, talking to the receptionist. Barbara was a beautiful lady, probably in her early forties at the time. I usually flittered in, got my roll book, and flittered out again, hearing only bits and pieces of Barbara's telling of one of her stories about how God had worked in her life or someone else's.

One day, however, I'd flippantly remarked, "I wish God would work in my life like that."

"Well, you know," Barbara had responded in her beautiful Southern accent, "there's more to being a Christian than *just* being a Christian."

I wondered what that was supposed to mean but didn't bother to ask. I'm sure she'd have been happy to tell me, but I just tossed off a quick retort of "I'll have to try that sometime," and then headed out the door with no idea what I'd just said I'd try.

Now here she was, smiling and telling me how happy she was to see me and how they'd been praying for me. She was interested in hearing all the details of the surgery and the trip to the Mayo Clinic, and somewhere in our conversation I remarked that God had done a miracle, and I wanted people to know that.

Barbara's blue eyes lit up. "I'm sure the girls in my Thursday morning Bible study would love to have you come and share with them, especially since they've been praying for you. Would you mind?"

I was surprised by her question, but it sounded like a good idea, so I agreed, and she said she'd call me with a date.

◇   ◇   ◇

It was a hot, humid August day in Alabama when I made my way to the house where Barbara's Bible study met. I was greeted by approximately two dozen young moms, all about my age. They seemed eager to see me, although I knew only three of them. One was a girl I hadn't seen since high school.

"Candy, when did you become a Christian?" Her question really got my attention. It wasn't that she asked in a way that indicated shock at my being a believer; it was more of a curious question from an excited friend.

Why did she ask that? What does she want, an exact date? I guess in some ways I still associated the word *Christian* with being good, and I figured she'd known me long enough to realize I was a good person. If really pressed for an answer, however, I'd have to say it was the night I'd had the packing pulled from my nose and had finally yielded my life to God. I knew my heart had changed that night, and I hadn't been the same since.

I was surprised that so many women had come for a Bible study on a Thursday morning in the summer. Since most of them were mothers, they must have gotten babysitters for their children so they could attend. I was usually at the country club with my children every morning, and we stayed most of the day. It also didn't seem to matter to these women that the lady in whose home they were meeting didn't even have her dining room decorated. Instead, she had two baby beds set up in there for her newborn twins.

Moments after I arrived, I was shown to my seat, and then Barbara introduced me. All eyes turned toward me, and it was obvious these ladies were eager to hear my story. Being a speech major, I wasn't a bit timid about speaking to a group of people, so I got started and was soon rambling on about every little detail of my un-thought-out presentation. I talked about how lucky I was to go to the Mayo Clinic, and how lucky I was to have Dr. Jackson as a surgeon. I told of the many coincidences that must have been God's interventions. No one seemed to mind that I talked too long, and they politely applauded when I finished.

When it was time to go, I looked around the group and smiled, confident I'd "done my thing." I had no idea what else they did at their meetings, but I imagined it included praying and studying the Bible.

On my way out, Barbara pulled me aside and thanked me for coming. Then she sweetly said, "Candy, be careful when you use the word *lucky*. There's no such word in God's economy. Everything is under His sovereign hand. Also, it would be a good thing to back up what you're saying with scripture."

"Okay," I said. "Thanks." I hugged her goodbye and walked to my car, thinking, *Great! I don't even know any Scripture—well, except for some of the Ten Commandments, the Lord's Prayer, and a couple of Psalms.*

I drove away, wondering about that Bible study and why I hadn't known things like that went on. Those ladies enjoyed being there, and it was obvious they were all friends. I'd never been exposed to anything like that. I knew there were girls in my neighborhood who met at one of the group's home for what they called "Thursday Group," but I thought it was more of an invitation-only social thing. One of my friends went to the group, and I'd once asked her what they did there.

"We study a book or the Bible," she'd answered.

Remembering that event as I drove home, I wondered if my friend had actually said, "We study a book of the Bible." I also remembered my response to my friend's comment about the Thursday Group: "I don't really like to study the Bible. I don't like to pick it apart. I'd rather just take it as it is."

Now I wondered how I could have made such a comment when I didn't know anything about studying or picking apart the Bible—or just "taking it as it is." The only Bible study I'd ever done prior to that time was taking a mandatory New Testament course at Huntingdon, and that was more of a history course than a scriptural study.

More than likely the reason I gave that answer to my friend was because I didn't want her to figure out that I wished I'd been included in their Thursday Group.

Before I got home from the study that day, I realized I'd just been introduced to a different world than the one I'd lived in all my life—and I wanted to know more about it.

◇　　　◇　　　◇

"The Pig" was short for the Piggly Wiggly grocery store in our neighborhood. It was a friendly store, where everyone knew everyone else. I was shopping there one afternoon when I heard someone call my name from the end of the row. I recognized her as a woman named Lee, who also taught dancing at Steeple Arts.

"How are you doing?" she asked, walking toward me. "I want you to know I've been thinking and praying for you."

Lee had always been in the front studio with the three-year-olds, while I was in the back with the older girls. We didn't see one another much, except to pass in the hall between classes, so our relationship was limited.

"We've been praying for you in our Bible study," she announced, and it hit me—another reference to a Bible study. Was I the only Christian on the planet who didn't go to Bible studies?

"Would you like to come to our group?" she asked, almost as if she could read my mind. "We meet every Tuesday morning at my house. Barbara Barker teaches it." Someone had invited me to a Bible study! And it seemed Barbara taught on Tuesdays, as well as Thursdays. Absolutely I'd like to come!

◇　　　◇　　　◇

In September 1982 I attended my first Tuesday Bible study. I didn't recognize any of the women in attendance, other than Lee, who'd invited me, and Barbara. Everyone else was a few years older than I, having gone to the same high school but graduating before I got there. These ladies represented many churches in our area, so it wasn't a "Presbyterian thing." Lee and her across-the-street neighbor Mary Ruth had been best friends since high school. They'd lived a fun and wild life but saw there was something missing. They both became Christians and wanted to share their new life with their friends, so they asked Barbara to teach a Bible study at Lee's house.

I immediately noticed how cute the girls were and how cute they were dressed. I also noticed they all had their Bibles with them.

We piled into Lee's living room, some of us on the sofa and chairs, others on the floor. Barbara had each one introduce herself and then asked me to briefly tell my story. I did, and Barbara asked for prayer requests. The ladies asked for prayer for friends who were ill or going through difficult financial problems; one even asked for the Lord to help sell their house. They requested prayer for people who didn't know the Lord, which was a new one for me.

"Turn in your Bibles to Romans," Barbara instructed after closing the prayer time. Then she explained, "Candy, we're going to study the book of Romans this year."

I smiled and tried not to look too conspicuous as I searched for Romans. When I saw "Romans" listed in the contents, I turned to the correct page, wondering what an epistle was and who Paul might be. But I wasn't about to ask.

◇   ◇   ◇

I looked forward to those weekly studies. The girls were so nice, and I enjoyed getting to know them. And I liked Barbara, both as a friend and a teacher. Finally, I was learning things about the Lord that I'd never heard before. Some of the terms were new to me, and at times my curiosity was almost comical.

I'd raise my hand and ask things like, "Do you mean to tell me that...?" It seemed I was raising my hand at nearly every verse, but no one seemed to mind. In fact, they seemed to enjoy watching me thirst to know and understand the Word of God, even at the expense of slowing them down.

The biggest revelation to hit me as we studied Romans 3 was the necessity of Christ's death—for the sins of the world, but also for me personally. "All have sinned and fall short of the glory of God" in verse 23 meant *me*—moral behavior, church attendance, and all. We were all sinners, and we all needed a sinless Savior to die in our place, to take the punishment we ourselves deserved. The implications of what had happened to me in that hospital room a few months earlier were finally beginning to gel in my mind.

"Grace is God's enablement," Barbara said in answer to one of my questions.

So that's what people meant when they said, "God's grace is sufficient" or "God has given you the grace to deal with your illness." I'd received God's enablement. That made sense to me.

Then, in November, the *Birmingham News* ran a full-page article about me on the front page of the Sunday paper. Beside the full-color picture of me sitting in the living room of my home was my quote in big, bold print: "I wasn't the type to pray for parking places, but I prayed a lot."

The quote was my answer to the reporter's question, "Have you always been religious?"

It seemed everyone in Birmingham saw that article in the paper, and I couldn't help but wonder what they thought about my quote on prayer. Little did I know what "praying a lot" really meant. But I would soon find out.

A few days later, I was home alone. My head hurt, and I was tired. The thought of the tumor recurring terrified me. How would I handle it if I had to deal with it again? If I could figure that out and get it settled in my mind, I was sure I'd be alright. I decided to call Barbara and tell her my concern.

"Don't think about that now," she said. "God will give you the grace when and if that time comes. Just like Corrie ten Boom's father in *The Hiding Place* didn't give her the train ticket until she was ready to board, your Father won't give you the grace until you need it—and not a second too late."

I'd never heard of Corrie ten Boom, but I understood what Barbara was saying. Still, understanding and putting into practice the waiting and not fretting was easier said than done.

"My head really does hurt, Barbara—different than before, but worse."

"What does the doctor say?"

"He says it's normal after having so much work done. How could it be normal for it to hurt worse than before—and more every day?"

"Let's just pray about that," she said, and then prayed for me right there on the phone. It seemed Barbara prayed about everything, and I wasn't used to that.

11

◇　　◇　　◇

I TRIED DESPERATELY TO MAKE CHRISTMAS SPECIAL AND NORMAL, but I couldn't ignore the increasing pain. Each morning when I lifted my head from the pillow, I could fill my cupped hand with nasal drainage. A constant uneasiness lurked inside, telling me something was seriously wrong—again.

"My follow-up doctor told me I was worrying about nothing," I told Dr. Poynor, the E.N.T. who first diagnosed me. "He told me I was an intense patient. But I know I hurt and something isn't right. Will you just culture my nose?"

Dr. Poynor agreed, and after getting the results he told me, "I've never seen this type of infection in the nasal area. It's a good thing we cultured it. My personal opinion is that you go back to the Mayo Clinic."

I didn't waste time making arrangements. I'd known all along that something was wrong, and now I had confirmation.

◇   ◇   ◇

I laughed when my friend Lois showed up wearing an opossum-fur coat and bringing me a gift for my trip. Pointing at her coat, I joked, "That's what I need in Rochester."

Lois immediately took off her coat and handed it to me. "Here, take it. I don't need it. It isn't really cold here anyway."

"But I was just teasing," I argued, trying to hand it back to her. When I realized she wasn't going to take it, I gave in. "Okay. I'll only be gone a few days. I'll get it back to you when I get home."

Since it would be a quick trip and the children had already lived in such confusion over the past several months, I decided to fly to Rochester by myself. When I changed planes in Memphis, the news was out. People were talking. The legendary Coach Bear Bryant had just died. It was Wednesday, January 26. Everyone from Alabama remembers where they were that day.

Dottie and Raleigh picked me up at the Rochester airport.

"I'm going to look good when I go to the clinic, Dottie," I said. "Dr. Jackson's going to see how well I'm doing."

As always when I was worrying, I talked as if I weren't. I knew I wasn't well or I wouldn't have been sent back to the clinic, but this was my coping mechanism. When I prepared for my meeting with Dr. Jackson the next morning, I put on makeup, making sure my cheeks were pink with blush. I dressed in red and black, which were good colors for me, and my hair had grown out on top enough that I no longer wore scarves. I always thought if I looked good and healthy on the outside, I'd get a better report from the doctor.

"He's going to be so proud," I told Dottie, thinking how glad I was that Lois had convinced me to take her coat, as temperatures were in the single digits.

It was good to see Dr. Jackson again, despite my reason for being there. I liked and trusted him, and I knew he'd be able to give me some antibiotics for the strange infection I had.

He poked around with his finger across my forehead and mashed the bridge of my nose with his thumb and forefinger.

"Does that hurt?"

"Yes, but not because you're pushing on it. My whole forehead hurts all the time."

He turned to three residents standing behind him and explained my medical history. Like everyone who heard my story, they were astounded. Dr. Jackson then discussed the infection with them, as well as my options. As I listened, I realized I wasn't going to get some antibiotics and return home. My heart began to race, as that familiar sick feeling invaded my insides.

"The infection is rampant in the forehead, Candy," Dr. Jackson announced, disappointment evident in his voice. "We'll have to go back in tomorrow."

My heart sank. "Surgery again? What kind of surgery?"

"We need to go in and clean out all that infection."

"How do you go in? Through the nose? Where?" I tried to think optimistically, but inside I knew better.

"Eh, just like I did before—across the top of the head." I could tell he was trying to add an optimistic note to his voice, but it wasn't working.

The residents stood listening, not asking any questions. I tried to read their faces to see if it sounded bad to them, but I couldn't tell.

"Will you have to shave my head again?"

"Eh, I don't know. We'll have to see."

Everything was becoming a blur. It was so quick and unexpected. I hadn't even been thinking about surgery, and now I was being rushed in within a matter of hours.

Here we go again. I knew something was wrong....

Dr. Jackson was talking again, and I tried to focus.

"You'll need to go to photography first. My nurse will take you."

Each of the residents gave me a sort of "I'm-sorry" smile as I got up to walk past them.

"Do you have someone with you?" Dr. Jackson asked.

"Yes, sir. Dottie Kent is with me." I was an adult, and Dr. Jackson probably wasn't that much older than I, but I still said "sir," as I felt young and vulnerable at the moment.

Photography was right down the hall, and I already knew the way. They took front and side pictures of my face, and by the time Dottie picked me up to take me to their apartment to gather my things for the hospital, I was numb.

"You know everything will be alright," she said. "Dr. Jackson knows what he's doing." I didn't know if she really believed that, but her soft voice and gentle manner were soothing, and I needed that.

◇　　　◇　　　◇

The nurses on Second Francis had written on my Styrofoam pitcher, "Welcome back, Candy." It was all so familiar, and to some extent re-assuring to be remembered.

"Is your family here?" one of the nurses asked.

"No. I didn't think I'd be here long. I didn't know I'd have to have surgery. My mom is flying up. She'll be here later tonight." I smiled. "But Dottie's here."

After dinner, Dottie left to go to the airport to pick up Momma. In between nurses' visits, I was alone. Everything had happened so quickly that I hadn't had time to get anyone back home to pray for me. I wanted the girls in my Bible study to pray; I just hoped it wasn't too late to reach someone.

I called Barbara and was so relieved when she answered. "Would you mind seeing if everyone could get together tomorrow to pray for me while I'm in surgery? I'm going in at nine."

She wanted the details to pass on and promised to get everyone together to pray. Soon Momma and Dottie arrived. With Momma there, I knew everything would be alright.

12

◇　　　◇　　　◇

SURGERY WAS SCHEDULED FOR NINE THAT MORNING. I'D HAD NOTHING to eat or drink since midnight, and I wasn't prepared mentally or spiritually for what I was about to face. I wished I knew some appropriate scriptures for the situation. So many of the Christians I'd been meeting lately seemed to know just the right verses to apply to any occasion.

Since the night in May when I'd surrendered my life to Jesus Christ, the Bible had suddenly begun to make sense to me. Verses seemed to jump off the page and speak to me at exactly the right time and circumstance. I still wondered if God worked that way, but I'd seen it happen too many times to doubt it.

"What time is it?" I asked Momma, who'd been there since six that morning.

"It's nine-thirty. They must be running behind."

I needed to do something, but what? I couldn't just sit there with Momma and Dottie and wait. What would we talk about?

"I want to call my Bible study group. I need to talk to someone who can give me some scriptures. They're meeting at Paula's house today, and I know I wrote the number down somewhere."

While Momma looked for the number, a nurse came in to tell me they were almost ready for me and to give me a shot of Demerol. I had to hurry if I was going to make the call before the shot kicked in and made me drowsy.

Momma dialed the number and handed me the phone. A little girl answered.

Hoping she'd hurry, I asked, "May I speak to Paula, please?"

"No, ma'am," her polite little voice answered. "My momma's praying for someone."

"I know. It's me. She's praying for me. So will you get her?"

"No, ma'am. My momma said that under no circumstances am I ever to interrupt her while she's praying."

I wanted to say, "Who cares? Why mind your mother? I didn't always mind mine!" Instead I urged, "Just go get your momma, okay?"

I heard her put the receiver down, and within a couple of minutes she was back.

"My momma said no."

In the meantime, the orderly came to take me to the holding area. I was mad as he transferred me from my hospital bed to the gurney. I wanted to talk to my friends before I went to surgery, and I wasn't about to lie down on that gurney.

"I want to sit up," I said, as the orderly pulled the lightweight blanket over my legs.

I wasn't really mad at the attendant, of course; I was mad at God, and I told Him so—out loud. "All I wanted was to talk to my friends, to have someone read scriptures to me. Why didn't You let that happen?"

The nice young man in the white orderly's coat didn't say a word. He continued to wheel me down the long corridor while I huffed and puffed at God, my arms crossed over my chest and my aching forehead puckered in a frown. My appeal made perfect sense to me, and I wanted God to know He was wrong in not seeing things my way.

"I don't think it's fair," I grumbled. "In fact, I think it's mean! All I wanted to do was talk to my friends and hear some scriptures. After all, You wrote them! I don't see why You wouldn't let me hear them, especially since You know they're the only thing that comforts me. I just don't know any by heart yet!"

I was afraid, and like a child with her parent, I wanted some attention. I was still mad when I arrived in the holding area, still sitting with my arms crossed over my chest while they situated my stretcher in a row with other waiting patients. Lined up with our heads against the wall, we faced about seven more patients lined up against the wall across from us.

I'd been told the clinic had fifty-three operating rooms in use, and all the patients waited in the same holding area to be taken to one of them. The area had speakers in the corners of the room, with piped-in elevator-type music to help calm the waiting patients. Most of us had some sort of pre-op medication to calm or sedate us, but that day I was not calm, and I was not sedated. I was still mad at God—and very much afraid.

I looked across at the patients facing me. Their eyes were closed. They all wore the typical hospital gowns and disposable green shower caps, and they were covered with green surgical sheets, tucked in around them. I wanted to comfort them somehow; actually, I wanted to comfort myself.

"Y'all," I called in my Southern accent, the Demerol slurring my words. "Idn't it goodaknow that God..." I paused, did my best to sit up straight, and then stretched my arms out wide, "can take care of *all* of us..." I brought my arms into my chest on the word *all* to show what I meant and then finished my sentence. "...at the same time?"

Exhausted, I fell backward onto the bed.

A man's voice answered from across the room, "Honey, isn't it the truth?"

"Mrs. Wood," the nurse asked, leaning over to speak to me and pointing in the direction of the man who'd spoken to me, "would you like me to move your stretcher next to his?"

"Yes, ma'am. Please." The Demerol had taken effect and I was looped, but I knew I wanted to talk with this man.

With my gurney next to his, I turned my head toward the older man and introduced myself as best I could. "I'm Candy. What's your name?"

"I'm Hank."

"What's wrong with you?" I asked, my voice sluggish.

"Kidney stone. What about you?"

"They're gonna cut my head open."

Hank's eyebrows raised slightly. "Are you a Christian?"

I laughed. "You don't think I'd let them cut my head open if I wasn't a Christian, do you?" At least I knew I'd go to heaven if I died while I was in surgery, and I wanted him to understand that.

"Are you afraid?"

I trusted that God would take care of me, but I was still afraid. "I know God'll take care of me," I said, wanting to believe that.

He seemed totally alert and lucid, but I thought I was, too. Then he talked to me about being involved in some sort of Christian businessmen's group in North Carolina. I was drifting in and out of consciousness, so I didn't quite hear everything, but I understood the part about his being a Christian.

Still wishing I'd had a chance to hear some scriptures from my friends, I asked, "What's your favorite Bible verse?"

"It's funny you should ask. Just last week I decided not to listen to the radio or watch television, but to memorize scriptures instead. I'll tell you what I memorized." Then he began to quote Romans 8: "There is therefore now no condemnation for those who are in Christ Jesus.... I consider that the sufferings of this present time are not worth comparing with the glory that is to be revealed to us.... We know that in everything God works for good with those who love him, who are called according to his purpose" (vv. 1, 18, 28).

I was sleepy, but I was catching most of what he was saying, and I was excited because I knew I really did love God and I wasn't mad at Him anymore.

"If God is for us, who is against us?" Hank continued. "Who shall separate us from the love of Christ? Shall tribulation, or distress, or persecution, or famine, or nakedness, or peril, or sword?" (vv. 31, 35).

Then I heard him say, "No, in all these things we are more than conquerors through Him who loved us" (v. 37).

I interrupted his recitation and exclaimed, "You're right, Hank! I am more than a conqueror!" At that moment, Demerol or not, I could have conquered the world. Nothing could separate me from the love of God. Nothing!

I'd heard the scriptures I needed, and I was ready to go to surgery—ready to go to battle.

"Candy," Hank said.

I looked at the man who'd shared thirty-nine verses of scripture with me, not to mention with all the other patients and medical personnel in the room that day.

"Nothing can touch you that hasn't already been sifted through the hands of a loving God first." He stretched out his arm to me, separating his fingers with his palm up, as they came to take me to the operating room.

> *Nothing can touch you that hasn't already been sifted through the hands of a loving God first.*

"Bye, Hank," I called. "I'll pray for you till they put me to sleep."

"I'll pray for you too, Candy!"

The vision of his outstretched hand went with me into surgery.

◇　　◇　　◇

"The bandages are too tight, Momma. Can't they loosen them?"

Instead of being placed in intensive care after surgery, I'd been taken to a four-unit room with a nurse assigned to the four of us. Even so, I was glad to have Momma beside my bed, watching out for me.

"I'll ask again," Momma said, "but the nurse already checked and said they're alright."

My eyes were nearly swollen shut, but I could tell when the nurse arrived and was standing beside my bed. I repeated my complaint about the bandages, but she assured me they were fine.

I complained throughout the night, and by the time I was moved to a private room the next morning, the pain was unbearable. One of the nurses finally made a call to a resident, rather than calling Dr. Jackson on a Saturday. The resident granted permission to loosen the bandages, which eased my pain only slightly.

That evening a young couple came to see me. I was still hurting and not able to talk much, but Momma was there to talk with them while I listened.

"I'm Edwin Morris," the man said in his deep south Alabama accent, "and this is my wife, Mary. My grandmother lives down the street from your grandmother in Wetumpka, and she wanted me to check on you."

It was obvious my mother was excited to meet someone from her hometown. "Wetumpka? Is your mother's name Theresa? We went through school together!"

As it turned out, Edwin's mother, Theresa, had grown up in Wetumpka but moved to Headland, Alabama, when she got married. Both Edwin and Mary had graduated from the University of Alabama, and now Edwin was doing his residency in internal medicine at the Mayo Clinic, while his wife worked at the clinic as a secretary.

Edwin, Mary, and Momma had a nice long visit, and then this friendly couple left, promising to return when I was feeling better.

They were just two of the steady stream of visitors that came to see me over the weekend, but I really couldn't enjoy them much, as I was still in a lot of pain. However, they helped pass the time for me, and they were good for Momma too, as she was there all day with me, usually until around midnight.

◇　　　◇　　　◇

Monday morning arrived, and with it came bad news. Dr. Jackson came to check on me. When he removed the bandages, he discovered my forehead skin had begun to necrose, or die, due to lack of blood supply to the area.

I heard him tell my momma, "She may need a skin graft on her forehead." He didn't replace the bandages before he left, and that helped ease the pain and tightness I'd been experiencing across my forehead and temples, but my spirits continued to sag. I didn't know what a skin graft would involve, but I knew it meant another surgery. After hurting all weekend, I was very teary and emotional, knowing I had to face another operation.

It seemed every day brought more bad news, and I found myself crying a lot and questioning God. Just seven months earlier He'd performed a miracle, using Dr. Jackson to not only remove the tumor but also to restore my face. Now everything was going wrong. I'd been talking and praying with my friends back home; the girls in my Bible study were praying, as were people in many churches; I listened to praise music on my cassette player; I read the Scriptures. I still loved the Lord, but I was very confused.

Why did He perform a miracle and then take it back? My children needed me at home, yet it seemed I'd never get there. I didn't want to appear ungrateful, but nothing seemed to be working. Wasn't God in control of that? Why didn't He do something?

◇　　　◇　　　◇

It was late on Monday evening, and Second Francis was quiet. The visitors had gone home—except for Momma, of course. The nurses worked quietly at their station, and the TVs were either turned off or way down. No one was in the halls. Patients were allowed to get drinks and ice from the small kitchen if they wished, so I decided to go down the hall to get a drink. On the way I glanced into the waiting room and noticed someone sitting in the dark. As I got closer, I saw it was a girl with extremely long brown hair. Her bowed head kept me from seeing her face, but I could tell she was crying. I sat down beside her.

"Are you alright? Is there anything I can do?"

Without looking up, she shook her head no.

"Are you having surgery tomorrow?"

She nodded.

"Are you scared?"

She started to nod, then shook her head no again.

"Who's your doctor?"

"Dr. Jackson."   ·

"He's my doctor, too. He's really good. What are you having done?"

With her head still down, she answered, "My face."

"He operated on my face, too," I said, taking it upon myself to be the veteran surgery patient and comforter. "Twice. It'll be okay. I had cancer surgery back in June. Now I have an infection. I had surgery again last Friday." I paused. When she didn't move or lift her head, I said, "Stay here. I'll be back in a minute."

I went to my room to tell Momma about the girl and how I needed to go back and talk to her about Jesus. Forgetting my own despair at the thought of more surgery, I was now on a mission.

"She's having surgery tomorrow," I told Momma, "and I need to know if she's a Christian."

I went back to the waiting room, relieved to see she was still there, right where I'd left her. I soon discovered her name was Sharon. She was married and lived in northern Minnesota, and she had children the same age as mine. When we started talking about our children, she finally looked up, though her long hair still covered one side of her face.

"What kind of surgery is Dr. Jackson doing tomorrow?" I asked.

She pushed her hair back, revealing her disfigurement. "I had a normal face until I was seven or eight, and then the bones began to dissolve—but just on one side."

"So what's Dr. Jackson going to do tomorrow?" I asked, knowing it couldn't be any worse than my first surgery and hoping I could be of some comfort to my new friend.

"He's going to build my face back with some bone and tissue grafts. Did they have to shave your head?"

I nodded. "Only across the top. It's grown back some." I thought I was being encouraging, but she began to cry again.

"Are you upset about having your head shaved and losing all your beautiful hair?"

She nodded, admitting she hadn't cut her hair in years. It hung below her waist, but tomorrow it would be gone.

"I'm…sorry," was all I could think to say. I tried to talk to her about spiritual things, but she wasn't interested. She stated that her parents were Catholic, and that seemed to close the subject.

"Let me pray for you," I offered.

She didn't argue, and after praying, I hugged her, and then we said goodnight and parted ways to our separate rooms.

◇   ◇   ◇

Thursday marked nearly a week since I'd been in the hospital, and on Wednesday a heavy snowstorm blew through the area, preventing Mary and Dottie from coming to see me. Momma was in a motel directly across the street from the hospital, so she came every day. Trudging through the snow in the early morning hours, she made it a point to be there when the doctors arrived to do their rounds. She didn't return to her motel room until late at night.

Dr. Marsh and his team of neurosurgery residents came daily to check on me, along with Dr. Jackson and his team of residents.

"Candy, you may lose your forehead bone later," Dr. Marsh informed me on Thursday evening, after seeing the films of my CT scan and skull x-rays.

What did that mean? Dr. Jackson had said I might need a skin graft, but now Dr. Marsh was saying I might lose the entire forehead bone. What was happening?

Later that afternoon, a neurosurgery resident named Fred who'd been involved in my first surgery seven months earlier came by to explain.

"Candy, the forehead bone is hot. It needs to be removed. Infection is rampant."

Dottie tried to make me feel better, but I was very emotional and teary. My whole body was a wreck. I wasn't hungry even for the red beans and rice that Mary brought when she and Edwin came that afternoon. It was becoming noticeable that I was losing weight, which in turn made me weaker. It seemed to be a downhill spiral that no one was able to stop.

On Friday morning, February 4, one week after my surgery, all the doctors involved came in to examine my forehead and scalp. Some of the stitches across the top of my head were removed—then more bad news.

I was sent back to the operating room, with no time to prepare myself. Once again the scalp was pulled down to irrigate the area of infection. Somehow the incision down the side of my nose from the week before had burst open and needed to be re-stitched.

When I returned to my room after my short time in surgery, I had a new incision across the top of my head and a drainage tube with a bulb at the end to collect the infected fluid from my head. I couldn't stop crying, no matter what I did. I tried calling friends who were taking turns watching Colley and Elliott until Lee got home from work in the evening. I missed my children and wanted them to hear my voice and know I loved them. But even that made me sad.

When people called to see how I was, I got sad thinking how sweet they were to check on me. Each time I received flowers or balloons or a card, I cried. I cried when Raleigh and Dottie left that day for the Cayman Islands, although I was happy for them and hoped they'd have a wonderful time.

I was still crying when the nurse came in to check on me and discovered my tube wasn't draining properly. I cried as she explained the situation to my momma.

"Candy may need some blood. That may be one of the reasons she's so teary and blue. I'll check on that."

Later that evening I received a pint of blood, and it did seem to lift my spirits.

The one bright spot in the middle of all this was the Bible verses I received from so many people, even if I didn't always understand them. I'd call Barbara, and she'd patiently explain them to me.

On Saturday morning I received another pint of blood. Lee was due in late Saturday afternoon, and Mary went to the airport to pick him up. By the time he checked into the motel and got to the hospital, I felt like a new person. Apparently the extra blood really helped.

I felt well enough to go to the floor lobby with Sharon, one of the patients I'd met earlier, and Bob, a burn patient from Iowa. The three of us, all about the same age, were quite a sight in our hospital gowns, dragging our IV poles beside us. Sharon and I still had our drainage tubes coming from our heads and pinned to our gowns. We called ourselves the "gruesome threesome," and it felt good to laugh again.

Although I wasn't better physically, the pain medicine was working, and after having the blood transfusions, my spirits were a little better—at least for the weekend.

◇   ◇   ◇

On Monday, Dr. Schultz removed the drainage tube and said I might be able to go home for a visit the next weekend, since my temperature was down. That was some of the best news I'd heard in a long time.

Lee's flight to Birmingham left at six on Tuesday morning, so he came by early to say goodbye. The next day, February 9, would be Elliott's seventh birthday, and I so wanted to be home to give him a party. Lee and his dad, along with my dad, were going to take Elliott and his friends to Chuck E. Cheese, which I knew he'd enjoy, but it didn't seem right that I couldn't be there to help.

I also knew my hopes of going home without more surgery were fading fast. I wasn't improving. The stitches on the side of my head were still draining instead of healing. I had no appetite and continued to lose weight. The IV was problematic and had to be changed almost daily, meaning they had to find new places to stick me. My scalp had patches of dead, black skin, and I looked almost as bad as I felt. I knew I was going downhill. It was time to fight or give up.

After almost two weeks in the hospital, becoming thinner and weaker each day, I began to notice a cycle. When I kept my eyes focused on Jesus, I did better. When I took my eyes off Him, I began to focus on circumstances. Then I lost my appetite and didn't want to eat. I became teary and depressed, and weaker by the day. The only thing that broke that negative cycle was to once again fix my eyes on Jesus. It was like riding a spiritual roller coaster, and I knew I needed to get off that ride once and for all.

I started picking out where I was in the cycle, and then I'd make a concentrated effort to read my Bible and see what God had to say. The Scriptures told me that God would never leave or forsake me; He'd be my strength; He'd carry my burden…. Then something would go wrong. The IV would stop, or I'd get some disconcerting information on my condition, and my eyes would move from Jesus to my circumstances. Depression and discouragement became my constant companions.

Dr. Michael See, who'd been on Dr. Jackson's service during my first surgery at the clinic, was so good about stopping by to see me.

"Things aren't going so well, Mike," I told him when he came on Thursday.

"It's real unusual to find sarasha infection in the head," he commented, his tone sympathetic but puzzled. "It's usually found only in old, debilitated people."

Dr. See wasn't the only one puzzled by my condition. No one seemed able to get a handle on it, no matter how much they pumped me with antibiotics. I could see the concern on their faces, which didn't do much to help my outlook. I had to stop looking at the circumstances and keep my eyes where they needed to be—on Jesus.

I continued to read the Scriptures, and each time I came across one I didn't understand, I picked up the phone and called Barbara. Graciously, she took the time to explain them, helping me grow stronger in my faith and understanding of God's Word.

◇   ◇   ◇

During my time at the hospital, I made friends with other patients and their families, and they often stopped by to see me. Sharon had been released but was still in town. Her surgery had gone well, and Dr. Jackson didn't have to shave her head. Sharon and her husband, Richard, visited me every day, as did Mary and Edwin and a new friend, Linda Longshore from Birmingham. Raleigh and Dottie were still out of town, but their friends made sure I didn't feel abandoned.

News had spread back home that I was in the hospital, and cards, gifts, and flowers poured in. The steady stream of visitors, which primarily consisted of ten couples who were doing residency programs at the Mayo Clinic, continued in and out of my room. Dottie and I had christened them the "Southern Connection" because they were all from the South and friends of Dottie and Raleigh's.

However I might be feeling, I always perked up for visitors. It was as if God sent them to cheer me up. If people didn't come to see me, I walked down the hall to introduce myself to the other patients and visit with them.

I decided I needed to have a schedule. I wasn't going to allow myself to grow weaker by lying around in bed all day, so I planned everything. Mornings were busy, with doctors making rounds and breakfast trays coming and going. I didn't eat much, just some hot cereal and juice, but it was something, and it was the only meal I liked.

After breakfast it was time for one of my two daily baths. The warm water felt so good on my sore body, and it also made me feel better to be clean.

Following my bath, I watched *Love Boat* and then took a nap before lunch, which I rarely ate. Visitors broke up most of the afternoon and evening, and then I watched *M*A*S*H* at nine. A bittersweet comedy, set in a mobile Army surgical hospital (thus M*A*S*H) unit in Korea, the long-running comedy kept me laughing, something I really needed to do.

◇   ◇   ◇

On Friday morning, Dr. Schultz came to check on me, and I told him, "I was supposed to go home today."

"I know. I'm sorry that didn't work out. I'm afraid I have some bad news for you. I know how much you like getting out to visit the other patients, but you're going to have to be put in isolation because of your infection."

"Isolation?" Hot tears sprang to my eyes as I spoke the word. "What does that mean?"

"It means you'll need to stay in this room and not go out anymore. You can't receive any patients as visitors. You can have other visitors. They'll need to wear the yellow gowns that they can put on before coming in here and then discard them in a receptacle outside the door when they leave." As he checked my incisions and the skin on my forehead, he went on to explain that I was contagious to other patients with open wounds.

"The middle area seems to be leaking air," he commented.

Leaking air? I'd barely stopped reeling from hearing the word isolation, and now he was telling me I was leaking air? The implications of that fact scarcely registered, as I focused on his first announcement. I was devastated about being isolated from the other patients. That meant I couldn't visit with them in their rooms or mine, or even in the sunroom at the end of the hall, and I couldn't take baths or go to the kitchen to get the grape juice and crushed ice I liked so much. It seemed I had so few pleasures left, and now even those were being taken away.

God, what's going on? I love meeting everybody, and now You've taken that away. And my baths are such a luxury! Why did You take those away too? What else are You going to take away? I don't mean to whine and complain, but are You trying to teach me something? Because if You are, I'm not getting it. It looks like I'll be stuck here in my room with nobody to talk to. I won't get any exercise, and I'll just wither away.

It was a definite setback, and I easily slipped into the martyr role. I wasn't rejoicing as the Bible instructed me to do, and I certainly wasn't thankful in my circumstances. As soon as Momma arrived, I told her exactly how I felt.

Momma, as always, did her optimistic best to cheer me up. "Well, you can still have visitors, just not the other patients."

"Yeah, but that's not all. I miss Colley and Elliott, too. I was just going to come up here and get some antibiotics; instead, I've been here two weeks, and now I'm in isolation. Couldn't the children fly up with Daddy tomorrow? It would really help if I could see them."

Momma reminded me that Daddy already had his ticket; we also discussed the situation and agreed it might be best for the children not to see me in my current condition.

"Momma, what if I die?" I wasn't trying to be dramatic; I was asking a very serious question.

"Oh, Candy, you're not going to die. Remember the Bible verse God gave you at Tricia's house that night? You're going to live and declare the works of the Lord."

Sometimes I thought that verse was more for her than for me. She never wavered in believing it.

"Besides," she reminded me, "you've got to live to write that book. I'm already taking notes."

She was right. Momma kept a daily, detailed journal. She recorded every visitor, every gift, and every phone call in the red spiral notebook. She took pictures of me in each stage, and she took pictures of everyone who visited me. Momma had a way of making everything special—even an extended stay in the hospital.

13

◇　　　◇　　　◇

VALENTINE'S DAY, MY FAVORITE HOLIDAY, WAS ONLY THREE DAYS AWAY. I couldn't imagine spending it in isolation!

Each year as a little girl I looked forward to February when my teacher set aside time for us to make something special to hold the Valentines from our friends. One year it was a cigar box, adorned with hearts and cupids. My favorite was the year we made a cardboard mailbox out of a shoebox. It was so much fun to pull out our scissors and paste, the kind where the brush was attached to the lid of the plastic jar. It smelled so good! I liked everything about making those masterpieces. Cutting hearts out of red and pink construction paper, using white paper doilies, ribbons, and hearts—I liked it all!

The room mother, usually my momma, brought homemade cup-cakes and red Kool-Aid, and we each got a box of little sugar hearts with

"Be Mine" or "I Luv U" on them. As I got older, Valentine's Day meant sending and receiving specially chosen cards, red roses, and even a box of chocolates from someone special. Valentine's Day, 1983, however, was spent in isolation, waiting for another surgery—anything but exciting.

As I lay in bed feeling sorry for myself, I looked up and saw Mr. Weipert standing in the doorway. Mr. Weipert's son, Bob, stood out in the hallway, behind his father. Being a burn patient, Bob wasn't allowed into my room because I was in isolation.

Dressed in a flannel shirt, jeans, cowboy boots, and Western hat—most of which were covered by the required yellow gown—Mr. Weipert struck a rugged pose. His leathery face showed years of hard work on their Iowa farm. He seemed out of character with the gift he held in his dry, suntanned hand—a big heart-shaped box of chocolates, covered in red satin and trimmed in frilly white lace with artificial roses on top, not what I would have expected from this tough but dear man.

"This is from Bob and me," he said, smiling as he walked over to my bed and proudly handed me an early Valentine gift, while Bob looked on from outside my room. Though they didn't stay long, their gift touched me more than any of the many other Valentine's gifts I received over the next few days.

◇   ◇   ◇

Dressed in a shirt, tie, and slacks and covered with a yellow gown, Daddy wasn't prepared for the way I looked when he arrived on Saturday. "What are they doing to my little girl?" he asked, hugging me and giving me a kiss.

"I'm okay," I insisted, not wanting to worry him. "I'm doing fine."

He frowned. "What do we have here? What's all this black on your forehead?"

"It's where the skin has died, Bill," Momma assured him. "They're going to take care of it if it doesn't get better."

"I know that's where the skin died," Daddy said, "but what are they going to do about it?"

"They're going to do a skin graft, Daddy," I told him, wishing I felt as confident as I tried to sound. "Martha's back here at the clinic, and she just had some grafts done last week. She's doing okay, and I'll be alright, too." I smiled, hoping to encourage him to do the same. "Look, Daddy." I held my nose and blew lightly. The black skin on my forehead bulged.

Daddy's face turned ashen, and he turned to Momma. "Bett, we're in trouble."

Even Momma looked worried now. "What do you mean?"

Seeing the concern on Momma's face and hearing it in her voice, I became frightened. Maybe I was worse off than I realized.

"Air isn't supposed to be under the skin," Daddy said. "There's a leak somewhere."

A wave of faintness swept through me, as I recalled Dr. Schultz's mention of a leak, and I realized Daddy was right. We were in trouble.

◇   ◇   ◇

Sunday, February 13, was the beginning of my third week in the hospital. I was in isolation, the infection was rampant, and no one seemed able to stop its spread. Raleigh and Dottie had returned from their trip and were there in their yellow gowns, visiting me and doing their best to cheer me up when Dr. Jackson arrived.

Dr. Jackson had also been out of town on a week's vacation, thinking he'd left me in decent shape. When he showed up that evening, I was relieved. I'd missed him, and I was more comfortable when he was there, even if it was just for short visits. Dressed in a smoky blue-gray sport coat and carrying my chart under his arm, he walked in and greeted my mom and me, but there was something different in his manner. His suntanned face was creased with concern, although he smiled as he sat on the edge of my bed. He didn't seem in the least bit pressed for time.

"Did you have fun on your ski trip?" I asked.

In an obvious attempt to keep the mood somewhat lighthearted, he replied that he would have except that he thought about me every time he got on the chair lift. He said he'd been checking in with the hospital and knew I hadn't been doing well.

"I wanted to come and talk to you myself. Everything we've tried has failed," he said, his voice somber as he enumerated all the things that had gone wrong during his week away. The forehead skin had begun to die, turning black and flaky due to probable lack of blood supply to the area. The forehead bone was still rampant with infection and was not responding to the mega-bags of antibiotics that were being pumped into my bruised arms.

Honest about my dire situation, he said he'd have to operate again. "The forehead bone and skin will have to be removed. There's no way to save them. The antibiotics haven't worked. I'm sorry; I feel totally responsible."

Speaking deliberately, he made sure I comprehended everything he said. "I'll rotate the skin from the back of your head to the front, to cover the brain, and then use a skin graft to cover the skull on the back of your head. The donor site will be more painful than the head itself...."

I lost him somewhere in the middle of his explanation, picking up only the word *donor*. I didn't realize he was referring to a donor site from which the skin would be taken from my body; I understood it to be from another person.

He looked at the chart in his lap, his disappointed face saying it all. Hating to see him that way, I took his hand in mine and told him I was sorry things didn't turn out. "Dr. Jackson, it's okay. God has taken care of me so far; He won't stop now."

He looked at me and said, "Candy, you'll have a skin graft on the back of your head. You won't ever have hair there again. You'll be bald."

"So I'll wear a wig."

"I don't think you understand. You'll look worse when you leave here than when you came."

Impulsively, I lifted his hand to my lips and kissed it. "It'll be alright. See, I'm already ahead of the game. Seven months ago I was told I'd lose the greater portion of my face—not to mention both eyes. No one in

Birmingham wanted to touch me with a ten-foot pole. You took a chance. You made a judgment call, and it worked. You saved my face and got the tumor. This time you made a judgment call again, and it didn't work. But I'm still ahead. I won't have my forehead, but I'll have the rest of my face. That's more than I thought I'd have."

"But, Candy," he said, obviously still struggling, "I have some pride here."

I knew some of his team thought the forehead bone should have been removed earlier, which might possibly have saved the skin. But Dr. Jackson had made the choice to try to save my entire face. It hadn't worked.

I kissed his hand one more time and smiled. "I'll be alright, I promise."

He stayed a moment longer, and then stood up to leave.

"I have one last request," I said.

"What's that?"

"Tomorrow before you operate, will you pray with me?"

He nodded and smiled, then walked out and pulled the door shut behind him.

◇   ◇   ◇

Dr. Jackson hadn't been gone long when I received more bad news. Martha, speaking from experience, called me from her room to tell me she was leaving. She'd been through so much, and she still had more surgeries ahead of her, but for now, she was going home. I was glad to hear that, but then she broke the news to me about what to expect regarding my upcoming skin graft. "It will hurt like heck, and the donor skin will come from your own body. I just don't want you to be surprised."

I appreciated her honesty. I would miss Martha and her family, but at least I knew what to expect.

◇   ◇   ◇

"Candy knows everyone in this hospital," Dr. Schulz announced when he and an unfamiliar resident made rounds on Monday afternoon. Most of the residents were about my age, and we were on a first-name basis by then.

"Paul," I said to Dr. Schultz, "do you know Martha, Dr. Iron's patient? She told me today that the skin graft is coming from me. What part of me does it come from?"

He explained it would probably be taken from the top of my leg.

"But what goes in its place?"

"Your skin will heal there. Only the top layer is removed. It'll be a little more sensitive there, and you'll need to protect that area from the sun, but it should heal just fine."

After they left, Momma and Daddy and I were alone. "I don't understand what's going to protect her brain if they remove her forehead bone," Daddy said, shaking his head as he thought aloud. "What's going to keep her from getting more infection if they open up that area again?"

"Try not to be so negative," Momma said. "She'll be alright."

"That's what they've been saying all along, and she isn't alright. She's had enough antibiotics for a lifetime. I don't like her having so many antibiotics. They're not good on her stomach."

Momma and I were used to Daddy's pessimism and worrying about worst-case scenarios. We knew it was because he loved me and felt frustrated over his inability to "fix" this situation.

"Daddy, I have an infection. I have to have antibiotics to clear it up."

"I know, I know," he admitted, his head drooping as he rubbed my knobby knees. "I just don't like to see my little girl not doing so well."

The nurse came in then to check my vital signs, patting softly around the red puffy place on my hand where the IV needle was taped.

"Your hands clean?" Daddy asked.

"Yes, sir, they are," she assured him, smiling as she inserted the needle. Then she turned to me. "I don't know if this one is going to make it, Candy. We'll probably have to replace it before you go to surgery tomorrow. Do you want a hot towel on it?"

"She's not going to have to have anymore blood, is she?" Daddy asked.

"I don't know."

"She's already had two pints. Do you know where that blood came from? The guy didn't have hepatitis, did he?"

Momma and I started to laugh. Daddy was usually the one who kept everybody in stitches, but that Valentine's Monday he didn't seem to think anything was funny.

"The Mayo Clinic has its own blood donors," the nurse assured him. "They're checked out pretty thoroughly."

"Bill," Momma suggested, "why don't you walk down to Baskin Robbins and get us some ice cream?"

I really didn't want any ice cream, but Daddy took our orders and walked the few blocks through the snow to the ice cream store.

"Thanks, Momma," I said. It seemed my momma always knew what to do, whatever the circumstances.

◇   ◇   ◇

Something had happened between Dr. Jackson and me the night he told me how he felt and I kissed his hand; we bonded. He may not have noticed it, but I did. I found myself deeply attached to him after that, and I couldn't get him off my heart.

Maybe it was because I saw him so disappointed that things didn't work out for me. Maybe it was because I knew God had specifically chosen him and worked through him to save my life, and that made him special to me. I'm sure other patients felt that way about him, too, but for me, there was more.

Spiritually, I had a burdened heart for him. In the seven months I'd been home after the first surgery, I found a deep, personal relationship with the Lord that I'd never before experienced. I had a craving for the Word of God, and I was excited when some new truth was revealed to me from the Scriptures. I underlined and marked verses and words, just like my friends who'd come to see me with their Bibles the summer before.

As hard, painful, confusing, and emotional as the last two weeks had been, I knew God loved me. I knew He was there. I knew I'd spend eternity with Him because Jesus had paid the penalty for my sin when He died on the Cross. I finally understood that being a Christian was more than being moral or even asking Jesus to come into my heart, getting baptized, and checking it off my to-do list. It was more than believing there was a God and Jesus was His Son. It was living a life surrendered to God's will, not mine. I didn't quite understand what that entailed, but I was sure that's what I wanted.

The circumstances of my life weren't any better; in fact, they seemed to be getting worse. But I had a peaceful assurance of where I was going if things didn't work out in the operating room. My life was totally different—inside. Because of that, I wanted the same for everyone else, especially those I loved.

Dr. Jackson had expressed his disbelief in a Supreme Being seven months before, and I couldn't shake that fact from my mind. This gifted man, who'd unselfishly done so much for me and others, didn't know the peace that comes with the assurance of one's salvation for all eternity.

Just like I was stubborn and persistent on a lot of other things, I was going to be persistent with Dr. Jackson as well. One of my required courses in college for my major in speech and drama was The Art of Persuasion. Persuasiveness came easy to me, and I did well in that class. I was going to persuade Dr. Jackson to believe in Jesus Christ. I didn't understand that I wasn't able to persuade or convince anyone to trust in Jesus as their Savior. It wasn't dependent on me to do a good sales job; I was merely to tell him that Jesus loved him and died on the cross for him. The results were up to God. Dr. Jackson could receive God's offer or reject it. That day, however, I didn't know that.

I wasn't scheduled for surgery until late Tuesday afternoon. I had a lot to do in the meantime. In between visitors, I was busy.

Friends had sent me scriptures to encourage me, and although I still didn't know a lot of them by memory, I knew more than I had in previous surgeries. I also had to figure out what to do about the skin graft, now that I understood it was coming from me.

"Momma, they said I couldn't get sun on the skin graft area," I said. "What about when I'm wearing shorts or a swimsuit? Do you have a ballpoint pen?"

She pulled a pen out of her purse as I was pulling up my nightgown to expose the upper part of my leg.

"Candy, what are you doing?"

"I'm going to draw a line on my leg where my shorts come to and tell them not to take any skin from below that line. I can get a swimsuit with a little skirt on it."

Any other time she probably would have told me I was being ridiculous, but not that day. It wouldn't have mattered if she had; I was determined. I drew a line about four inches below my panty line. "That should do it."

By that time, Daddy was there, too, and I spoke to both of them. "You know, if I have to die during this surgery for Dr. Jackson to become a Christian, I will."

Daddy was leaning up against the wall, his head drooping as he spoke. "You don't worry about Dr. Jackson, Candy. You just worry about getting better."

Well, then, if I'm not going to die for Dr. Jackson, I'll have to be sure to get him to pray with me before they put me to sleep, like he said he would. He'll see how much I care about him and how much the Lord loves him.

I was excited at the prospect, and I didn't want to risk falling asleep from the pre-op medicine before carrying it out. I asked the nurse to give me only half the shot before the orderly came to take me to surgery.

It was three o'clock when I got the half a shot and they began to wheel me to the holding area. As anxious as I usually was before surgery, somehow that day I almost looked forward to it—not the surgery part, but the fact that I was on a mission. I had a plan, and I already had my prayer memorized in case the Demerol made me forgetful.

When they pushed me through the double doors into the familiar holding area, I was sleepy, so I asked for a piece of paper and a pencil, determined to keep myself awake by writing down the things I knew about the Lord and His promises. It would also help to keep my eyes fixed on Him.

The nurse brought me a small notepad and a pencil, and I began to write, but I was only in the holding area a short time before they took me to surgery. It seemed like a smaller room than the other times, but the attendants were dressed in the same familiar green scrubs.

"Hey, Candy. Jesse Muir." A man wearing a surgical mask looked down at me, but I wouldn't have recognized him even without the mask, having met him only once when he stayed with me in the holding area before my first surgery.

The only other doctor was a resident who stood at my feet. I asked where Dr. Jackson was, and when they told me he was in the next operating room, finishing a surgery, I said, "Before you put me to sleep, I want to talk with Dr. Jackson."

"Candy," the resident said, "we need to get you to sleep so we can prep you."

"Not until I see Dr. Jackson. And I marked on my leg not to go below the pen line with the skin graft."

I could tell the resident was getting impatient. "We need to put you to sleep."

"Uh uh. No. I want to see Dr. Jackson first." I wasn't going to budge. No one was going to mess up my plan. I'd been looking forward to this all day.

Finally Dr. Muir said, "We have to respect her wishes. If she wants to speak with her surgeon before we get started, we'll just have to wait."

Before long, Dr. Jackson stood smiling down at me. "I hear you want to see me."

"I wanted you to be here to pray with me," I said, reaching out to take his hand.

There in the silence of that small sterile operating room, Dr. Jackson and his team were ready—but first I wanted to pray. "Dear Lord, I pray that everyone in this room will feel Your presence in a very special way. I pray that You'll give wisdom and guidance to this man I've come to love. Right now, I want to thank You ahead of time for what You'll do through his hands. I pray these things in Jesus' Name. Amen."

The room was silent until I said, "I'm ready to go to sleep now."

A nurse gently rubbed my forehead with something wet, as I looked into her eyes.

"That was a very nice prayer," she said with a Spanish accent.

Jesse told me to count to ten.

"One, two, three, four…"

14

◇　　◇　　◇

NOTHING COULD HAVE PREPARED ME FOR THE PAIN OF THE SKIN GRAFT. As I worked my way back into consciousness, the pain crashed in on me, escalating to unbearable levels.

"Please, God, take me home," I begged, not even considering that I would be leaving my family behind. I just wanted to escape the pain.

Using an instrument similar to a cheese slicer, the surgeon had removed the first layer of skin from the top of my leg, just above the line I'd drawn and up to my buttocks, an area about six by ten inches. A sheet of gauze was then laid on top of the bloody, raw wound, and a coat of something called "scarlet red" brushed onto the entire area. The scarlet red hardens over a period of several days, leaving a thick layer similar to a scab. During the drying and hardening process, the exposed site is left unbandaged, and a wire frame is placed over the area to prevent anything from touching it.

In all my previous operations and procedures, nothing had come close to being as painful as that.

Dr. Jackson had also removed all the dead forehead skin, along with a section of forehead bone about six inches in diameter. He'd made an incision behind my right ear to enable him to rotate the scalp from the back of my head to the front, covering the brain. That left no scalp to cover the skull on the back of my head, so that's where Dr. Jackson would place the skin from the graft at a later date.

As I lay on my side, the exposed area facing up, I continued to beg God to take me home. Daddy paced back and forth outside my room, while Momma tried to console him.

"Bill, she doesn't know what she's saying."

"Yes, I do," I called out. "I want to go home to be with Jesus!"

Then I heard Momma asking one of the nurses if there was something they could do to lessen my pain—a pill, a shot, anything to ease the intense burning.

"We can give her Tylenol," the nurse replied, "but that's all. Her blood pressure is too low to give her anything else. She could go into shock."

I knew Tylenol wasn't going to help, and I continued to cry and scream while Daddy paced and Momma did her best to calm and console us.

In the midst of that ongoing scene, the resident I'd met earlier in surgery came to check on me. He was alone, wearing camouflage pants and not looking at all like the doctors who usually popped into my room in their coats and ties.

"How's she doing?"

"Not good at all," Momma answered. "Can you do something? Isn't there something else she can take for the pain besides Tylenol?"

"Nope. Can't give her a thing. But don't worry. She'll get through it. That's just the way it is."

As I listened to what seemed his flippant reply, I decided I didn't like him very much. If I hadn't been in so much pain, I probably would have told him so.

After about eight hours, my blood pressure finally stabilized and I was able to get a shot of Demerol to take the edge off the pain. Once I'd settled down a bit, Momma sat on the edge of my bed and said deliberately, "Candy. Aren't you glad…God doesn't always answer our prayers," she paused, "the way we want Him to?"

She was right. That day, God's answer to my prayer was "no." And I was glad.

But that didn't change the fact that I still hurt—a lot. But at least I could have something every four hours for pain. I watched the clock closely and soon discovered that if I pushed the nurses' button at three and a half hours, it would be about three hours and forty-five minutes by the time anyone returned with the injection, and that seemed to be alright with them. That way I never had a lapse in the pain medication.

The graft area wasn't the only thing that hurt. My entire head seemed engulfed in a heavy, dull pain that made it difficult to lift it from the pillow. The right side of my head stung from where they'd made the incision, and the left side was thick with extra skin—not to mention that there was no skin at all in back.

Aren't you glad God doesn't always answer our prayers the way we want Him to?

"There was so much blood that we didn't try to attach the skin graft yet," Dr. Schultz explained. "We'll do that later."

"Later?" Momma looked concerned. "Where's the skin you took from her leg?"

"In the refrigerator. The skin will be kept alive in there. She won't have to go back to surgery for that. We can do it right here."

Momma's face went from concern to shock. "I can't believe this," she said, nearly overwhelmed at the thought of having the procedure done in my room.

Personally, I didn't care where they did it. I just wanted the pain to go away; all my energy was focused on the clock and my next shot of Demerol.

The constant pain in my head was annoying, but it didn't begin to compare in intensity to the agony I experienced from the skin graft. It was so bad I sometimes held my breath so I wouldn't move a muscle and increase the pain. I couldn't find a way to adequately explain it to Momma and Daddy.

"It's like when you fall on the pavement," I told them, "and you get a 'strawberry' on your knee. Or when you burn your finger touching a hot burner on the stove or the iron. Only it's bigger. It's what Martha and Bob have to go through all the time."

I had to lie on my left side, with the exposed graft under the cage and covered by the sheet. I couldn't get comfortable that way because I couldn't lay my head down completely. By the time the resident came back to check on me the next morning, I was ready for him.

Pointing to the chair beside my bed, I ordered, "Have a seat. We're going to have a session on Bedside Manners 101—of which you have none, by the way." Then I lit into him about his behavior the day before when my momma asked about pain medication. He didn't say much, but we understood each other from that point on.

Later that day, Sharon and Richard—both of whom were going home—stopped in to say goodbye, but they couldn't come into the room. They called to me from the doorway, as Dr. Schultz stitched the skin from my leg onto my head. Thankfully, I didn't feel a thing, as the skin was simply laid on the skull. When he was finished, he wrapped my head with a gauze and net covering. It would be a few days before we'd know if the graft took or not.

Then Dr. Jackson came in, with another doctor in tow. "Well, now, how are you feeling, Candy?"

I loved Dr. Jackson's accent, and his voice had a calming effect on me. Then he introduced his colleague, and my anxiety returned.

"I want you to meet Dr. Arnold. He'll be taking care of you while I'm away."

While I'm away... He was going on a trip to South America for three weeks to operate on disfigured children. He'd mentioned it before, but I hadn't known I'd still be at the hospital when he left. It was definitely not what I wanted to hear under the circumstances.

◇   ◇   ◇

The scarlet red hardened over the gauze on the graft area, but it seemed I was never free from pain. I had little or no appetite, and I continued to lose weight. I hadn't yet seen my head, as it was covered with bloody, wet bandages, which held the freshly applied skin in place. In addition, my skin had a sickly yellow, jaundiced appearance.

I continued to press the nurses' button for pain shots every three and a half hours. Even though I tried to wean myself from Demerol, it seemed all other pain medications had side effects, including nausea and hallucinations. My left hip was becoming a bruised pincushion from the never-ending injections, and the antibiotics being fed through the IV were burning my veins. The IV sites were changed daily, from one arm to the other, being inserted from the tops of my hands to the inside of my arms. Little white blisters had formed inside my cheeks, along the gums, on the tongue, and down my throat, so I couldn't swallow. Each day seemed longer and harder than the last. I was becoming weak and weary.

At the same time, I had many wonderful new friends who did everything they could to encourage me, stopping by to read scriptures to me and calling on the phone. But despite the scriptures and encouragement from friends, there never seemed to be any good news about my condition. To say I was in bad shape would be a serious understatement.

◇   ◇   ◇

My emotions felt like they were on a never-ending roller coaster ride. Someone came to encourage and pray with me, and I'd begin to feel a bit hopeful. Then the pain hit or I'd have a setback, and my heart plummeted right back to earth.

"I feel like there's some sort of tug-of-war going on in this room," I told Momma. "Like somebody's pulling one arm and somebody else the other one. The trouble is, I have to fight so hard not to be pulled down into the dark side. Could God be pulling one way and somebody else the other?"

Momma tried to help me find the bright side; other people did too. I especially liked it when Edwin came to see me. He was so upbeat.

"Hey," he said when he showed up one morning, "how's the celebrity patient doing today?"

I smiled, enjoying the nickname he'd given me. Edwin had a contagious, down-home friendliness. I thought he should have been a preacher. I asked him why he wasn't, and he told me he couldn't decide whether to go to seminary or medical school. He eventually chose medicine because he felt it would enable him to do a little of both—heal people physically and comfort them spiritually. And that's exactly what he did.

Mary and Dottie usually came to visit in the afternoons after work, while Raleigh and Edwin came later in the evening.

"Y'all don't have to come every day," I told them, wanting to be thoughtful but hoping they wouldn't take me up on it. "It's freezing outside! Y'all could go home and drink hot chocolate instead of getting out in all this snow."

Dottie smiled. "We can drink hot chocolate here, too. Isn't that right, Mary?"

Mary agreed, but I knew she didn't like blood and needles. If she was around when my IV was changed, she'd hold my hand and turn her head. She and Dottie were great about keeping Momma and Daddy company. Sometimes Dottie worked on a needlepoint picture frame while we visited. They were all so good at making us laugh. Anyone who walked by my room and heard us would never guess I was getting worse every day.

One day, as we were all visiting in my room, Momma surprised us by suggesting, "Let's take a picture of the skin graft."

"You are not taking a pornographic picture of me," I insisted.

"Just the donor site," Momma said. "That's not pornographic. You'll be glad to have it later."

I conceded and let her lift the cage from over my leg. The area was still wet, and the exposed raw nerves stung when the slightest bit of air touched it.

Though I no longer had any sense of smell, I knew the room reeked of the pungent scent of infection and bloody bandages, but no one seemed to mind. I took sponge baths, but they weren't the same as a good hot tub bath or shower. I felt dirty, and my mouth tasted bad from the ulcers, even though I swished with Lidocaine and Cepacol to numb my mouth so I could swallow. My dancer legs were beginning to atrophy.

Being on pain medication, I sometimes didn't know or care what time it was. If I had a question about something scriptural, I'd pick up the phone and call Barbara.

One day, after making several phone calls to Barbara, my daddy brought the bills to pay while he was visiting me in my room. Momma looked at them and asked, "Candy, whose number is this?"

When she read the number, I said, "Oh, that's the Barkers' number—Frank and Barbara's. Why?"

"Did you know you talked to them for thirty minutes one night—at two-thirty in the morning?"

I hadn't realized that. I just knew that the only way I was going to make it through my ordeal was to draw nearer to the Lord and learn what the Bible said about suffering. I wanted to know how, as a Christian, I was to view suffering, disappointment, setbacks, delays, and everything else that went along with the trials I was experiencing. When a question popped into my head, I asked whoever was in my room for the answer. If no one was there, I called someone—usually Barbara.

I knew God had written a lot about suffering in the Bible, and I wanted to know everything I could about it. People often sent me cards and notes with verses about suffering, and many of the daily devotionals I read in

Streams in the Desert talked about the value of perseverance in suffering and the lessons that could be learned from it.

But all that learning about suffering—and actually doing it—took work, and I was tired. "God, I just don't understand," I prayed one day. "Seven months ago I expected to lose the right side of my face and my eyesight. Then You did a miracle, and I thought I was healed. Now it's as if You're taking it all away. I think what You're doing is kind of mean."

I told Momma the same thing. "It's like God gave me an ice cream sundae seven months ago, and now He's taking it back, a little bit at a time. First He snatched the cherry; then He scooped off all the whipped cream, and then the nuts. What's He going to take next, the chocolate sauce? Is He going to leave me with nothing but a little bitty scoop of ice cream? I think that's mean."

Momma was good about listening. She'd let me think things out, but always have the right thing to say. "Candy, you know God isn't mean. This has been a hard week for you, but it'll get better."

"No, it won't. Momma, if I die, will you make sure Colley and Elliott know I loved them? Promise? And what about you and Daddy? How will you handle it if I die?"

Sometimes I needed to verbalize my thoughts about dying, and I didn't need someone discouraging me from doing so by saying things like, "Let's not talk about that." Momma knew me well enough to understand I needed to get it out and I'd soon be back to my stubborn, strong-willed self, fighting to recover.

◇　　　◇　　　◇

"Which pain shot will it be this time, Candy?" Sue, the nurse with the contagious laugh, asked one day.

"I don't know. Do I want to throw up, or do I want to hallucinate, or do I just want to hurt? It's a hard decision. What do you think?"

She laughed. "Whatever you want."

"I know. We'll put the names of my choices on pieces of paper, and I'll draw one. It'll be like a game!" We did, and she held them out to me like splayed cards in a deck, letting me pick.

Two days after the surgery, Dr. Laws from the neurosurgery department stopped by and said my head looked good. Daddy didn't seem too convinced.

"What's going to keep her head protected when she gets home?"

"She can come back in about six months and have a forehead bone put in. In the meantime, she can wear a helmet."

After they left, I heard Daddy talking to Momma about getting me a helmet.

"Daddy," I said, "he was kidding. I'm not going to wear a helmet!"

"You'll have to. That doctor was not kidding. You'll have to have something to protect your brain."

"I'm not going to wear some football helmet around town," I insisted, and that was that.

I still couldn't get comfortable, no matter what I did. The scarlet red gauze was hardening and tightening, and I understood why burn patients begged to die. My entire head throbbed where the bones had been cut. The incision down the side of my nose itched and pulled, and my entire face felt tight.

But I couldn't give up. Forget the game Sue and I played with the pain medicine. If Demerol was the only thing that worked, that's what I'd want to use. The dosage was increased, along with visceral medicine that enhanced the Demerol. This combination helped quite a bit—for the first two hours. After that the pain steadily increased, and I eyed the clock until it was time for another one. Pain consumed my thinking, but I was absolutely resolved to fight. It was exhausting, but the alternative was to lie there and give up, which was unacceptable. And so I continued to pray, "God, don't take me out of this until I've gotten out of it what I'm supposed to get."

One day I read an excerpt from *Streams in the Desert,* which stressed that if we are being tested by afflictions in order for God to be glorified, then the testing will end when we "bear witness to His praise." In the meantime, we are to be patient and know that we will be compensated for our trials.

"I don't quite understand this, God," I prayed, "but I trust You and want what's best for me."

One day Daddy stopped pacing and sat down on my bed, and I saw his frustration at not being able to help. "Bett," he said to my momma, "this is why I never wanted to break her spirit."

I'd always been stubborn and headstrong, persistent and determined, and though I know I tried my parents' patience—especially Momma's—Daddy always said there was a fine line between discipline and breaking my spirit, and maybe he was right. Maybe God was using my feisty temperament to help get me through my terrible ordeal.

◇   ◇   ◇

When the day arrived for the nurse to unwrap the bandages from my head, Dottie was the only one in the room with me. After the bandages were off, the nurse excused herself, saying she'd be right back.

Once she was gone, I said, "I want to see what my head looks like. Do you have a mirror?"

Dottie seemed a bit concerned. "Are you sure?"

"I'm sure. I want to see."

She got a compact out of her purse, sat on the edge of my bed, and held the mirror up to my face.

I felt my eyes widen, as I stared at my reflection. "Dottie, what is that?" I asked, pointing at a glob of shaved scalp hanging over my left ear.

"I don't know." She reached out and gently touched it. "I think it's skin."

I too reached up and touched it. We were like two squeamish little girls, touching a worm for the first time.

"It looks like a beagle's skin," I said, "with those folds of extra skin."

Suddenly the entire situation struck us as funny, and we started laughing, as I continued to examine my shaved head. There were stitches stretched across the area where my forehead had been, but it wasn't completely sunken in because of the swelling.

"What is that?" I asked, pointing to a roll on top of my head that resembled the curl on top of a soft-serve ice cream cone. "Is that skin too?"

Dottie touched it too and confirmed it was skin.

"I look like an elf," I said. "I want to see it in the bathroom mirror."

Dottie wasn't sure that was a good idea, since I hadn't been out of bed since the surgery, but I was determined to get the complete view before the nurse came back to wrap me up again.

"Just be careful," Dottie cautioned, as she held my elbow with one hand and the IV pole with the other, and we shuffled the seven or so feet to the half-bath in my room. She stood behind me while I looked into the medicine cabinet mirror.

"Oh, my," was all I could say. For a moment I stared at my reflection. Then I looked at Dottie in the mirror behind me and said, "I look like one of those cone heads on *Saturday Night Live!*" Then we really lost it, laughing until tears squeezed from our eyes.

"Dottie," I finally managed to gasp between giggles, "I look so pitiful I'm almost cute!"

It was an odd response for someone who was so into her looks just one year before. I wondered why I didn't crumble at the sight, as there truly was nothing funny about craniofacial surgery and the pain patients endure who have it, nor was there anything funny about being disfigured. But for that moment on that day, God enabled me to hold myself together with laughter.

◇　　　◇　　　◇

Three days after the surgery, Dr. Jackson came to check on me before leaving for his annual three-week trip to Peru, where he'd operate on children with facial deformities, something he'd been doing since he came to America and the Mayo Clinic. Helping children with horrendous deformities was his passion. One little boy named David had been brought to him in Lima after being bitten by a sand fly. The tissue and bone in his face had begun to die as a result, and by the time Dr. Jackson saw him, David's nose, cheeks, and mouth had all died. The only thing left was a large, gaping hole between his big, beautiful brown eyes.

Dr. Jackson was unable to help David immediately, but after returning to Scotland, he sent for the boy and began the long process of making David a face, a process that was still ongoing when I had my surgery. In the interim, Dr. Jackson and his wife adopted David into their family of four children. They lived in Rochester, and I'd heard David's story from Raleigh before I went to the Mayo Clinic.

Later that day, Momma handed me a letter. "This is from Dr. Jackson's wife, Marjorie."

I was surprised—and very touched. She wrote to tell me she'd heard a lot about me, and assured me I was in her family's thoughts and prayers. She said that whatever decisions her husband made concerning me had my best interests in mind, which I didn't doubt for a moment. She also said she hoped we could one day have tea together when I came back to the clinic for a checkup.

On Friday, February 18, just four days after my surgery, Lee flew up to see me. Raleigh and Daddy picked him up at the airport and brought him to the hospital late that afternoon. It was the first time he'd been there in ten days, so I'm sure it was quite a shock for him to see my head wrapped like a mummy and my bony shoulders protruding from my nightgown.

I felt like I was with a stranger. I couldn't put my finger on it, but something didn't feel right. Maybe it was because he hadn't been there to experience firsthand all I was going through, but he couldn't seem to identify with me. Maybe, too, it was because Lee and I had never had a deep emotional connection, and to a large degree, he'd increased that emotional separation throughout my illness.

Part of me felt guilty because I didn't miss him when he wasn't there. To be fair, he was concerned about my condition, and I could tell he was sad about all that was going on. I was glad, however, that Momma and Daddy and Raleigh and Dottie were there with us, and that I was on stronger pain medication, which made me a little less alert but much more comfortable.

"My head looks like an elf," I announced to Lee, "or an ice cream curl!" But no one seemed to think it was as funny as Dottie and I had.

◇   ◇   ◇

The next morning, Drs. Arnold and Schultz made their rounds.

"Your head looks okay," Dr. Arnold observed as he examined my forehead. "But you get an A-plus on the donor site!"

Thankfully the donor site was healing nicely. It was now almost completely hard, like a large ten-by-six-inch scab.

While examining my forehead, he commented to the other doctors, "This one spot needs to be replaced."

Replaced? What did that mean? Everybody said my head looked good, so why did something need to be replaced? Oh, how I wished I could talk to Dr. Jackson!

"What do you mean, replaced?" I asked.

"There's one place right here on the forehead that needs to be removed and replaced by a skin graft."

My heart sank. I thought I might be sick. "Another skin graft? Why?"

"It'll be a small one," he assured me. "Only the size of a nickel." He turned to the other doctors. "We'll schedule her for Tuesday."

Surgery again! Oh, Lord, no! This was too much. I couldn't possibly go through this again. Why, Lord? Am I fighting to stay alive and it's not Your will? Maybe I'm trying to live and You don't want me to. Is that it? But why now, with Dr. Jackson gone and Momma and Daddy leaving tomorrow? Oh, God, do You want me to stop fighting? Do You want me to lie back peacefully and let You take me home?

The more I thought about it, the more I was sure that's what I should do. *All right, God, I'll give in. I won't fight anymore. I surrender, Lord. Just bring me home.*

The rest of the day I was complacent, staring up at the ceiling and waiting to die. They could operate or do whatever they wanted; it didn't matter because I was going to die. I'd given it my best shot. I'd trusted the Lord and depended on Him, but it was time to give up. I decided to ring for another pain shot so I could take a nap. No sense staying awake if I was going to die anyway.

By that evening, I told God I'd changed my mind. "I've decided to fight after all, Lord. If You want to take me to heaven, then go ahead. But I'll go kicking and screaming the whole way!"

It was a good thing I'd made the decision to keep fighting because I discovered the next day I was in for something even worse than I'd imagined.

Martha had been home from the hospital for a week now, and she called me from Rockford, Illinois. "I just wanted to call and check on you—and to warn you about something."

I didn't like the sound of that.

"Have they taken the scarlet red off yet?"

"What…do you mean?"

"After the scarlet red dries and is hard enough, the nurse pulls it off. It hurts like crazy."

"What do you mean, pulls it off?"

"I mean, the skin underneath heals, and the scarlet red has to come off or it could get infected. They rip it off, usually after about seven days."

It had been five days. Rip it off? Infected? I was beginning to feel nauseous.

"You mean…" I swallowed and forced myself to ask, "…ripping it off like a bandage?"

"Exactly. But that's why I called. Tell them you'll do it yourself. That's what I do. Tell them you want a pain shot, and then pull off as much as you can stand. Then wait until you can get another pain shot and pull off some more. Make sure you don't pull off any of the new skin underneath. It'll take awhile."

My head was spinning. I had to have a break—from everything. This was too much! Dr. Jackson was gone, and Momma and Daddy had left too. After hanging up, I prayed, "Oh, God, You know I love You. And I trust You. But I'm so tired. Can't I check out for a couple of days? I can't even concentrate on prayer or reading the Bible. I can't fight right now, God. It's not that I'm giving up, but I need a break. Can I please do that, Lord? You can carry me, okay?"

As I pictured God carrying me while I rested in His arms, it gave me peace. I was resting, as I'd asked the Lord to let me do, and I decided to give my body a rest as well.

"Okay," I announced to the nurse that evening, "I'm getting off all pain medicine. My body needs a break from it." That lasted one night. By morning the pain in my head and leg was unbearable, and I

You're in the center of God's will. Where else would you want to be?

was tired and depressed. When Edwin stopped in to check on me, no one else was in the room. I watched him as he read my chart, and I could tell by the look on his face that he didn't like what he saw.

"Edwin," I asked as he came near my bed, "I'm going to die, aren't I? I'm not going to make it, am I?"

He could tell I was serious. "I'm going to be honest with you." He sat down on the edge of my bed and took my hand. "Candy, you're in the center of God's will. Where else would you want to be?"

"Nowhere," I answered, gazing into his compassionate brown eyes. I shrugged my shoulders and dropped my eyes. "Nowhere."

He was right; I knew it. The only safe place was in the center of God's will. Edwin had been honest with me, and I appreciated it.

"Why don't we pray?" Edwin asked.

We bowed our heads, and in the stillness of that little room, he called on the mighty name of Jesus Christ on my behalf.

15

◇　　◇　　◇

"AM I STRONG ENOUGH FOR SURGERY AGAIN IN THE MORNING?" I ASKED
Kathy, my night nurse. "It's only been a week since the last surgery, and I
feel so weak."

Kathy's assurance and another pint of blood helped a bit. Then I
thought, *I need to get in shape for tomorrow morning. I haven't had any
exercise at all. I could walk around and around the bed, but I'd get tangled
up in my IV.*

I pushed the nurses' button. When Kathy arrived I said, "If I wait until
the middle of the night when all the other patients are in bed asleep, can I
get out of my room and walk up the hall and back for some exercise?"

Kathy agreed, and I silently prayed, *Lord, thank You for carrying me
these past few days, but it's time to check back in. With another surgery in the
morning, I can't be on a break any longer.*

I watched *M*A*S*H* like I did every night, and then I waited until after midnight. Kathy came in and unhooked my IV so I was free to walk without the IV pole.

I was determined. I thought that by getting some exercise, I'd be in better shape for surgery. With my hands clenched into fists and my arms bent at the elbow, I shuffled all the way to the nurses' station and back— twice. When I completed my trek and collapsed back into bed, I went right to sleep, believing I was ready for yet another surgery.

◇   ◇   ◇

I was taken into the operating room at eight-thirty and back out again by nine-thirty. This time the donor site was small—about two square inches on the top of my right leg. I was in unusually good spirits and not in nearly as much pain as the last time.

When I returned to my room, Lee was waiting for me, and I told him I was hungry for lunch. He'd been worried about my continuing weight loss, and I could tell he was pleased by the possibility of my returning appetite.

The next day, however, Lee walked in right after I finished breakfast, took off his heavy coat and laid it on the chair, and demanded to know, "Where's my cup?"

"What cup?"

"The cup that was on your bed tray last night. The Styrofoam cup of water." He pointed to the hospital bed table. "Where is it?"

Why is he so upset about a cup of water? Then I remembered. "Oh, I cleaned up last night after you left and threw some things away."

His face took on a hard, chiseled look, and his eyes went cold. "What have I told you about throwing away things without consulting me first?"

Consult. He'd been using that word a lot lately, demanding that I "consult" with him before doing things.

"It was just a cup of water," I said, keeping my voice calm.

"By God, Candy, it wasn't just a cup of water!" he yelled, his face turning red. "It had my contacts in it!"

We'd been through these confrontations before, and I knew the best way to defuse them was to remain calm and to apologize. It didn't necessarily prevent his becoming mad, but it sometimes curbed a full-blown rage. "I'm sorry. I didn't know."

"Of course you didn't know," he said, exerting effort to control his voice, though it rose a notch anyway, "because you never *asked!*" As he spoke, he sliced the side of his right hand down into his left palm, over and over again with each word, as if to emphasize his point.

Inadvertently I found myself pushing farther back against the pillow on the elevated hospital bed. It was a vain effort to get away from him, but I was hooked to an IV and there was nowhere else to go.

Oh, Lord, I can't deal with this. Not now!

Lee's behavior was nothing new. It had been going on for a long time, seeming to escalate as I got sicker. The slap of his right hand into his palm could be heard even over his raging words, so I decided to try again.

"I'm sorry, Lee. I told you I was sorry." I pressed my feet into the mattress, hoping to inconspicuously push myself away from him. I was afraid, but I didn't want him to know that. I didn't want him to see me squirm.

Finally, as he continued to rage about his lost contacts, I began to cry. I tried so hard not to give in to the tears because I didn't want to give him the satisfaction of seeing how much he'd upset me, but also because crying made my head hurt so much worse.

Then, as quickly as it began, the storm was over. His rages never lasted longer than a few minutes, and then *poof,* they were over. He acted as if nothing had happened, but I knew it had. Another brick had been added to the thick wall I continued to build around my heart. Soon he'd be gone— back to Birmingham—and I was glad, though I felt guilty about it. I was supposed to love Lee and want him with me, but I didn't even like him, and I didn't want him around. I was supposed to be able to lean on my husband for comfort, but I couldn't and had no desire to even try.

◇   ◇   ◇

By Saturday night, Lee had been there an entire week. Everyone else had gone home, and it was just the two of us. I told Lee he could leave too so he could prepare for his morning flight, assuring him I was fine and feeling much more encouraged since Dr. Arnold had told me I could go home Tuesday or Wednesday. But Lee opted to stay awhile.

We watched *Love Boat* on TV, and for the first time I found myself becoming depressed over it. As always, it was a love story about two passengers who met on the cruise, and this particular show had the ship stopping at the port of Cabo San Lucas. The couple, now madly in love, got off the boat and frolicked on the beach, as the beautiful waves splashed on the shore. Everyone seemed happy and carefree, and suddenly I began to cry.

"Look at all the happy people," I said.

Lee was sympathetic in a quiet kind of way. The entire mood of the program was romantic and fun, nothing like the reality of my life. While they enjoyed the sand and surf and sun, I was stuck in a hospital bed in freezing Minnesota, fighting to stay alive. The characters in the show were lovely and tanned, while I was skinny and pale, with a shaved head.

Right then and there I had a pity party—the first one I'd really allowed myself since all this began. Maybe it was because I hadn't compared my life to anyone else's until that moment. Before that I'd been grateful to have made it through alive and knowing I'd soon be going home. But that night the music and images from the TV were too much for me, and I was actually sad that Lee was leaving the next morning. And in all fairness, he really did try his best to comfort me.

◇　　　◇　　　◇

Not long after Lee left Sunday morning, there was a tap on my door. "Candy?"

It was Raleigh. He'd been to church and out for lunch, and then decided to drop by and see how I was doing. "How are you feeling?"

When I assured him I was feeling somewhat better, he grinned. "Good, because we're going to an antique auction. Do you think you're up to coming along?"

My heart raced at the thought of getting out of that dreary room, even for a little while. "I can do that?"

"Absolutely—if you want to."

Oh, I wanted to! But then the practical side of me kicked in. "But I don't have anything to wear—at least, nothing that fits."

"That's alright. Wear what you have on. Who cares? It'll do you good to get out."

I laughed. "Go out in my nightgown?"

"Why not? Nobody will notice."

Though I imagined he was wrong about no one noticing, I couldn't turn him down.

While Raleigh went to arrange a pass, the nurse came and unhooked my IV. Dottie was there by then, helping me "dress up" as best I could. We laughed as I put on my black tights and black patents. Then I donned my turquoise-magenta velour robe over my nightgown, and I was nearly ready. We covered my bandaged head with a floral cotton bonnet, and then completed the colorful ensemble with Lois's opossum fur coat. What a sight!

Once Raleigh had secured my pass, he went to get the car while Dottie walked me to the elevator and down to the patient pickup area. The cold Rochester air stung my face, but it felt so clear and fresh that I didn't mind a bit.

When we arrived at the auction, we found the room crowded with people wanting to make a deal on all sorts of china, paintings, jewelry, and furniture. We also found that Raleigh had been right—everyone else was so caught up in the activities they didn't even notice one skinny lady in multi-colored clothes.

"People around here are used to seeing patients from the clinic around town," Raleigh said.

By the time I got back to my room a few hours later, I was exhausted but happier than I'd been in weeks. It had been quite an adventure, and I collapsed onto my bed, knowing I was one day closer to going home.

◊   ◊   ◊

The next day I decided I'd had so much fun that I'd try to get another pass. Raleigh arranged for me to go to lunch with Dottie and Mary, but when I started to get dressed, I knew I was in trouble. My black pants fit like a tent! I'd lost twenty pounds, one-fifth of my entire body weight, but I was so excited about having lunch with my friends that I wore the pants—saggy, baggy, and all.

It was worth it. Lunch was wonderful, and afterward we went to the mall to buy some clothes that would fit me. Then I was so tired that they took me back to the hospital for a nap. When I awoke, Edwin brought me home for dinner. When we opened the door to their cozy little home, we were welcomed by the aroma of Mary's home-cooking.

"Lookahere, Mary," Edwin announced in his down-home way. "I've brought home the celebrity patient!" He walked up behind her as she stood at the sink, put his arms around her waist, and hugged her. Then he turned to me and asked, "Don't I have a beautiful wife?"

Mary laughed as I voiced my agreement, and Edwin added, "I'm a blessed man!" It seemed those two were on a continuous honeymoon, and I was glad for them, although I couldn't help feeling a little envious.

After a delicious dinner, we watched the last episode of *M*A*S*H*, the one that wound up the long-running series. I was especially excited to view it with friends in their home, rather than alone in my hospital room.

I returned to St. Mary's late that evening and began some preliminary packing. I was only two days away from Birmingham and home.

◇   ◇   ◇

Mary and Dottie took me to lunch again on Tuesday, and I realized how much I'd miss their company. As anxious as I was to get home and be with my children, I knew I'd miss St. Mary's. I felt at home there—safe and cared for—and it would be hard to leave my friends.

By Wednesday, the excitement of going home had built to a climax. I'd counted the weeks, the days, the hours … even the minutes. Finally, the time had arrived.

I did everything I could to make sure I looked healthy before Dr. Marsh made rounds that morning; I didn't want to risk anything holding me back. I put on a dab of lipstick and some pink blush on my cheeks. I threw away all my flowers and cleaned up my room. Then I packed my suitcase, including my family pictures, my Bible, and the pile of notes and letters I'd received throughout my five-week stay. All I needed was the discharge papers so I could call Dottie and tell her to take me to the airport for my morning flight. I'd land in Birmingham at three that afternoon, and Colley and Elliott would be waiting for me, along with Lee and my parents. At last I'd see my precious children again!

I smiled, picturing our reunion. Elliott had celebrated his seventh birthday in my absence. He sounded so grown-up on the phone, and I was sure he'd gotten taller. And I couldn't wait to snuggle and hold my little Colleybug!

I was eating a bowl of hot cereal when Dr. Marsh came in. I knew I'd have plenty of time to call Dottie and to get dressed. Other than that, I was ready to go.

"Are you flying out today?" Dr. Marsh asked.

A shot of excitement zinged through me. "Can I?"

"You can. But what time is your flight?"

"Eleven."

"You might want to check to see if it's been cancelled. It's pretty foggy out there, and sometimes they cancel flights in this kind of weather."

My soaring heart crash-landed at my feet. After five weeks of waiting, I might not get to go home because of fog! As I sat there, stunned, Dr. Marsh checked my head and the bandages, pronounced me ready to go, and gave me my discharge papers. I was looking up the telephone number for the airport before he was out the door.

He was right. My flight was cancelled.

I hung up the phone and looked around the room, wondering what to do next. As the frustration, anger, and self-pity came flooding in, I turned it all on God.

"I've had it!" I shouted, not caring who heard me. "You've gone too far this time. I've done everything I'm supposed to do. I've praised You. I've been thankful in my circumstances. I've prayed. I've trusted. And now this! You know what, God? It's not just me that's upset. My children will be, too. They're expecting me home today. They're planning to meet me at the airport. Think how they're going to feel!"

I was determined to lay a guilt trip on God. If I'd had the strength, I'd have jumped up and down and stomped my feet. It just wasn't fair!

"And by the way," I added, feeling the need to get in one last word, "if You could part the Red Sea, You could lift the fog and let me go home!"

There was another flight going out at three, and I imagined the fog would lift by then and I'd catch that one, but I really had my heart set on catching the morning flight. "And another thing," I fumed. "I haven't had any exercise. I'm tired! If I wait till three, I'll be exhausted by the time I get home—and Colley and Elliott will be asleep."

I switched gears then, going for the martyr role. "Oh, well, that's okay. You've made up Your mind, and I'm not going to change it."

Somehow I made it through until lunchtime. By then Dottie had gone to work, so Mary took me to the airport for the afternoon flight. It had already been a long day by the time I checked in and walked to the gate. I collapsed into my seat on the prop plane for the short flight to Minneapolis. Snow covered the fields beside the landing strip, and I was so weak I could scarcely lift my carry-on bag filled with surprises for Colley and Elliott.

Republic Airlines was one of two carriers that flew into Rochester, and it was obvious I wasn't the only Mayo Clinic patient onboard. The attendants were used to carrying special-needs passengers with wheelchairs, oxygen, and other medical paraphernalia, so I didn't feel out of place with my flowered nightcap covering my bandaged head. It was a loud thirty-minute flight, with the propellers roaring in my ears, and I had quite a headache by the time we landed.

A long layover in Minneapolis gave me time to get to my next gate without hurrying. I sat down, leaned my head back, and closed my eyes. Every part of me hurt, and I was anxious about leaving the security of the clinic and my doctors. I'd come to know and care about many of the nurses, and I'd miss them and their attention and care.

"Candy?"

The voice sounded familiar. I opened my eyes to see Dr. Laws sitting in the seat across from me.

"Are you going through Memphis on your way home to Birmingham?"

"Yes, sir," I answered, thrilled to see a familiar face. I'd liked Dr. Laws from the first day I met him with Dr. Jackson the summer before.

"So am I," he answered. "I'm giving a lecture in Memphis tonight. Have you checked in yet?"

I'd been so tired when I arrived at the gate that I hadn't even thought about it. "No, I haven't."

"Well, here," he said, "let me have your ticket and I'll check you in." He glanced down at my ticket, then looked up and smiled again. "This is great! You and I are both in first class. We can sit together."

"Oh, no, sir," I answered, disappointed that he had misread my ticket, as I'd have loved to sit next to him on the flight. "I don't have a first-class ticket. I've never flown first-class before."

"Your ticket says first-class."

I checked, and he was right. I had no idea how I got a first-class ticket, and I was pretty sure I hadn't had one for the morning flight, but I had one now, and that was all that mattered.

Dr. Laws took my bag, and I followed him onboard. We were seated in the first row of the front of the plane. We talked awhile, mainly about my going home and seeing my children. We also talked about how rough it had been the past five weeks, but that things seemed to be settling down now.

We had just quieted for a minute when—*phhhttt!*—I heard a strange noise in my right ear. I grabbed it, knowing something had happened. It was more than my ear popping from the air pressure, and it hurt terribly. *Oh, no! What now?*

It was obvious from the look on Dr. Law's face that he'd heard it too.

"What just happened?" I asked, still holding my ear and trying not to panic.

"Do you have tubes in your ears?"

I told him I did, but just in the right ear.

He smiled. "Then it's nothing to worry about. The tube just blew out, that's all. It can be fixed when you get home."

Because Dr. Laws didn't seem concerned, I wasn't either. I relaxed, grateful he was sitting next to me. I doubted I could have dealt with another incident by myself.

It wasn't long before I noticed Dr. Laws was taking a nap. As I watched him sleep, I thought, *Oh, Lord, I've done it again, haven't I? I'm so sorry! I didn't trust You like I should have. I was mad at You this morning, and now look. I have someone to escort me home. And not just anyone, either—my neurosurgeon! You had a better plan all along, didn't You? You always do.*

I felt terrible that I'd been so mad at God, that I hadn't trusted Him, even after He'd been faithful to me through everything. *I'll never not trust You again. Time after time, You've shown me You're in control. When will I ever learn?*

◇   ◇   ◇

My connection in Memphis was tight, and I knew I couldn't make it on my own. Dr. Laws ran ahead, checked me in, and held the flight till I got there. I hugged him goodbye and told him I'd see him in a month—but *not* in a helmet! He laughed and waved me onto the plane.

It was late, and I was exhausted by the time I arrived in Birmingham, but Colley and Elliott were there, waiting for me with Lee and my parents. Lee had told the children they could stay up late for this special occasion, and they were so excited. Elliott ran to me as soon as I stepped up the corridor to the gate. My little boy seemed so grown up!

Then I saw Colley. Momma was holding her, but when my daughter saw me, she buried her head in Momma's chest.

"Colleybug, it's me," I said, trying to turn her head to see me, but she buried it even deeper. It was obvious she didn't recognize me, and she was afraid of the person she saw. The scars were still visible down my face, and the nightcap covered my head. It's no wonder she didn't know me!

I decided to let her be, even though I ached to hold her. It would take time, and I'd have to be patient. At least I was finally home.

16

◇　　◇　　◇

When I walked into the dining room of our cozy cottage, I felt welcomed by the warmth of the lamps against the peach walls. What struck me most were the daffodils and roses. They were everywhere! Daffodils are my favorite flowers, and all I could think of was Ethel Merman singing about everything coming up roses and daffodils.

Hot tears of joy and gratitude pricked the back of my eyelids, as I realized my friends had filled my home from front to back with vases of freshly picked daffodils, which bloom about two weeks out of the year. The timing was perfect! Bright yellow blooms with orange centers, white blooms with yellow centers…. Though I had no sense of smell, I knew the house must be permeated with the fragrance of those lovely flowers, which seemed to smile at me as I admired them.

Already tired from the long day and grateful to the Lord for providing me with the perfect escort home, my heart now swelled with gratitude for thoughtful friends and family who'd given so much of themselves during this long ordeal and who'd now given again to make my homecoming perfect.

I was also overjoyed at being able to once again tuck my precious children into bed, though Colley was still a bit uncomfortable with me. I sat on Elliot's bed and thought of all the grown-up situations he'd had to deal with in the past couple of years. He'd overheard the adults' conversations, and he knew the seriousness of my condition. He understood he could lose his mother, and that possibility was reinforced by the way I looked. I did my best to be cheerful and encouraging, but all the makeup, scarves, and bonnets in the world couldn't hide my physical appearance.

That continued to be my biggest challenge with Colley. As much as I wanted to rock her to sleep that first night, I realized she just wasn't ready, so Momma rocked her instead. After Colley was asleep, I stood over her bed, watching her in the dim light of the bathroom.

For a two-year-old, Colley was already showing signs of being insightful. She'd sensed something was going on, even before my first surgery. She somehow understood I wasn't feeling well, though I tried to hide it from her. For seven months Colley accompanied me twice a week to the allergist for my shots. She was only one year old at the time, and throughout those months, she clung to the security of my momma.

Later, even when Momma was away at the hospital with me, Colley remained close to her. Their bond had continued to deepen, even when I was home, since Momma was with us much of the time then as well. I was thankful for that, but I was also a bit jealous. I wanted that sort of bond between Colley and me, though I understood why that wasn't the case. Now that I was home and ready to take over my nurturing role once again, I prayed Colley and I would quickly draw close.

It was late when I finally crawled into my own bed, under my own comforter, and lay my hurting but grateful head on my own pillow.

The next morning reinforced my gratitude, when I awoke to a bright spring morning. With the draperies always opened, the sun shone through the windows, glistening on the hardwood floors of the living room, dining room, and sunroom. The trees outside burst with the life of new green leaves—quite different from the cold, snow-covered ground I'd left behind the day before.

It truly was the beginning of a new day—no more shots or tests or surgeries or isolation. I was home with my family, where I belonged.

◇　　　◇　　　◇

In early March, 1983, though still weak, I was anxious to get back to Bible study. That group of twenty girls was more than just a gathering of acquaintances who attended a Bible study with me; I was a Christian, and they were the first group of believers I'd ever been a part of—and I missed them! More than any kind of social or special-interest group, there was a deep bond between us that I'd never experienced before. It didn't take away from my relationships with the girlfriends I already had, but something different happened when we studied the Bible together.

Getting ready to go to my first study was difficult and getting dressed was exhausting, so I went in my pajamas. Mary Ruth and Lee Whatley picked me up to take me the few blocks to the meeting. The warm welcome of the group made me feel right at home, even dressed as I was. We laughed about my calling and not being able to talk with them before I went to surgery, and I told them about Hank and how God used him to give me the scriptures I needed to hear.

We all agreed that God was teaching us about His sovereignty and faithfulness, and that He was playing it out right before our eyes, allowing us to be part of it. Barbara was able to use the many things that happened during those five weeks as examples in her teaching about the importance of prayer and of trusting in a sovereign God and knowing His Word.

"When I think about the past five weeks," Barbara said, "I think of the scripture in 2 Corinthians 4:8-10, which says, 'We are afflicted in every way, but not crushed; perplexed, but not driven to despair; persecuted, but not forsaken; struck down, but not destroyed, always carrying in the body the death of Jesus, so that the life of Jesus may also be manifested in our bodies.'"

"Wait a minute," I said. "Where was that again? I want to underline it in my Bible."

I was underlining a lot in my Bible those days, and that's the way I wanted it—a Bible that was underlined, marked, starred, and very obviously used. I had a long way to go, but I was committed to doing it, and my Bible study girlfriends were just the ones to help me along the way—even if I had to be there in my pajamas.

◇　　　◇　　　◇

Lee Whatley, one of the ladies in the group, seemed determined to help in another area as well.

"We've got to do something about those hats!" she announced one day.

"What?" I asked, feigning surprise but determined to defend my cloth shower caps. "You don't like my Little-House-on-the-Prairie hats? They're loose on my head, and I think they're cute. Well, maybe not cute, but they serve the purpose." I had two or three of them, covered with tiny pastel floral prints. They were far from fashionable, but they covered my bandages and kept Colley happy.

"Don't take it off!" Colley would say if she happened to pass the bathroom when I was standing at the sink, getting ready to remove it.

But Mary Ruth backed Lee up. "We have to change your headgear if you're going to keep going out in public."

Then one day a woman flounced into my bedroom, followed by Lee and Mary Ruth—no one ever knocked in our neighborhood; they just announced themselves as they entered—and the woman introduced herself as "Gregory" (her maiden name) and informed me that "those hats have got to go!"

Gregory was even more dramatic than I, and that's saying a lot. She was strikingly beautiful, with dark brown hair swept over one eye—sophisticated, like a model, but fun. Everything she had on that day was purple and expensive, including funky earrings and jewelry. I liked her right away.

She set a box down on my bed and pulled my hat off, expertly hiding the shock of seeing my head for the first time, and then whipped all kinds of sizes and shapes of brightly colored scarves out of her box and wrapped them in various ways around my head. Each time I looked in the mirror, I couldn't wait to see the next creation. I was comfortable wearing "do-rags," as we call them in the South—bandanas tied at the back of the neck, Aunt-Jemima style—but Gregory's creations were high fashion to me!

"Let's take pictures," I suggested. "But first, let me put on my lipstick." It was the most fun I'd had since I got home. My head wasn't healed enough to wear the wig I'd bought, and I didn't like it anyway. Most everyone in my community knew of me by then, as the story had been on Sunday's front page of the *Birmingham News*, so I wasn't embarrassed or self-conscious in the little cloth shower caps. At the same time, the look did portray a kind of pitiful appearance. Though my lack of a forehead bone was obvious with the scarves, I couldn't wait to go out with my new look.

"Now look," Gregory ordered.

I peeked in the mirror and was thrilled to see the scarf tied in a loose knot over my ear, perfectly matching my purple robe. It was like a party, with the four of us in my bedroom, pulling out scarves and tossing them on the bed and over to Gregory to see what she would do next. Mary Ruth and Lee were egging her on and commenting that I needed some big hoop earrings so I'd look like a gypsy.

I wouldn't mind that. Looking like a gypsy would be fun! I'd always loved playing dress-up when I was a little girl, so why not now? I loved the costumes I'd worn over the years for dance recitals and musicals, and

I somehow sensed this was a turning point. I could still look cute—at least to me—not like the poor girl who had cancer and was covering up her mangled head.

"Okay, y'all, which one can I wear tonight?" It was Wednesday, the night for dinner at church. Wouldn't everyone be surprised to see the new Candy?

"I'll wear something basic," I decided. "What about black pants and a white sweater?"

Before I knew it, Gregory whipped out a solid red scarf and tied it like a bandana, then tucked in the ends at the back of my neck. She then wrapped a long black and white silk scarf around my head, making a flowerette over my ear.

"This is it!" I exclaimed. "I love it!"

"Oh, Lord, what have we done?" my girlfriend Lee drawled, and then laughed. "She's on stage now!" We all laughed with her, aware that the entire mood had changed. We were gleefully happy, glad to be having so much fun together.

Not even Lee could spoil my mood when he got home from work. Though it was obvious he wasn't thrilled with my new look, nor was he interested in hearing about my afternoon with the girls, I didn't care. I felt cute and happy and excited—and I was going to dinner at church!

◇   ◇   ◇

My excitement mounted as Lee and I and the children neared our historic Tudor-style rock church. It was dusk, and people were out walking their dogs along the winding, divided street that curved through the beautiful old Birmingham neighborhood. It had been two months since I'd seen the people who'd prayed diligently for me and my family. I couldn't wait to thank them and let them see the answer to their prayers!

Photos

"Therefore, if any one is in Christ,

he is a new creation;

the old has passed away, behold,

the new has come."

II Corinthians 5:17,18

Me as Raspberry Tart, age 5

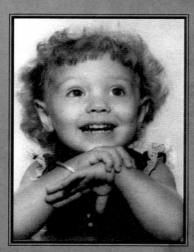

Age 2

With Daniel Boone,
my first dance partner

Another birthday and another reason to get all dressed up, age 8

With Granddaddy Williams, I picked me a bouquet at the end of the red dirt road

"Yet, O Lord, thou art our Father; we are the clay, and thou art our potter; we are all the work of thy hand."

Isaiah 64:8

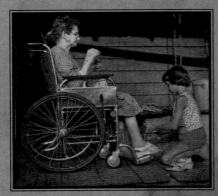

MaMaw Williams. I loved to lace her shoes

Robert, my first love, and me in my cheerleading outfit

Shades Valley High School, senior picture, 1969

With my University of Alabama college roommate, Kathy Willis, 1972

Huntingdon College,
Montgomery,
Alabama,
freshman year

University of
Alabama,
sophomore year

Posing on a rock,
college days

Elliott, age 3

Colley, age 6 months

Bridesmaid for my best friend Tricia (1981)

Colley, age 1

Lee and Candy, New Year's Eve 1981

First Surgery

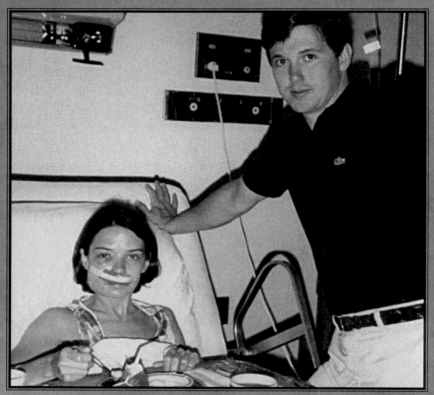

Pivotal day. Biopsy. Our 10-year anniversary
and the day I surrendered my life to the Lord. May 20, 1982

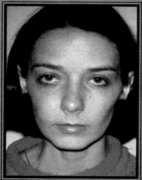

Before my surgery at Mayo Clinic,
immediately after leaving
Dr. Jackson's office

Pre-surgery in pink robe and my
lovely white stockings

Before surgery, Dr. Jackson marked my face to show where he would cut.

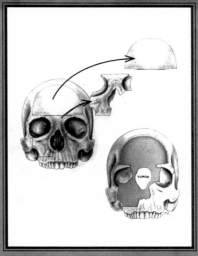

Arrows indicate the two bones to be removed. The original plan was not to replace them.

"A new heart I will give you, and a new spirit I will put within you; and I will take out of your flesh the heart of stone and give you a heart of flesh. And I will put my spirit within you, and cause you to walk in my statutes and be careful to observe my ordinances."

Ezekiel 36:26,27

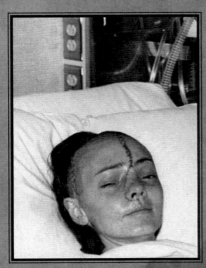

After surgery

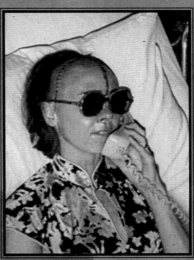

My eyes couldn't take any light at all, but there was no problem talking on the phone.

Dr. Jackson
I'm leaving Rochester

Dr. Laws
Released from the clinic

Raleigh and Dottie, Momma and Daddy and me leaving the hospital

Post-surgery antique
shopping with Momma

Six weeks after surgery,
having fun

Home, one and a half
months after surgery

My playgroup, a month after returning home

"The king is enthralled by your beauty; honor him for he is your lord."
Psalms 45:11 NIV

Interview with the *Birmingham
News,* November 1982

Infection. Back at the
Mayo Clinic, January 1983

Next Trip to the Mayo Clinic

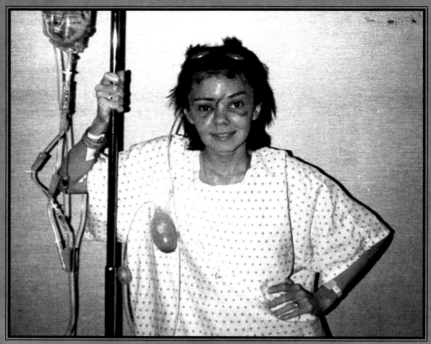

Back in for yet another surgery

Patty, my nurse, after the
first surgery

Dr. Jackson and Candy

Dottie visits,
second surgery

The first of many innovative head coverings. Nurse Sue gives me my choice of pain medicine.

Mary, Edwin and Daddy

Scalp rotation completed

Skin graft from my upper thigh

My field trip in my black patent shoes with Raleigh and Dottie after all four surgeries

Hats & Wigs

Candy and Dr. Creagan, May 1983

Candy and Dr. Dahlin, May 1983

"...for the Lord sees not as man sees; man looks on the outward appearance, but the Lord looks on the heart."

I Samuel 16:7b

Having fun, getting out

I visited burn patient Martha in Rockford, Illinois. My wig is Donna #8.

From left, my "colorful" and outrageous friends, Lee Whatley, Lynn Letson,
Mary Ruth Caldwell and me.
Can you tell the one who taught me how to do the scarves?

"Create in me a clean heart, O God,
and put a new and right spirit within me."

Psalms 51:10

Easter 1983, with Colley

Candy and Janice Hill. Photo taken at
a theater gala (first hairpiece)

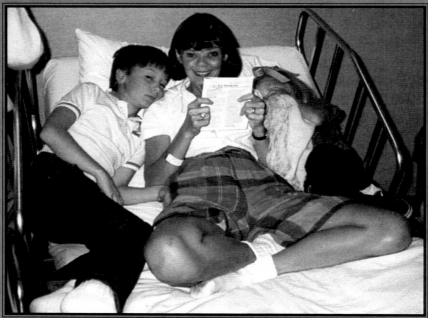

The tumor returns, May 1985. I return to the Mayo Clinic for another surgery.
This time, Colley and Elliott accompanied me.

My favorite visitors

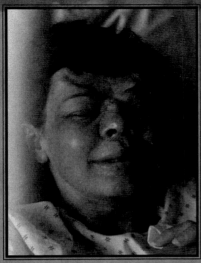

Back from surgery

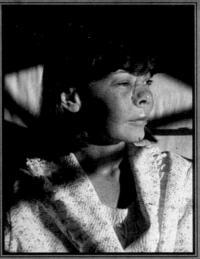

Pensive moment

*"For thou hast delivered my soul from death, my eyes from tears,
my feet from stumbling: I walk before the Lord in the land of the living.
I kept my faith, even when I said, 'I am greatly afflicted.'"*

Psalms 116:8-10

Leaving Mayo Clinic. Southern girls
never go out without their red lipstick.

Christmas photo with family, 1985

Makeovers

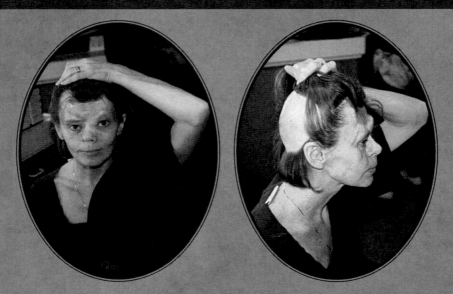

This is me even now, without my makeup and hairpieces
– and the tape that holds my eyebrow up.

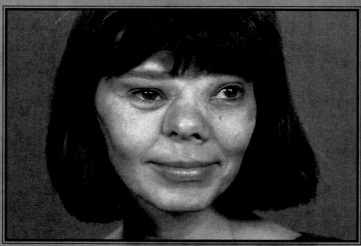

The makeovers begin. The "before" photo on my *Let's Face It* video

The "after" photo. Makeup by Sharon Myers

"Charm is deceitful, and beauty is fleeting,
but a woman who fears the Lord is to be praised."

Proverbs 31:30

After makeover with makeup
artist Leslie Christin

Marilyn Skiba,
makeup artist in NYC

My Family

With Elliott

Daddy takes the lead,
my favorite dance partner

Momma and me

With Colley

Daddy and me, Roll Tide!

All dressed up for the Ball of Roses, from left, Sara and Elliott, me, Gilder and
Colley, Daddy and Momma

"A glad heart makes a cheerful face."
Proverbs 15:13

Colley and Gilder's wedding, 2003

Elliott and Sara's wedding, 1998

Elliot and Sarah, 2013

Colley and Gilder in
New York, 2013

My family at the beach, 2005

John, Candy and the grandchildren, 2013

The Hatchett family, Colley's in-laws
(we are family!)

Cal, Candy and Nathan

The Lindleys – Margaret, John Jr., Mary Gailor,
May May, Candy and John

*"I will restore
to you the
years which the
swarming locust
has eaten...."*

Joel 2:25a

Candy and John with
Davis and Mallie Tate

Dearest friends, my minister
Frank Barker and his wife, Barbara,
my Bible study teacher

With my cheerleader, the queen of
encouragement, Sandra Aldrich

If it's Tuesday, it's Bible study.

Dr. Jackson and his wife, Marjorie, accompanied me when I
received the American Society of Plastic Surgery *Patients of Courage* award.

"Prayer warrior" Elizabeth Ray,
welcome home from the U. S.
Paralympic Bocce team!

Junior Miss Pageant Director,
Eddie Macksoud, and Ginger Roberts,
Choreographer of Jefferson County
Junior Miss Program, my successor.

Faces of Broadway

Faces of Broadway, a charity performance by Broadway's leading ladies and men, benefitted the Cleft and Craniofacial Center, operated by Dr. John Grant, Children's Hospital in Birmingham, Alabama

Red Mountain Theatre Co.

I ♥ New York!

When I was Associate Director
of Red Mountain Theatre Co.
youth programs

Wedding Photos

Raleigh and Dottie hosted our wedding
in their home.

As always, I made a grand entrance.

*"Now unto him that is able
to do exceeding abundantly
above all that we ask or think,
according to the power that
worketh in us."*

Ephesians 3:20 KJV

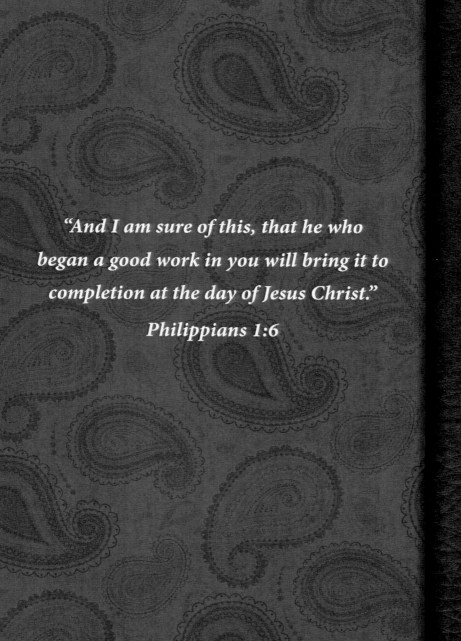

"And I am sure of this, that he who began a good work in you will bring it to completion at the day of Jesus Christ."

Philippians 1:6

I opened the heavy glass-paned doors to the great hall and marveled at the warmth of the rich wooden walls. *So much like the people who worship here! Warm and beautiful.*

We made our way up the stairs to the fellowship hall, where dinner was about to be served. On the way we passed the senior pastor's office, a warm, library-like room, where Dr. McClure had spent many hours on the phone with me while I was in the hospital. I peeked inside, and he was there.

He looked up and smiled. "Well, isn't this wonderful?" he boomed, his deep voice sounding a lot like I imagined God's would sound. We hugged, and I thanked him for all the prayers and phone calls. He assured me he was glad to have been able to be there for me. It was obvious he was amused at my childlike excitement about my newfound spiritual growth and love for Jesus. Although ours was a reserved and somewhat formal congregation where outward expressions of faith were rare, I was "on fire," and I wanted everyone to know it and to know they'd been a part of it.

The warm welcomes continued, as we entered the fellowship hall and gazed at the tables, covered in starched white tablecloths, lined up under the beamed ceiling and surrounded by the old English sconces that adorned the walls. But it was the people—their smiles, their words of welcome and expressions of joy—that made it seem like we'd come home from a long trip.

"Candy, you look so good," they remarked. "It's so wonderful to see you here!"

I was surrounded by senior citizens, young couples, singles, and children of all ages, welcoming me and telling me how good I looked. It was encouraging to receive their hugs and hear their words of affirmation, rather than getting my usual pitiful "poor dear" stares. I knew it was because of the bright scarves and the little bit of blush and lipstick I was wearing, but I didn't care. I was happy to have people respond positively to me again. The more they did, the better I felt.

"You like all the attention," Lee told me later. "Otherwise you'd wear the wig and try to be normal."

"This is how I have to deal with it," I said, determined not to let him put a guilt trip on me or bring me down from the emotional high I hadn't felt in so long. *I'm going to get attention no matter what I wear or how I look, so why not get positive, encouraging attention instead of the other kind? Why can't he be glad for me? Oh, well, I'll just do what I have to do....*

◇   ◇   ◇

Oh, no, not again! What's he mad about now?

I'd been home about two months, and Lee's negative moods were getting worse. I hadn't heard exactly what he said, but I could tell he was angry. I'd just hung up the phone and settled onto our bed, and was arranging the pillows behind me. Lee was sitting on his side of the bed, watching TV, and the children were asleep.

Keeping my voice calm and hoping to defuse his mood, I asked, "What are you so mad about?"

"What do you mean, what am I so mad about?" he demanded, turning his attention from the TV to me, his voice escalating with each statement or question. "You don't even know, do you? If you really knew me, you'd know why I'm mad. But then, how could you? You don't even talk to me anymore."

Daddy always said it takes two to argue, so I decided I wasn't going to be the second person. Softly, I said, "I talk to you, Lee."

"No, you don't. You were on the phone—again."

"Yes, I answered the phone."

His voice was louder than the TV by now. "It's always someone on the phone."

"But I didn't *stay* on the phone," I said, hating that I had to defend myself. "That was Christy. She called to see how I'm doing. We didn't talk long."

"I wish you talked to me like that. That just goes to show where I am on your priority list."

I was getting desperate to find a way to stop this conversation from deteriorating further. "I'm sorry. I did hang up, though. I'm off the phone now, Lee. Let's talk."

"Can't you see I'm in the middle of watching a show?" His face drew close to mine as I inched back. My fear level was rising, and I scarcely heard what he said. Still, I didn't want him to know I was afraid or he'd get worse.

He got up and stood at the foot of the bed, pounding the edge of one hand into the palm of the other as he emphasized certain words. *Pound, pound, pound.* The sound was becoming quite familiar, as he was doing this more and more often.

"Lee, the children are asleep," I said finally, my voice nearly a whisper.

That did it. He began kicking the boxes of clothes that were stacked on the floor as charity donations, kicked harder until the boxes burst and the clothes began to fly around. His face was red, his lips tight, and his veins popped out in his neck.

I was trapped. I couldn't even slide out the bedroom door without going past him, and I wasn't about to try that. We didn't have a headboard on our bed, so I pressed my back against the wall. *What if he hits me? What if he hits my face? What will happen to the grafts?* I pulled my knees to my chest and put my arms around them, deciding to duck my head into my thighs if necessary.

He came and stood next to my side of the bed. "Look at me!" he demanded, moving then to stand in the doorway. "Look at me, Candy!"

I looked at him, standing there in his shorts and t-shirt, with his right forefinger pointing to his temple. "This is what you're going to cause me to do! Do you hear me? This is what you're causing me to do!"

Still pressed against the wall, I listened to his heavy footsteps as he exited the room, trying to track them so I'd know where he was. He went down the hall toward the front of the house, and then…where? I was too afraid to get up and find out, but I couldn't sit there forever.

What now, Lord?

I looked around the room at the scattered clothes and torn, upside-down boxes. For the past four months we'd been seeing one of our pastors for weekly counseling. We both had such a myriad of emotions to deal with, Lee's anger being one of the primary ones. That anger was escalating and becoming more unpredictable, his outbursts seeming to come out of nowhere. I couldn't predict them, so it was hard to prepare or know how to react. His anger was like a tornado that suddenly appears and wreaks havoc, then just as quickly disappears.

I tried to be sensitive to the added attention our family was receiving, but our situation was difficult and people were naturally concerned. I wanted to scream, "It's not my fault that I got sick! It's not my fault that it was my face and it's noticeable! I can't hide it like some other cancers. Yes, I like the attention. It's encouraging to me that people care. And whether you believe it or not, Lee Wood, God is in the middle of all this, and it's not an accident. I want people to be a part of what He's doing; in fact, they *are* a part of what He's already done. I want them to know their prayers have been answered. I'm alive! Why can't you be glad I didn't die? What do you want me to do, stay in a corner of my room and never go out? Not answer our phone?" Of course, I didn't say any of those things; it would only have made the situation worse.

Now, as I sat on my bed, listening for any sounds coming from Lee and wondering what to do next, I thought that if I knew for sure he was in the front of the house, I could sneak out the back. But that wasn't an option because I couldn't leave Colley and Elliott. I was amazed but grateful that they were still asleep.

It was obvious I had to stay but I had to have help, so as quietly as possible, I called our pastor's home number. "Carl," I whispered when he answered, "can you hear me? This is Candy. I can't talk any louder. Lee may hear me. Carl, he's gone crazy. I mean, crazy! I can't talk long. He may come in, and I'm afraid. What do I do?"

Never having seen Lee in this condition, Carl did the best he could with what information he had. "Just try to remember that he's mad at the illness, not at you. He takes it out on you, but it's really not you."

Suddenly I heard horrible noises coming from the living room—wailing and banging. I hung up and slid out of bed, then tiptoed a few steps down the hall, stopping and hoping he wouldn't hear the occasional creaking of the old hardwood floors. What if the children awoke? What would I do?

I continued tiptoeing, a few feet at a time, until I was able to peek around the corner of the door facing into the living room. My heart nearly stopped when I saw Lee on his knees, wailing and banging his head on the floor. Terrified, I scurried back down the hall and into my bed, pressing myself against the wall with my knees pulled up in the same position I'd been in before.

"Oh, Lord, God, please! What's going on? Help me, Lord! Please!" I was too afraid to cry. "Just get me out of this, Lord! Please, please, please!" I held my breath, feeling my heart pounding inside my chest. "Lord, I've made it through cancer. I've made it through infections. But I can't make it through this!"

My head throbbed, and my insides quivered as I sat there in the silence.

Silence? Suddenly I realized Lee was no longer wailing or banging his head. What had happened? I sat there for what seemed like forever, waiting and praying.

Finally Lee dragged himself into the bedroom. My heart rate escalated, but he didn't say a word. He walked past me and collapsed into the club chair in the corner of the room. All energy seemed to have seeped out of him. He dropped his head into his hands. Neither of us said a word.

"Oh, God," he said finally, "help me. Help me!"

I tucked my head against my legs, praying silently. *God, he's asking for help. Please help him! But, God, please get me out of this marriage. Isn't there some way out? I can't keep doing this. Can't I please get out? I know You hate divorce, but this is different, isn't it? You can figure out a way; I know You can.*

I was hopeful, knowing God could do anything and not believing He'd leave me in such a horrible situation. I had no idea how He was going to do it, but I was confident He would. Then I'd be free—free of Lee, free of this craziness and these terrifying episodes. There was light at the end of the tunnel, so long as I held on to the hope that God would get me out.

Then my heart sank, and all hope seemed to *whoosh* right out of me like air out of a popped balloon. *There's no way out, is there, God? I have no biblical grounds for divorce. He's never committed adultery, and he hasn't abandoned me. If only he'd committed adultery! Or if he'd just leave me... But I can't pray for that because that isn't Your will, and I can't pray for something that isn't Your will. So I guess I'm stuck.*

I risked a glance at Lee and saw he was limp and no longer agitated or out of control, so I broke the silence. "Do you want me to call Carl?" I asked, not daring to tell him I already had.

"Do what you have to do," he mumbled, his head still bowed.

I had his permission, so I picked up the phone and dialed. "Carl, this is Candy. Lee's had an explosion. I'm afraid he's going to have a heart attack."

Carl asked what he was doing right then, and I said he'd collapsed into a chair. "It's like all the energy drained out of him."

Carl repeated that it wasn't me Lee was mad at; it was the illness. *But what about all the other times, even before I was sick? What made him so mad then?*

As I hung up, Lee crawled into bed, rolled over, and promptly went to sleep. I turned out the lamp on my bedside table. The crisis was over—for that night.

17

◇　　　◇　　　◇

IN MAY 1983 I RETURNED TO THE CLINIC FOR THE FIRST OF SEVERAL
checkups during the next two years. I could hardly wait for everyone to
see me! I'd even bought new clothes—smaller ones that fit. I still weighed
about ninety pounds, but I knew I looked a lot healthier than when I'd left
the clinic two months earlier.

I carefully picked out my clothes and matching scarves, eagerly
anticipating everyone's surprise at how well I was doing. Any anxiety I had
about CT scans and blood tests was overshadowed by my excitement at
going back to Rochester and seeing my friends. I missed Dottie and Raleigh
and Mary and Edwin. I considered my doctors and nurses friends too, and
I looked forward to seeing them as well.

My heart raced when the pilot announced our descent into Rochester. I
was sorry it was nighttime and I couldn't see the fields of corn surrounding
the airport. I thought about how this trip would be different than the last.

It was hard to believe it had been only two months since Dr. Jackson was actually inside my head. I was cancer-free then, and they didn't expect it to recur this soon. I knew the infection was clear because of all the follow-up visits in Birmingham; the skin grafts looked good and were healing nicely, and I was slowly gaining my weight back.

"Candy!" It was Dottie, standing next to Raleigh and calling to me from the top of the stairs in the airport. "Look at you! Aren't you something? Raleigh, doesn't she look good?" She reached out and drew me into a hug, and I knew she was right. I did look good, at least compared to eight weeks before.

"Yeah, you do," Raleigh agreed, smiling. "You feeling okay?"

When I assured him I was, he gave me a quick hug and took my carry-on bag, as we turned and made our way toward the baggage claim area.

When we entered the warmth of their apartment after a brief but pleasant drive, fresh flowers, carefully arranged in a small, clear glass vase on the kitchen table, welcomed me. Raleigh put my bags down in the room with the antique sleigh bed, where a zebra skin rug lay on the floor. It was almost like coming home.

◇   ◇   ◇

Monday morning started with a CT scan. I was comfortable going to my tests by myself, so Raleigh, dressed in a coat and tie like all the Mayo Clinic physicians and residents, brought me along to the clinic with him. Once there, I found myself looking forward to finishing my morning tests and having my afternoon visit with Dr. Jackson. When I finally walked into his office, he responded just like I hoped he would.

With my chart in hand, he smiled and said, "Well, now, you look quite a bit better than the last time I saw you." I loved his accent and the twinkle in his eye, and I thought how much he sometimes reminded me of a little boy with mischief on his mind. "I must say," he continued, "you had us worried there. But it's good to see you looking so well."

He stood by the examining table, where I sat with my legs swinging over the side. "Let's see how things are looking up here. This kerchief is a bit more flattering than the bandaging, eh? It looks nice."

I was glad he noticed, and I untied the turquoise bandana as he carefully lifted it off my head. Puzzled, he frowned and asked, "What do we have here?"

I laughed, realizing he was referring to my makeshift forehead padding, which I'd inserted under my scarf to help fill in the missing bone. "Oh, that's half a Kotex pad. It has a sticky back."

He laughed. "I'll have to remember that one."

Then he began his exam. "Well, now, the graft has healed nicely. It looks quite good. So does the one on the front." When finished, he asked, "When are you going back?"

"Friday morning."

"Marjorie wants to meet you and introduce you to David. Would tomorrow be good?" When I assured him it would be, he picked up the phone to call his wife. In a moment, he relayed her question: "Can you come for tea tomorrow?"

I eagerly nodded. *Tea? That sounds so English. I get to meet his wife and David. He's told them about me. I wonder if he does this with all of his patients.*

◇   ◇   ◇

I'd never been in this part of Rochester before, but I took a taxi to the outskirts of town. It was like being in the country, with clean, fresh air and no humidity—completely unlike Alabama that time of year.

This time last year I was so sick and didn't know why. I didn't even know if I'd live. Yet here I am, seven surgeries later, feeling fine and going to meet Dr. Jackson's wife and David. I'm going to have tea!

The driver turned onto a two-lane road, and I sat quietly, gazing out my window and wondering when we'd arrive. He slowed down and turned onto a long, tree-lined driveway, finally stopping at a modest white ranch-style house.

Marjorie greeted me at the door and apologized for the mess in the foyer, then led me to a glassed-in room overlooking the pool. She didn't seem to mind that things weren't exactly in place; she wanted me to feel at home, and I did. She was completely unpretentious, clearing off a place for me to sit on the sofa and asking how I like my tea.

Even without the accent, I would have known Marjorie was from Scotland or England. She was tall and fair, with strawberry blonde hair and little makeup. Her look was natural and kind, and she didn't try to impress me. We talked about my family, and I told her I was an only child.

"It must be very hard for your husband and children, and for your parents," she said, her interest obvious and genuine. "How have they dealt with everything?"

They were fine, I assured her. Momma was a rock, and Daddy was okay as long as he knew I was okay. Lee was doing…alright. It was a good thing we had excellent insurance, I explained, so my illness hadn't been a financial strain on him. Daddy had worked hard to build a successful Allstate agency and was financially able to pay for all our airline tickets and other expenses.

"You know," she said, "Ian felt absolutely terrible that you had such a difficult time. He felt responsible. He was very concerned about you when we were on holiday."

I remembered the day he sat on the edge of my bed and told me that nothing was working. I remembered the look on his face and the tone in his voice, but I didn't blame him for anything. How could I make her know that?

"It's all okay now," I assured her. "God has been faithful. I'm thankful for Dr. Jackson. It was a judgment call that didn't work. But he tried, and I'm okay. Really!"

We heard the dog bark then, and Marjorie smiled. "The school bus is here."

Two boys soon joined us in the sunroom. The older one, Andrew, dropped his backpack on the floor, said hello, and went off to find something to eat. Then Marjorie turned to the second boy, who had sunk into a chair.

"David, this is Candy, one of your father's patients. Your dad has operated on her several times."

"He has?" David asked, his slight speech impediment noticeable.

So this was David. I'd heard about him from Raleigh and Dottie. I remembered the commotion at the clinic the year before when the BBC was there with their crew, doing a special program about him.

I looked into the young boy's face, obviously rebuilt with a multitude of surgeries. He had the darkest, biggest, most expressive eyes I'd ever seen. He was short and muscular and dark, an Inca Indian from somewhere on the Amazon. I was immediately drawn to him, not because we were both facially disfigured but because he had a certain quality about him.

"Yes," I said, "but nothing like you. I've only had six or seven surgeries. How many have you had? "

He looked at Marjorie for confirmation. "Fifty-seven?"

When he noticed the astonished look on my face, he laughed and his eyes shone with amusement.

"That's right." Marjorie smiled. "David is a very brave boy."

Obviously unimpressed with himself, David changed the subject. "Do you want to hear a joke?" Before I could answer, he launched into one of those why-did-the-chicken-cross-the-road jokes, and I laughed—but not nearly as much as he did. I was pleased to have made a new friend.

I noticed David's laugh was unusual. His entire mouth, gums, palate, and lips had been remade from various other parts of his body. It wasn't yet noticeable that he had no teeth, as he couldn't make a smile big enough to tell. He just smiled with his eyes.

"How old are you, David?"

"Eight."

"My son is seven. He has brown eyes and brown hair, too."

Before David could respond, a beautiful teenage girl entered the sunroom, pushing the dog back out the door behind her. "Hey, Mom!"

"Candy, this is Sarah," Marjorie said. "This is one of your dad's patients."

"I know." Sarah smiled shyly. "I've heard about you. Hi."

Then she turned to her mother, announced, "I'm going to get dressed for work, Mom," smiled again, and left the room.

I knew Dr. Jackson and his wife had other children and they were trying to legally adopt David, but I wasn't sure of the exact count. "How many children do you have? They just keep coming!"

"Two more. There's Susan, who's away at school...in Georgia." She dragged Georgia out, attempting a Southern drawl—a Scottish Southern drawl! "And Linda. She's the oldest and lives in France. That's all."

Marjorie then suggested we take some pictures. She got her camera, while I pulled mine from my purse, and we each snapped some shots. When Sarah stepped back in, she finished the photo session by taking pictures of David, Marjorie, and me together.

"Do you want to hear another joke?" David asked when we were finished with our photo session.

It was obvious he was on a roll, and I couldn't help but think of Elliott and how hard it would be if he, like David, were—different. *Children can be so mean. How does he handle it?*

I smiled at him and said, "Yeah, David. Tell me another joke. Is it going to be as funny as the other one?"

The afternoon passed quickly until I realized I needed to get to Raleigh and Dottie's because we were going out to dinner, so I called a cab and excused myself when it arrived, but not before hugging David and Marjorie, knowing we would always be friends.

◇　　　◇　　　◇

I got up early Wednesday morning and chose a red, white, and black outfit with my scarves dramatically tied around my head, then hitched a ride to the clinic with Raleigh. I quickly found my way to the Pathology Department, wanting to meet Dr. Dahlin in person. As in Birmingham, not many pathologists meet the patients they diagnose.

"Are you Dr. Dahlin?" I asked, knocking on the door of a room where all the walls were lighted with strips of slides in rows. When he said yes, I smiled and said, "I'm Candy Wood." I was about to elaborate when he interrupted, just like the day I'd called him on the phone.

"I know who you are." He smiled, and I knew he remembered. He was a very handsome man, in his mid-fifties. His eyebrows were dark, almost black, and a white physician's hat covered his hair, but I imagined it to be dark as well.

Though his expression was pleasant, he looked perplexed. "Did you come to see me?"

"Yes, sir. I wanted to meet the famous Dr. David Dahlin!"

"Well, I don't know about that. Come in; have a seat." I did, and he said, "You know, you're a very lucky young lady. Most people don't live with that type of sarcoma—especially in the location of yours."

I knew he was right. "I don't want to keep you from your work, but may I get a picture with you?" I was already peeking out the door to find someone to take it. Spotting a nurse, I motioned her inside.

He seemed genuinely surprised. "You don't want a picture of me. I was just the pathologist involved in your case."

"Dr. Dahlin, God used you mightily in my life. That telephone call last year was one of the first signs to me that God was in control. Even as bad as the news was, I knew He was there—in charge! So, yes, I want my picture with you."

Instead of protesting further, he inched closer to the slides behind him. "Then let's get over here. It's a better background." When we were finished, he said, "You know, we seldom hear what happens to the patients we diagnose. Thank you for coming to see me."

I had some time before my appointment with Dr. Jackson, so I took the clinic shuttle ten blocks to St. Mary's. I then took the elevator to Second Francis and passed my former room on the left. I didn't want to stop and stare, knowing another patient was in there, but a deep sense of awe ran through me as I passed—awe at the time spent in that room with the Lord.

I stopped just past the room to take a breath and absorb the feeling of being loved and cared for, a feeling beyond words to adequately describe it.

I looked down the hall toward the nurses' station. I wasn't in a hurry, so I walked slowly like I'd done two months before, when I dragged my IV pole with me. I wanted to remember how far I'd come in such a short period of time.

"Candy!" That familiar voice came from behind the desk. It was Shirley, the head nurse. "You look so good!" Something about her Midwestern accent touched my heart. "Just look at you! Are you here to see Dr. Jackson? I bet he was glad to see you. And look at your scarves! I remember those bonnets you had." She laughed. "Let's go into the break room. I'll tell everyone you're here."

It didn't take long for the news to spread. "We don't always see patients again," one of the nurses observed. "Sometimes we never know how things turn out. Remember the time I came in to introduce you to my aunt? You were in isolation, and I'd told her about you. You were so sick. We walked into the room, and you were doing some sort of ballet exercises—lifting your leg up and down. You said, 'Cancer isn't going to get me! I'm not going to give in!'"

It seemed everyone had at least one Candy story, some of which I didn't even remember—but they surely did. "Remember the day you took Harold back to his room, with his backside exposed?" We all laughed, and I was glad to hear Harold was better and had gone home.

Then Sue showed up, laughing as she entered the room, and gave me a hug. *How odd that I feel so at home here. Is it just because of all the attention? Then it dawned on me. I'm totally myself here. It's so...different. I'm free... but free of what?*

⋄   ⋄   ⋄

Then it was time for my meeting with Dr. Jackson—a highlight of my trip.

"Well, I hear you had quite a nice visit with Marjorie and David yesterday," he commented when I walked into his office. "David doesn't meet a lot of other patients like yourself." Then he switched gears. "Your tests look very good. Things seem to be settling down quite nicely."

That was good news, wasn't it? So why did I suddenly feel sorry that I had to leave? I knew it would be awhile before I could have plastic surgery to replace the forehead bone, but Dr. Jackson didn't seem concerned about the fact that there was no protection there, and I wasn't eager to return to the operating room. So we left that question alone for the time being, and our appointment came to an end.

As I sat in the oncology department waiting room for one of my last appointments on Thursday morning, I studied the other patients. I saw a lot of slick heads—radiation patients. Many of the women chemotherapy patients wore turbans, and I felt a rush of reality. My appointment was with an oncologist named Dr. Edward Creagan, whose name I had read on the directory plaque on the wall but I had never met. I was in the *oncology* department. What an ominous word!

Suddenly the excitement from the previous three days escaped me, and a feeling of dread settled into my gut. What if it was back? Dr. Jackson said everything looked good, but what if my oncologist found something on the CT scan or chest x-ray? *Lord, I don't think I can deal with another setback!* My heart raced, and I wanted to run away, back to yesterday when I was laughing with Dottie and Mary, without a care in the world. In the waiting room, I realized I was one of the cancer patients and there was a care in the world—lots of them.

I decided I liked the plastic surgery floor better. Raleigh had thoughtfully tried to caution me that oncologists can sometimes be very direct and abrupt, but he said, "Just remember, Candy, that is what you want." There were disfigured children who broke my heart, and other disfigured patients who'd been through various traumas. But they were alive and on the road to recovery. There were also those whose surgeries weren't so obvious, but this—the oncology department—was different. These people—myself included—were cancer patients.

"Candace Wood?"

Finally! The unfamiliar nurse stood at the door, looking around the room for me. When I walked up to her, she smiled and asked how I was doing as she led me to an examining room. I said I was fine, although that wasn't true. She wasn't excited to see me because she didn't know me. I hadn't thought about this visit being difficult by myself.

Oh, Lord, help me calm down! When is he going to come in? What if it's bad news? Oh, please don't let it be bad news! What about my children? I took a deep breath. *It'll be alright. They were just inside my head two months ago and didn't see anything. But it usually metastasizes to the lungs. What about my lungs?*

The door opened interrupting my thoughts.

He reached his hand out to shake mine before sitting down at the desk and turning to face me with his total attention. "I'm Dr. Creagan. Well, Mrs. Wood, everything looks good." He was the only doctor who referred to me as Mrs. Wood; everyone else just called me Candy.

"You had a pretty rough go of it, didn't you?" he asked. I could feel that he was genuinely interested.

I wasn't even thinking about how rough a go I'd had. He'd said everything looked good. What else was there to discuss?

He talked politely as he examined me, commenting repeatedly that things looked good. "How are things on the home-front? How's the husband, and the rest of your family?" I answered as best I could, but when he asked how I was, I knew he didn't mean physically. In my most convincing tone, I told him I was all alright.

"My head hurts, but the doctors at home are on top of that."

"How do you feel about being followed at home for your oncology checkups?"

I hadn't thought about that. I'm sure the possibility had been mentioned to me, but with the infection problem to deal with, having the oncology checkups locally hadn't been addressed again.

"How often do I need to do that?"

"About every three months—initially." He didn't gloss over the fact that osteosarcomas were mean and typically recurred or spread to the lungs. "I'd prefer to be here, then. I feel more comfortable here."

It was settled. I'd return in three months. And Raleigh was right, Dr. Creagan was very direct, but I liked him and I trusted him.

◇   ◇   ◇

Mary fixed a huge dinner on my last night in Rochester, including fresh vegetables and homemade whipping cream pound cake. Edwin was home, and he bounded up the stairs from the basement, calling her name when we arrived. He picked her up off the floor when he hugged her, and she laughed. They were like two teenage lovebirds.

"Candy," he said, "what do you think of my little wife? She's something else, isn't she?" He patted her stomach. God had answered all our prayers; Mary was pregnant.

"And how is the celebrity patient? We're so glad you're eating with us." He laughed and lifted the pot lid to smell the simmering black-eyed peas. In a crazy sort of way, I realized how much I hated leaving to go home the next day.

◇   ◇   ◇

I buckled the seatbelt and looked out the window of the small prop plane. The corn was growing, and a field of yellow flowers glistened in the distance. Tears clouded my view, but I blinked them back. Rochester. What was it about that place? Or was it the people? Yes, but…not just the people…

My emotions were jumbled as the plane took off and the perfect squares of different colored green crops grew smaller. A red barn, a silo… the Midwest. Hardworking people, mostly from immigrant families. It was good to be alone with my thoughts.

Oh, God, You're amazing. I don't know what to say. Look what You've done for me! I can hardly take it in.

I continued to stare out the window as we lifted above a few sparse white clouds. I was leaving the people I'd grown to love. *But what was that all about, God? I know it was You. You put them there for me.* My eyes welled up with tears. *And I thank you so much. But then…my whole life is still in limbo. Nothing seems for sure. Maybe it's not supposed to. My ordered little world isn't so ordered anymore, is it? Or is it ordered by You now and not by me? I should find comfort in that—and I do—but what does my future hold, God?*

18

◇   ◇   ◇

"Girls, you are all so talented, smart, and beautiful," I told the thirty-five girls participating in the Junior Miss program that fall of 1983. "But if that's where your confidence lies, it can all be taken away at any moment. The only thing that lasts is a personal relationship with Jesus Christ. That can never be taken away."

I'd been the choreographer of Jefferson County's Junior Miss Scholarship Program since 1979. Although it isn't called a beauty pageant, and grades and interview count for at least half the voting, these high school seniors were all cute, pretty, well-spoken, smart, and gifted.

The Junior Miss program and its staff of volunteers were a huge part of my life. It was one way to keep doing what I loved—dancing. I enjoyed every part of picking out music, costumes, and sets, as well as teaching the numbers and getting to know the girls.

This year was different. I was thankful to be alive, and I wanted to be more than just the choreographer. I wanted to teach and share things that really mattered, things that at age thirty I was just beginning to learn. I wanted to help them understand the only way to receive eternity in heaven, but also how to live their lives on earth. I wanted to help them learn where to place their priorities.

> *The only thing that lasts is a personal relationship with Jesus Christ. That can never be taken away.*

With my new face and the dowdy wig I'd begun to wear in the fall because it kept my head warmer than the scarves, I could easily have become discouraged, looking at all those girls with their normal, pretty faces. They were the same age I was when I participated in the program as a senior fifteen years before. But somehow, someway, God was changing my heart to care about the things that mattered to Him. He was moving my focus from outer beauty to the real beauty inside, and that's what I wanted to convey to these girls.

The Junior Miss Program was by no means a religious organization or related to any particular religion. I simply told my story and let it speak for itself. It became a ministry for me, as did volunteering my time to anyone who had cancer. This resulted in our phone beginning to resemble a counseling hotline, which didn't make Lee very happy. But I knew how much I wished I'd had someone to help me through my own trials, so I was more than willing to donate whatever time and energy I had to others who needed a friend who'd "been there."

◇　　　◇　　　◇

"John prayed to ask Jesus into his heart today," Elliott announced one day when I picked him up at neighborhood Bible study. It was the summer of 1984, and Elliott was eight. Thinking he was too young to understand the gospel, it never occurred to me that he too might have prayed to receive Jesus.

"Elliott, have you ever asked Jesus into your heart?"

To my amazement, he answered yes, so I asked him when that happened.

"One day when you were at the Mayo Clinic. I was by myself in bed."

As I got used to the idea that my son had already received Jesus as his Savior, I began to pray that God would help Colley, who'd just turned four, understand how to do the same. Not long after that afternoon, Colley and Elliott were sitting in the backseat of my car when Colley excitedly said, "Guess what, Momma? I asked Jesus to come into my heart today!" Then, before I could respond, she added, "And into my stomach and my arms and my legs!"

Elliott chimed in ahead of me. "Colley, you don't ask Jesus to come into your stomach. You just ask Him to come into your heart. When you do, He promises to come in—and Jesus doesn't break His promises."

That settled it for me. Whether or not Colley understood what she'd done or why didn't matter. I knew my children would always know and love Jesus, which made it easier to face my uncertain future.

◇   ◇   ◇

Throughout this time, I went back to the clinic for tests every few months. Those were always bittersweet times for me. Two or three weeks before the trip, I made my appointments and airplane reservations, fearful of what the doctors might find. I'd seek the Lord more often than usual, determined that my relationship with Him would be close and vibrant, regardless of the outcome of the tests. My life was clouded with an underlying fear of the unknown, but I was also learning how to trust the Lord, even with those unknowns.

At the same time, I looked forward to my trips to the clinic, eagerly anticipating staying with Raleigh and Dottie or Mary and Edwin, not to mention the time I knew I'd spend with the Jacksons. We'd become so close over these months and years that I was eating dinner with them at least once during each of my visits.

I felt at home in Rochester—medically safe and secure. I always made those trips by myself. Either my parents or Lee's or my friends took care of Colley and Elliott during the day, and Lee was home with them at night. I didn't have to think about caring for the children or Lee—or anyone. I was responsible just for me.

My visits with my oncologist, though stressful, were encouraging as well. He was upfront and honest about my evaluations, assuring me that things looked good for that visit but never offering hopeful words for the next one.

It was during that time that I really drew closer to the Lord, as if I couldn't spend enough time with Him, learn enough about Him, tell enough people about His love and what He'd done for me. I had to make up for lost time and was sometimes attending three Bible studies a week, trying to learn as much about this God and His Son as possible. I'd experienced His awesome power, his hand upon my life, the realness of a relationship with Him, and the bond of fellowship with other believers. As I now began to read the Bible, I noticed an amazing thing: It made sense where it hadn't before. People told me that was because God's Holy Spirit lived inside me, enabling me to understand spiritual things.

In the midst of all this, I had to deal with my situation with Lee. I was trying to fit him into the physical and spiritual aspects of my life, but spiritually, he just wasn't there. He was annoyed at all the attention people gave us, especially me. He wanted our life to be normal again—whatever that meant—but it would never be the same.

I was a different person. I clung to those who could provide the truth of God's sovereignty and perfect plans; Lee wasn't able to do that. His skepticism and negative ways were of no help or comfort to me. I couldn't join him in his negativity or I would sink. Even though I tried to include him in my new life, my attempts often served to push him farther away. His anger, whether seething or raging, was obvious.

"Sometimes it would be easier if you'd died," he told me one night.

I was stunned, but I knew he was right. Life—at least for him—would have been easier, but I couldn't allow myself to dwell on that.

By that time I was increasingly being asked to speak at various churches and organizations. Having graduated with a speech-and-drama background enabled me to do that easily, and I had an encouraging story of God's faithfulness, which people were anxious to hear. The local newspaper kept up with me, with Candy Wood's story becoming well known and God's name being glorified.

In fact, as I eventually found myself doing occasional talk shows, I developed a signature statement that seemed to summarize what I'd learned about relying on God: "Everything can be taken away except a relationship with Jesus Christ." However, if it had been left up to Lee, I would have come home, recuperated, and melted back into his version of a normal life, with no attention to any of us and no chance to glorify God in the telling of my story. But it just didn't happen that way.

During that time, I began experimenting with makeup, as well as with the creative use of scarves and wigs for people going through chemotherapy or experiencing other reasons for hair loss. As a result, I began work on two videos for patients. This was before everyone had a VCR in their home, and not many doctors' offices had them either. All this took time, as I investigated makeup lines and techniques, drawing on my theater background in the process. I knew this was a project that could be beneficial to many patients, and there was nothing like that available at the time.

Dr. Jackson was encouraging and helpful, caring about the "whole recuperation" of the patient. Interest in the project mushroomed, and it was still in process and at the forefront of much of what I was involved in when I went for my checkup in May 1985.

19

◇　　◇　　◇

THOSE TWO YEARS BETWEEN 1983 AND 1985 WERE FILLED WITH JOY
and tears, laughter and disappointments—all the normal events of everyday
living, as well as some not-so-normal activities. Typically, my type of tumor
would have recurred within the first year in the same place or metastasized
to the lungs. It had been three years, and I had beaten the odds.

One night, I woke up with the sense that I needed to write something
down. I flipped on the bedside lamp and fumbled in the drawer for a pencil
and a piece of paper. Glancing at Lee, I was relieved to see he was sound
asleep and not roused by my movements.

The thoughts I recorded that night were allegorical. I'd always wanted
to be a star. I wasn't, of course, but I was a dancer—always had been
and always would be. Here is what I wrote down: One day the Director
presented me with a part, and I accepted it. Had I known the script, I

would have turned it down. Yet the Director promised to walk me through the part, leading me—even carrying me—every step of the way. As in so many shows I'd done over the years, the Director had given me the "blocking," meaning He was onstage with me, walking me from one place to another and instructing me when to enter and when to exit the stage. All I had to do was follow His lead.

The curtain closed after the first act. I had found the Director easy to follow, and when I messed up, He was patient and gentle with me. The second act was more difficult, and there were times I felt abandoned on the set. Sometimes the Director was backstage, behind the scenes, working with someone or doing something else that needed to be done to bring the production to completion. Sometimes He stood at the back of the theater, watching, while I wanted Him right at my elbow, showing me where to go or what to do. I wanted clear directions: "Walk downstage"; "Slowly walk stage-right and sing directly to Me"; "Keep your eyes fixed on Me. Above the audience! You're not playing to the audience now. You're playing to Me."

There were times I became frustrated with the part, times I wanted to throw down the script and yell, "I quit!" But when I got to that point, the Director walked up onto the stage with me, leaned over and picked up the script, and gently put it back into my hands. "You can do this. Just trust Me, and follow My directions."

End of second act. The final curtain closed. No more acts ... or was there?

The next week, when I arrived in Rochester for my checkup, Edwin was getting ready to set up his internal medicine practice in Dothan, Alabama. He and Mary were busy packing for their move, so I checked into a hotel across the street from the clinic. I put my luggage in my room, sat down on the edge of the bed, and took in my surroundings.

I was lonely. I stood up and opened the curtains to look out over the downtown streets of Rochester. It was a beautiful day in late May, and I decided I wasn't going to spend it inside a hotel room. I figured I could browse the specialty shops and talk to the sales clerks who were used to entertaining out-of-town patients.

After spending an enjoyable afternoon window-shopping and stopping for a light supper, I went back to my room, pulled out my Bible, and reread the familiar, underlined verses. It was time to get into battle mode—my "let's face it," "God is with me, so I shall not fear" mode. All the usual tests were scheduled for the next morning—blood work first, then CT scan with and without dye. I knew that would take awhile, and I couldn't have any food until they were finished. After that I could eat something and then go back to radiology for my chest x-ray. I prepared as best I could, reading the Bible and praying, and finally drifted off to sleep.

The next day, after all my morning tests, I was sitting in the radiology waiting room when I spotted a young teenaged girl across from me, reading a book.

"Hey," I said, and she looked up.

I was right. She'd had an operation similar to mine. "You don't have a forehead bone," I said, pulling up my bangs. "Neither do I."

We began talking, and I learned her name was Angie, she was from Germany, and she spoke fluent German and English. She explained what happened to her forehead when she was young and how the physicians in Germany had removed it. She was at the clinic having tests before her appointment with Dr. Jackson the next day.

"He's my doctor, too," I told her, then added, "You'll like him a lot."

◇   ◇   ◇

It was a full house at the Jacksons' place that evening. There was a couple from South America visiting, as well as a surgeon from the Middle East who was there to work with Dr. Jackson for a few weeks. The surgeon, whose name was Medhi, was a funny little man with black hair and a thick black mustache and black glasses—a sort of Middle Eastern Groucho Marx.

I set the table while Marjorie finished preparing dinner. It was a clinic day for Dr. Jackson, so he got home early. My thoughts of the day's tests were distracted by our hearty conversation. I enjoyed listening to Dr. Jackson and Medhi talk about plastic surgery procedures and medical problems. I'd actually learned quite a bit from the many nights I sat around their table in the past. I asked questions and felt smart that I even knew enough to ask in the first place.

After the company left, I helped Dr. Jackson put the dishes in the dishwasher. "What are the chances the tumor could be back?" I asked.

He appeared surprised. "You seem to be doing well, are you not?"

"I am—at least, I think I am. But I feel some little something in my nose that's small and crusty."

"Is that so? When do you go to oncology?"

"Tomorrow morning at nine-thirty."

He handed me another plate. "Well, I wouldn't worry too much about it. It's been how long now—three years?"

Before I could answer, Marjorie joined us. "Why, Candy, he's got you working," she teased.

Dr. Jackson laughed. "Absolutely! She's got to earn her keep, you know."

I smiled. I liked helping; it made me feel like part of the family.

◇   ◇   ◇

"Good morning. How are you, Mrs. Wood?"

Dr. Creagan's cheery greeting couldn't mask the concern on his face. I'd seen him enough times to know that when things were alright, he opened the examining room door saying everything looked good *before* he said hello. Since that wasn't the case this time, I was nervous.

"Fine," I answered, determined to convince both of us that there was nothing wrong with me. "Don't I look good? I've gained all my weight back. And look—my hair has grown back too! I even have a new hairpiece."

"Yes, you do look good. But..." He paused, and then snapped the CT scan on the wall and pointed with his pen to a spot on the scan. "The tumor's back."

Those three words were the last I heard. He continued talking, but I'd checked out. I don't remember leaving his office or the clinic or how I got to the Jacksons' house. I do know I stayed there until it was time to go to Mary and Edwin's for dinner. Right before I left, Dr. Jackson called to tell Marjorie he'd be home earlier than usual. It was his surgery day, and he usually didn't get in until after eight at night.

"Ian will be home soon," she said. "You can talk to him. He'll make you feel better."

I was waiting for him in the foyer when he arrived.

"Dr. Jackson," I said, breaking into tears when he walked through the door, "the doctor saw something."

"Now, now," he said, setting down his briefcase and putting an arm around me while steering me toward the kitchen. "What did he see?"

As the three of us sat at the Jacksons' kitchen table, I explained what had happened. "He said the tumor's back. He saw it on the CT scan."

Dr. Jackson's voice was calm. "It could be scar tissue. Let's not be concerned quite yet."

"If it isn't scar tissue, the tumor can't be too big, can it?" I asked, trying desperately to regain at least a glimmer of hope. "My scan was clear six months ago. It can't have grown too much since then, right?"

"Well, let's wait and see what it is first. What time do you see me tomorrow?"

"First thing—nine-fifteen in the morning."

He asked if I was staying for dinner, but I said Edwin was picking me up to take me to their house for dinner and to spend the night. I just couldn't stay by myself at the hotel again.

"Don't worry," he repeated, "not until we know what it is for sure."

His suggestion that what Dr. Creagan saw might be scar tissue was the only bright light in the conversation, and I chose to hang on to it until I knew otherwise.

◇　　◇　　◇

It hadn't occurred to me that Dr. Jackson would have to biopsy the place Dr. Creagan had seen on the CT, but as I sat in his office the next morning, he explained to me and the two residents and Medhi that he would do the biopsy in the examining room.

"Here? But I'll be awake. I'll feel it!"

My heart raced, and tears pooled behind my eyelids as he left the room to prepare for the procedure. Medhi took my hand and patted it. "It will be over fast."

"But I don't want to be awake!"

Dr. Jackson returned and began setting up some utensils on the tray next to me.

"Are you going to deaden it like they do when they put the tube in my ear?" I asked, eyeing the long tweezer-like instrument on the tray.

"You don't have any feeling in there. It shouldn't hurt."

"Yes, I do. I can feel in there!" It was true I didn't have feeling on the right side of my face and head, but I could feel in some of the places in my nasal cavity.

"Is that so?" he asked. "Well, then, we'll have to do something about that." He swabbed the inside of my nose with some sort of Novocain. "This will only deaden the surface of the tissue."

I braced myself against the back of the chair, pressing my head against the headrest. Grabbing the chair with my right hand and squeezing Medhi's hand with my left, I froze. "Be careful, Dr. Jackson. Tell me when. Don't do it until you tell me when, okay?"

Opening the nostril with the instrument in his left hand, he gently inserted the tweezer instrument with his right. "Be very still," he cautioned, his voice soft. "Now."

I felt the tug of the chunk of tissue he'd grabbed with the tweezer, and I let out a groan. But I didn't open my mouth, and I didn't move. Tears fell from my eyes. I whimpered as blood flowed down my throat, remembering the times I'd experienced something similar before I knew what was wrong with me and the doctors thought I just had allergies.

"Is it over?" I asked, feeling woozy from holding my breath and trying not to burst into tears.

"Yes. All done."

Medhi pulled his hand away from mine and held it up like it was broken, and then shook it. He scrunched his nose like he was in pain, and we all laughed, lightening the moment.

"We'll send this off and see you back here this afternoon," Dr. Jackson announced, putting his arm around me and then, accompanied by Medhi and the two residents, walking me out of his office.

"Make her an appointment for this afternoon," Dr. Jackson instructed his nurse. Then he turned to me and asked how I was feeling.

"I'm still swallowing blood, and it tastes terrible. But I'm okay."

It was lunchtime, but the last thing in the world I wanted was food, though I did want something to rinse out my mouth. I had time to go back to the hotel before returning to the clinic that afternoon, so I decided to go to my room and call Momma and Daddy and Lee to let them know what was going on.

What's this all about, Lord? I'm not having surgery again. If the tumor is back, then it'll just have to stay. No more surgeries!

◇ ◇ ◇

Later that day I stood alone in the examining room, staring blankly out the window at the overcast sky. If the tumor was back, I'd let it run its course, and then I'd go home to be with the Lord. If it wasn't, I'd come back to be checked every six months for the rest of my life—however long that might be.

I heard the door open and turned to see Dr. Jackson walking toward me. He was alone, and when he stopped and put his arms around me, his words confirmed what I already knew.

"Well, Candy ... it looks like we're going to be in one more act together."

One more act together? What an odd way for him to tell me he was going to have to operate again. I'd never told him about the night I'd written my analogy between surgeries and acts in a play, and yet ...

It really did seem that life was like that—some tragedy, some drama, some comedy, some heavy, some light—one act after another with short intermissions in between. Shakespeare said it so well: "All the world's a stage, and all the men and women merely players."

20

◇ ◇ ◇

"So, Candy," Dr Jackson said, his smile as fatherly as his tone, "do you see Dr. Creagan today?"

I said I'd be seeing him later that afternoon, but otherwise I was free for the rest of the day.

"Well, then, why don't you go ahead with your appointment and then come back up to my office? You can ride home with me for dinner."

I appreciated his attempt to be positive, but I knew he was as discouraged as I was, though there was nothing he or anyone else could do to change the situation.

"Okay," I agreed, giving him a hug. "I'd like that."

I admired the way Dr. Jackson was able to be both a friend and a doctor to me, setting aside his personal emotions to care for me as a physician. I was sure that was no easy task.

The nurse came then, meeting me in the hall, and I could tell she already knew.

"Don't make any surgery arrangements for me, Claire," I cautioned. "I'm not going back. I'm serious!" I might have been tough enough to survive all the previous operations, but I wasn't tough enough for another. The thought of having my head cut open again was too much! I planned to inform Dr. Creagan of my decision as soon as I saw him.

"You were right," I said, when I went to his office for our scheduled appointment. "It's back. I saw Dr. Jackson, and he confirmed it. He wants to operate Tuesday, but I'm not going to do it."

He advised me to use the long Memorial Day weekend to consider my decision. He may have suspected that while I continued to insist that surgery was not an option, I knew better. I would have the surgery, but my mind wasn't ready to accept that yet. Besides, the children were older now, and they'd remember me if I died. I also knew I'd done my best over the last few years to be a better wife to Lee, so I could die without feeling guilty.

Momma, Daddy, Lee, and the children were scheduled to fly up over the weekend. No matter what I decided to do, this time I wanted Colley and Elliott with me. They were old enough to handle it now.

◇   ◇   ◇

Dinner at the Jacksons' was more somber and subdued than usual. Everyone knew how Dr. Jackson's patients felt before surgery. Their son David had experienced more than fifty surgeries, thanks to his father's ability to separate his emotions as a dad from his professionalism as a surgeon.

Marjorie was being honored as "Woman of the Year" in Scotland the next week, and I knew Dr. Jackson was proud of her, although she seemed to take the whole event in stride. Mary was still busy packing for their move back to Alabama, as well as taking care of their one-year-old daughter, Amy. It was David, with his big black eyes, who seemed the most focused on empathizing and encouraging me through this incredibly difficult time.

After dinner I returned to Edwin and Mary's house, glad to be staying with them rather than locked away in a hotel room alone. I lay under the covers in the downstairs guestroom, trying to sleep. It was after midnight when I finally got out of bed and went upstairs to knock on their bedroom door, being careful not to waken Amy across the hall.

"Edwin, I'm scared," I said after they invited me in. "Will you and Mary pray?"

They sat at the head of their bed, while I sat cross-legged at the foot. We'd done this before, when I was nervous about having tests, but never because I was facing cancer again. It always made me feel better when Edwin prayed for me.

◇   ◇   ◇

Colley was staying with my friend Tracy when Lee picked her up on Friday afternoon. He told Tracy the tumor was back and the family was flying to Rochester the next day.

By the time Colley got into the car, she was crying. She was old enough now to understand what was going on, and I hoped I was doing the right thing by having them come. I thought it would make them feel better if they were able to see me, rather than risk their overhearing the news from adults back home. I knew adults sometimes talked openly in front of them, not realizing the children were listening and absorbing their words. I didn't want them to overhear comments like, "I heard Candy may not make it," or "I heard Candy wanted to die because she was in so much pain." But if they came to the hospital and I didn't make it, that wouldn't be easy for them either. Even if I made it through the surgery, how would they feel when they saw me immediately afterward? I knew from past experience that it wouldn't be a pleasant sight. Still, it was a chance I had to take. I desperately wanted them near me, to see and talk with them right up until time to go into surgery.

We cooked out at the Jacksons' on Saturday night. Lee, Colley, and Elliott had arrived earlier that afternoon, and my parents would fly in on

Sunday. I still looked the same as when I'd left home, and I did my best to be upbeat and keep things as normal and happy as possible.

We tried not to be preoccupied with my situation. The children swam in the pool with David, Dr. Jackson, and the dog. I loved the Jacksons as if they really were family. I knew it was going to be a long weekend of waiting, and I was thankful for Marjorie's calm demeanor and Dr. Jackson's care for me. I also felt a bond with David, though he'd experienced far more in his short nine years of life than I ever would.

The next day, Susan, the Jacksons' daughter who had lived in Georgia and recently moved back to Rochester, took us to their house for lunch before going to the airport to pick up Momma and Daddy. Susan, with her rosy cheeks and sweet laugh, kept Colley and Elliott occupied. It was obvious she loved children, and my two took to her immediately. I couldn't have asked for a better babysitter!

That night, with the children staying in Momma and Daddy's room, I lay awake, staring at the ceiling and thinking, *I can't do it, Lord. I just can't do it again.*

"Lee," I said, still staring at the ceiling but aware that he too was awake, "if I die, do you promise you'll marry a Christian?"

He didn't want to talk about it, but I wanted to cover all my bases and make sure my children would be brought up in a Christian home.

In a crazy kind of way, cancer took my mind off the fact that I wasn't happy in my marriage. What seemed to be a death-sentence diagnosis was, in many ways, an escape for me, though no one knew that. Everyone thought I was so brave, when actually it was easier to deal with the cancer than with the pain of emotional and verbal abuse. At least I could take a pill for the pain in my head; there was nothing I could take for the pain in my heart. And that made my love relationship with Jesus Christ all the more special, sacred, secure, real, and unconditional.

◇　　　◇　　　◇

Lee played an early nine holes of golf on Monday with Dr. Jackson and his son Andrew before we met Mary and Edwin and Amy at Silver Lake.

When we arrived at the lake, I watched several couples, strolling hand-in-hand, and I thought, *They must be in love.* Bikers on the trails passed joggers along the way. Children put quarters in the machine for handfuls of birdfeed to throw to the geese that scurried after their offerings.

Momma enjoyed watching the geese. She loved animals of any kind, as well as drawing pictures of them. In many ways she was like a child. I guess that's why Colley and Elliott liked being with her so much. She did fun things with them, even making pink mashed potatoes and placing green peas in the middle. "Like a bird's nest with eggs," she'd tell them, making eating their vegetables a much more pleasant experience.

The sun shone down on us, as picnickers spread their blankets on the grassy areas and arranged their food in front of them. But even with all the enjoyable activities going on, I couldn't get my mind off the impending surgery. Would I go through with it? If I did, would I come through it okay? Whatever happened, I wanted to give my children one more sweet day to remember with their mother.

"Take a video, Momma," I suggested. "Come on, Colley. Let's slide!"

She clambered up the steps to the top, and I climbed up right behind her. We waved at the camera and slid down, laughing.

"I want to do it again!" Colley announced, then ran back to the ladder to repeat the procedure several times.

"Push me, Daddy!" Elliott called, and Colley saw her brother on the swings and ran to join him. She squealed with delight, throwing her head back as Lee pushed her higher and higher. They were having such fun and making such wonderful memories. Was it possible this would be the last time we'd all be at the park together? I wanted it all on tape, and I wanted it to be a happy time—every minute of it—so my children could look at the video years later and know their mother enjoyed her time with them. If they ever doubted that, they'd have the video to prove it.

Mary and I hooked arms, sang, and did a kick line, right there in the park for all to see. There was nothing about me that looked sick that day, and that's the way I wanted it. Besides, I didn't feel sick. I was all smiles and laughter, as Colley played in the sand pile with Amy while Elliott hung upside down from the jungle gym.

Truthfully, I did feel sorry for Lee, especially since he had to go through all this again. I knew it was hard for him to juggle work and caring for the children while I was away.

"I want to take Elliott for a walk by ourselves," I told Momma. I'd decided he was old enough to know what was going on. While we walked, I explained that Dr. Jackson wanted to operate again. Elliott already knew that, but I wanted to be sure he was clear on the details. I told him I didn't know how much Dr. Jackson would have to remove during the surgery, or even if he'd be able to remove the entire tumor. I explained to Elliott that there was a possibility I could have the surgery and end up looking even more different than I already did. I also told him there were no guarantees that the surgery, with all its risks, would fix the problem. Finally, I told him there was a small chance that I wouldn't make it through the surgery at all.

I didn't want my son to have any surprises. Elliott was grown up for his nine years, and though he hadn't verbalized his fears, I knew he had them. I assured him that he and Colley would be taken care of, no matter what, and by the time we'd walked about two-thirds of the way around the lake, we sat down side by side on a tiny section of sandy beach. I put my arm around him, and he rested his head on my shoulder. Wordlessly, we stared at the lake, watching the geese take a swim. When I asked Elliott if he had any questions about everything I'd told him, he didn't say anything.

"You'll still get to go to Camp Alpine with your friends next week," I told him. "I haven't packed your things yet, but somebody will." This was his first time to go away to camp, and I didn't want to mess that up for him.

"Elliott," I said, "God has been very good to me. He's let me have much longer than anyone thought I'd have. If things don't work out, I'll be in heaven with Him. In the meantime, I'm so thankful He let me see you and Colley grow up. I'm so proud of you. Did you know that? I'm so glad God allowed me to have you."

I hugged him and asked, "Do you know how much I love you?"

Elliott nodded.

"Well, good. And are you all right?"

He nodded again. I understood this was a lot for a little guy to take in, and nodding was about all he could handle. Maybe one day he'd look back and remember that day at the lake, as we sat there side by side, my arm around him while he rested his head on my shoulder.

"Okay," I said, "let's go see what everybody else is doing. We're going to the Jacksons' to cook out again tomorrow. That'll be fun, won't it?"

He nodded one more time, and we stood up and headed back to join the others.

◇   ◇   ◇

Memorial Day dawned sunny and warm, with families all across America turning out to remember and honor our veterans by flying American flags, attending parades, and cooking out. We all joined the Jacksons for another cookout, and I so enjoyed watching Colley and Elliott swimming, their squeals of laughter ringing out over the chatter of adults' voices. But as the day progressed, I felt the need to get away by myself. I still had some decisions to make.

I slipped away to the freshly-cut grounds of the ranch-style home and found a spot in the sun where I could sit, with my feet outstretched, leaning back on my elbows. It was time to deal with the inevitable. For three days I'd been saying I wasn't going back for more surgery, knowing that sooner or later, I'd have to concede. First I had to reach some sort of peace with that decision. The only way I knew how to do that was to get away and be alone with God.

By this time I'd seen too many surgery patients, experienced too much surgery myself, and knew all too well the complications that could arise. I sat there, discussing my arguments and concerns with the Lord: I didn't want more of my face taken away; I didn't want to acknowledge the word *cancer* again; I wasn't up for the whole ordeal.

This time was different from the last two. Before the other surgeries I'd felt so horrible and was in such constant pain that I was willing to take whatever steps necessary to feel better. This time I couldn't make myself do that again—at least not with a good attitude. And that was the problem. Without a good attitude, I knew I'd never make it.

I could hear the *whir* of the lawnmower in the distance, where Dr. Jackson was cutting the lawn on the other side of the long dirt driveway. I hoped he'd see me sitting there by myself and come and talk to me. I don't know what I wanted him to say, but surely he would say something reassuring.

Instead, he continued to cut the lawn, and I continued my conversation with God. *Lord, I can't do this again and be okay.* That was true—at least not by myself. But after much agonizing deliberation, I came to a conclusion.

"Lord," I said out loud, "I can do this one more time, either with You or without You. I can do it with You and be victorious, or without You and who knows how I'll be? Now it's my choice."

I'd surveyed all my options to finally conclude that it was my choice.

That was a pivotal point in a pivotal day. By being victorious, I didn't mean I'd survive the surgery; I simply meant that attitudinally I'd be victorious, believing that I could accept whatever the outcome as God's will for my life. I had to think about it some more before making a final decision—a final commitment—and then it came.

"Okay, Lord," I said at last. "I choose to do it again—with You."

The struggle was over. The decision was made. Now it was time to get in "surgery mindset." Like a soldier going into battle, I was going for it!

Dr. Jackson finished cutting the grass, and I was glad when he came over to talk to me. Still in his shorts and t-shirt, he sat down beside me.

"What are you doing—getting your ducks in a row?" he asked.

I'd never seen him so "laid back," and I watched him for a moment before answering. "Actually, I'm sitting here, having a talk with the Lord."

Though he openly professed not to believe in any such deity, I always felt comfortable talking to him about my faith, and he seemed not to mind.

"Oh, really?" he answered in his endearing brogue.

"I decided I can do this again, either with the Lord or without Him. And I'm choosing to do it with Him."

"Eh, well...that's good."

"And by the way, there's something I need to tell you."

"What's that?"

Though many of our conversations were lighthearted, that afternoon I think he sensed the seriousness in what I was about to say.

"I want you to know that should things not turn out the way you want tomorrow, don't worry about me." I looked over at him, lying on his side with his head propped on his elbow. "I serve a sovereign God, who's in total control of my life. If I don't make it, I'll be in heaven, face to face with Him."

"Candy," he said, sitting up, "I don't know that any of that makes me feel a lot better. But I'm certain things will turn out fine."

"Well, if they don't, I don't want you to blame yourself. You do the best you can, but remember that God is in control, and you're really not responsible for the outcome." I knew he probably didn't understand, but I had to tell him.

After a brief pause, he said, "Well, now, are you about ready?"

I was scheduled to check into the hospital about six that evening, and it was already five-fifteen. It was time.

As we walked toward the house, I took his hand. Feeling childlike, I asked, "Dr. Jackson, will you do me one favor tomorrow?"

"What's that?"

"Will you pray with me before surgery?"

"Candy." His voice was hesitant. "You know how I—"

I interrupted him. "I know you don't believe like I do, but will you do it anyway?"

We kept walking.

"For me?" I pressed.

He didn't say no.

◇   ◇   ◇

A short time later, I sat at the kitchen table, talking quietly to Marjorie, who had a late flight to Scotland.

"I'm sorry I won't be here for you," she said. "But don't you worry. Ian and the girls will take good care of you and Colley and Elliott. I'll call to check on you tomorrow."

David came into the kitchen then, holding a stuffed animal known as Ruby Rabbit. Ruby Rabbit was tan with a red shirt, and David always took her with him into surgery.

David didn't speak; he simply smiled with his big black eyes and handed me his cherished friend. In that brief but wordless exchange, I knew he understood how I felt. He'd chosen to show me that he cared in the one way he could, and I loved him for it.

21

◇　　　◇　　　◇

"LOOK AT THIS!" COLLEY EXCLAIMED.

She and Elliott thought it was great fun to pile on the hospital bed with me. As I sat cross-legged and watched them, they took turns pushing the button to raise and lower the head and foot of the bed, squealing with delight and saying how they wished their beds at home could do that. I also showed them how to press the nurse's call button.

"When I want something to drink, all I have to do is push the button, and they come to my room, or they ask me over the intercom what I need. Pretty neat, isn't it?"

They agreed it was, and then I laid back against the pillows with a child on each side, as Colley clutched her blanket and sucked her thumb. We were all getting tired.

Momma noticed it right away. "Time to let your momma get some rest," she announced. "We need some, too; it's been a busy day. You can see her in the morning."

Everyone kissed me goodnight, as Momma took Elliott by the hand and Lee picked up Colley and carried her out of the room.

I was alone, other than when one of the nurses popped in to say hello. They were glad to see me, but disappointed I'd had to come back.

"Is Angie, the girl from Germany, here yet?" I asked when one of the nurses stopped by.

"She's right down the hall and scheduled for surgery in the morning."

It was late, but I decided to take a chance and see if Angie was still awake.

I was pleased to find her awake and alone. Her parents had gone back to their hotel, and this gave us a chance to talk privately.

"Angie," I said as soon as I'd settled into a chair beside her bed, "if you die, do you know where you'll spend eternity?"

Her answer was no, and she really wasn't interested. "I'll think about that when I get older."

"You mean to tell me you're willing to let someone cut your head open, not knowing where you'd end up if something went wrong?" That may have seemed a bit of an invasive question, but I felt comfortable asking because I too was facing surgery in the morning, and that gave us a common bond.

She shrugged. Like many sixteen-year-olds, she had other things to think about. She wanted a normal forehead. She wanted to go home, to go to school and just be a teenager. She talked about dances and boys and things I thought and talked about when I was her age.

I understood, but I prayed we'd have another chance to talk about things that really mattered.

◇   ◇   ◇

When the morning nurse came on at seven, I asked her what time I was scheduled for surgery.

"You're number two on the list this morning, Candy. I'll be in with your pre-op shot later."

I was glad. I'd waited long enough and was anxious to get on with it. I had time to think and pray and read my Bible, and I was glad for that too. I pulled out my daily devotional and began to read but was interrupted by a call from my friend Jean.

"I'm going down in just a minute," I told her. "I'm afraid, Jean."

"No, not you!" she exclaimed.

That made me mad. Yes, me! Just because I'm vocal about my faith and love for the Lord doesn't mean I can't be afraid.

"Just read 2 Corinthians 1:3-4," she suggested, trying to encourage me.

After we hung up, I opened my Bible to her suggested verses:

Blessed be the God and Father of our Lord Jesus Christ, the Father of mercies and God of all comfort, who comforts us in all our affliction, so, that we may be able to comfort those who are in any affliction, with the comfort with which we ourselves are comforted by God.

Then I opened my daily devotional and continued to read.

Tuesday May 28

Wholly His

Christmas and Easter. Sundays and Sabbaths. The very words turn your mind to thoughts of God. But what about the other days of your life? Is Christianity a segment of your schedule or the focus of your existence?

If God asks for the first day of your week, does that mean that He doesn't care about the other six?

In His Word God absolutely forbids every inclination and every attempt to break up your life into two parts, one part for yourself and the other part for Him.

There must be no cleavage, no division. Not six days for you and Sunday for God. Not a secular life sprinkled with godliness.

Never with less than your whole life does God take pleasure.

You have only one life to live for God—and he is vitally interested in all of it.

Agreeing that you and all you have are wholly His is one of the best ways of saying with your life—as well as your lips—"All that God wants is all of me, and that's all he gets!"

Okay, Lord. All of me. I get the message. I'm not quite there yet, but I know that's where I need to be—totally surrendered to whatever Your will is for my life. Here I go again, Lord. I surrender everything to You. Whatever You want is Yours.

◇   ◇   ◇

By the time my family arrived, everything was settled and I was at peace. Whatever happened was in the sovereign hands of God.

"Do you want to ride on the stretcher with Ruby Rabbit and me, Colley?" I asked when the orderly came to take me to surgery. She nodded and snuggled up next to me while we rode down the hallway, but partway there she changed her mind and got off. Elliott continued to hold on to the side of the stretcher until we reached the elevator, and then we all said our goodbyes.

I didn't want to talk to anyone in the holding area that day, but I didn't want to sleep either. I wanted to pray and read the Bible. I asked the nurse if she could find one for me, and she did.

My eyes were getting heavy, and reading was making me sleepier. "Do you mind getting me a piece of paper and a pencil, please?" I asked the nurse, as soft instrumental music played in the background, lulling the other waiting patients to sleep.

Fighting the urge to join them, I began to write.

May 28, Holding Area: Dr. Jackson came by to say hello. It's 8:40
a.m. My eyes are on the Lord Jesus for my strength. Nothing can
keep my eyes off Him. I've had Demerol, so instead of praying and
possibly falling asleep, I'll write.

Lord Jesus, thank You for giving me these extra four days to be able
to get to the point of being willing to accept Your will. But, Father,
You tell us to ask whatever we want but be willing to accept Your
plan—which is better than our plan—Your thoughts are greater
than our thoughts.

Father, I'm praying for and expecting something wonderful and
glorious to come from this! I'm trusting You. You know I get a little
nervous, but the song that's on in the room right now is "Day by
Day" from the musical Godspell.

Lord, I want to see You more clearly, love You more dearly, follow
You more nearly, day by day! Amen! Now there's another song—"All
of Me"—like my Bible study this morning on how the Lord doesn't
want part of us; He wants all of us.

I'd filled the front and back of the paper, so I asked for another piece.
The nurse brought it and asked, "Have you had something—any pre-op
medicine? Everyone else has."

I assured her I'd had my Demerol, and continued to write. Puzzled, she
walked away.

- *God is faithful 1 Cor. 1:9a*

- *Father, please comfort Lee, Colley, Elliott, Momma, and Daddy.*
  Take care of them. Show them how You love them!

- *Lord, I'm still fighting the good fight with Your help. I'm*
  thankful they brought me to the holding area where I won't

> *be tempted to talk on the phone but to talk to You, my real*
> *comfort.*

- *Dr. Marsh just walked through. It's 10:00, and we're off....*

The only thing I remembered after being wheeled into the operating room was when I said, "Amen!"

Apparently I'd prayed because Dr. Jackson echoed my "amen," and that was it.

◇　　　◇　　　◇

Before long Dr. Jackson reported to my family that he was able to get all the tumor, as well as the tissue surrounding it. He told them he'd gone in the side of my nose, as well as through the roof of my mouth, and that he'd taken some chips of bone from my skull and used them to build up my right eye.

"The quality of her voice may be different for a few days," he explained, "but that will eventually get better."

I was back in my room by dinnertime, and the phone was already ringing. Word of my situation had spread throughout Birmingham, and from that moment on, if someone wasn't calling in, I was calling out.

"Candy, what you need is rest," Momma cautioned. "Everyone understands you've just had surgery. You need to be quiet and let the medicine work."

Elliott and Colley were with the Jacksons, watching David's soccer game, but even when Momma and Daddy and Lee left, I didn't mind being alone. The nurses were like extended family by then, and they were always good to me.

◇　　　◇　　　◇

Dr. Jackson and Medhi arrived on Wednesday morning, all smiles.

"Hello, Holy Willy," Dr. Jackson laughed. (Somehow "Holy Roller" got lost in the Scottish translation!)

"She's already been preaching on the phone," Medhi added, having popped in earlier and overheard one of my conversations.

Elliott and Colley came in with Lee and my parents right after that. It was important for them to see that their momma was really alright. Elliott agreed I looked good, but Colley wasn't so sure.

"I don't think she looks too good," she said, speaking her mind as she always did.

I hoped I didn't frighten them, with my swollen face and eyes, my stitches and IVs and other hospital paraphernalia.

"You had one of these when you were little, Colley," I said, indicating the IV drip.

"I did? How old was I?"

"One. You were in the hospital with a virus. This gives you fluids. It's a good thing."

That seemed to reassure her, and soon they were back on my bed, playing with the buttons. It was exhausting, but I was glad they were there, though they didn't stay long. Momma stayed to answer the phone and keep me company, while Daddy and Lee took the children to see the Jacksons.

Right after lunch, Dr. Creagan arrived. "All obvious signs of cancer were removed," he announced, though I noticed he guarded his words. "Dr. Jackson had to use both approaches, through the face and through the roof of the mouth. The mucosa membrane didn't have to be removed, but the back of the hard palate did."

So that's what was different back there. The roof of my mouth hurt, and across the top of my teeth and the right cheek I felt a sharp, stinging sensation.

"Only a handful of people in the world have ever had this," he explained. "Most who had it in 1982 aren't here anymore."

He was very candid in his assessment, and I wasn't sure whether I should be encouraged that I was one of the few still alive or be discouraged by the prognosis. If I was anything like the rest of them, it sounded as if I was living on borrowed time—which I had been for years now. I understood that having come through the surgery successfully was no guarantee I was cured. What was ahead for me? No one really knew. That was something I had to resolve on my own.

I knew that apart from cancer or any other deadly disease, my future— like anyone else's—was not assured on this earth, and I was the type who liked things resolved, neatly tied up in understandable, predictable packages. No one could offer such a gift. All I had was today—and even that could end at any moment.

"Dr. Jackson and I are considering radiation follow-up," the doctor announced, information that was a bit difficult for me to assimilate, but I was glad he'd told me.

"This time I'm not going to try to hold out on pain medication," I informed Momma. "I'm going to get a shot every four hours. I want to be in good shape when Colley and Elliott come." The plan was that the children would visit me each morning, and the rest of the time they would be with the Jacksons or Daddy or Lee.

When Angie came for a visit later, I said, "After everybody leaves, do you want to do movie night in my room? Right now I need a nap."

Angie was recovering faster than I, but she understood I was tired. She didn't seem to be in nearly as much pain as I, and I asked the nurse why.

"She's sixteen, and you're thirty-three. The older you are, the longer it takes."

That explained it, so I took a nap. By that evening, Angie and I had a box of candy and soft drinks, and we were ready to watch TV. We didn't have a movie channel, but *M*A*S*H* would be on at ten-thirty. While we waited for it to start, we saw a commercial for a Billy Graham Crusade. Right there, in the middle of our conversation, Angie heard the words, "I am the Way, the Truth, and the Life," spoken in the familiar accent of the famous evangelist from North Carolina.

"Do you want to watch that?" she asked.

"No, it's just a commercial. But since you brought it up, do you know what that means—that Jesus Christ is the Way, the Truth, and the Life?"

She admitted she didn't, and then she said no one had ever talked to her about Jesus before. "I know the name," she admitted, "but I don't really know anything about Him."

I couldn't let her get discharged the next day without telling her everything I could about my wonderful Savior. Before the evening was over, Angie prayed with me to ask Jesus into her heart, though I can't say how sincere she was. That was best left up to her and the Lord. I'd done my part, and I promised myself I'd follow up with her after we went home, which I did.

◇   ◇   ◇

Dr. Jackson came in early the next morning with an entourage of residents and visiting surgeons, one of them from India.

"Well, there's nothing left between your ears," he teased, "but everything looks good." His eyes twinkled as he spoke, and I was encouraged by his words and attitude. He was right—I really did look good. After he removed the tumor, he'd used some bone chips to raise my right eye and make my face more level. I actually looked better than I had one week earlier before the surgery!

"I think you're good to leave this afternoon," he told me.

That meant I could move into the motel with Momma! My only concern was the pain that continued to sear through my right check, but the roof of my mouth was doing better. The last of the stitches had been removed, and I was able to eat.

When I expressed my concern, Dr. Jackson wrote a prescription and explained that the nerves and some of the muscle were damaged but would be better in time.

Before being discharged, I was escorted out of St. Mary's in a wheelchair to catch the hospital van to the Mayo Clinic, where I had an appointment with the radiation oncologist. Momma and I sat together and listened to his advice.

"We recommend six weeks of radiation. You must understand that this would be strictly for palliative reasons, not for cure." In other words, this would add a little quality of life, but only temporarily.

"I thought osteosarcomas didn't respond to radiation," I said. "Besides, Dr. Jackson said they got it all. So why radiation?"

His face was expressionless. "They removed all *visible* cancer. That doesn't mean there aren't microscopic cells still there—or elsewhere."

I wondered if anything he said ever sounded positive or encouraging. I doubted it, though I knew he was just doing his job.

"How would you know if radiation did any good if you don't know whether or not there are cancer cells there in the first place?" I asked.

"You wouldn't. It's more of an insurance policy."

"Well, God has taken care of me so far, and He'll continue to take care of me." I hoped he'd pick up on my optimism, but he totally disregarded my comment and told me I needed to wait one month for the tissue in my head to heal and then come back—or consider having treatment in Birmingham.

I looked at Momma as we sat in the van on our way back to the hospital. "Well, shoot, if I listen to him, I might as well go stand in the road in front of this bus. But I'll pray about it and see what God says."

"He's shown you before what you needed to do," Momma answered. "I'm sure He'll do it with this too."

As I considered it, I spoke my thoughts out loud. "It's weird, Momma. I really don't think I'll end up having it."

"Maybe not. You don't have to decide today."

◇   ◇   ◇

After dressing, being discharged, and moving to the motel, I fell across the geometric seventies bedspread, exhausted. What about that radiation oncologist? I began to think about the things he'd said. Palliative. Not a cure. They removed the *obvious* cancer. That insinuated there was the *un*obvious kind. Radiation doesn't work with osteosarcomas. So why have it? Even with the unobvious cells, what good would it do?

I was confused. I wanted to talk to Dr. Jackson. I left word for him to call when he got home, which he did. We discussed the situation, and he assured me he would support whatever decision I made.

Later that night Momma asked, "Candy, can you believe it? Three years ago today, you were still in surgery."

Momma's statement was meant to be positive, but I couldn't help thinking that now I had another decision to make—and all because there *might* be some unobvious cancer cells floating around inside me somewhere.

22

◇　　◇　　◇

I WAS AWAY FROM HOME ONLY TWO WEEKS THIS TIME, AND IT SEEMED I recovered faster than before, possibly because I was in better physical shape.

I'm not going to let this setback take up any more days of my life, I vowed. My mind was made up, and I dove into all the activities that had previously been interrupted. I also needed to make the decision regarding radiation treatments within the next three weeks.

Okay, Lord. This is what I'll do. I'll get second opinions from the doctors here. Then I'll lay it all out before You and let You make the decision. I won't just sit around waiting for. You to drop a note or give me a feeling; I'll do my part, and You do Yours. I'll trust whatever You decide!

By then all my doctors in Birmingham knew about the case, and because of its medical rarity, many other doctors knew of it as well. I called four well-known radiation oncologists in town, and all four agreed I should have the radiation. With Dr. Jackson's, Dr. Creagan's, and the radiation oncologist's opinions, that made seven—six for having it and Dr. Jackson's saying he'd support whatever decision I made.

There You have it, Lord. Seven opinions—humanly speaking. Now I'll wait to hear what You have to say. We have three weeks.

Two of my Birmingham doctors asked if I'd seen Dr. Gunderson at the Mayo Clinic, reminding me that he was considered one of the best radiation oncologists anywhere. I said I hadn't, but I'd seen someone else who was also very good. Then I filed away Dr. Gunderson's name—just in case.

My friends too were concerned. "When do you go back for the radiation?" they continually asked.

"I don't know," I'd tell them. "I don't know if I'm going to have it or not. God hasn't told me yet."

Another week went by, and I knew I was pushing it physically. I didn't slow down, though, determined not to let anything rob me of one single day of my life, including the two-hour drive to pick Elliott up at summer camp. We'd spent the previous night at a friend's mountain house near the camp, and I was still on the pain medicine and Valium for the nerve pain in my cheek.

When Elliott and I finally arrived home, I took a shower, sitting on the tile floor and letting the water pour down on me. The warm spray felt good on my worn-out, exhausted body.

"Okay, Lord, it's time to talk. I only have two weeks left. I know You never come too late, but we have to discuss the radiation. I have to make plans. I have to make arrangements for the children. Six weeks of treatment, remember? If I have it, do I just rent an apartment in Rochester and take the children with me? Radiation only takes an hour of the day." I continued to talk to Him out loud, while the water hit the glass door, drowning out any noise from outside. Then I got quiet and listened. Before long I heard it—that faint, still, quiet voice inside me.

If I've taken care of the cancer, why would you want to be radiated?

My eyes opened wide. "What was that? Was that You? I'm not sure, God. Did you say not to have the treatment? Well, that's ridiculous. All the doctors said to have it."

If the doctors said yes, why would God say no? I tried to reason with Him. "It's alright, Lord. I don't mind having radiation. It can't be worse than surgery. And I don't mind going to Rochester. You know I like it there."

The water was still hot, washing over my shower cap and onto my shoulders. Then I heard it again.

If I've taken care of the cancer, why would you want to be radiated?

The very same words as the first time! That's when I realized it couldn't be me just thinking it because I wouldn't have thought it that way. I would simply have said, "Don't have it." But it wasn't me. Could it be Satan telling me not to have it?

"Is it You, Lord?" I asked again. Everything in me said it was. *My sheep hear my voice.* The Bible promises that. It was His voice, and I knew it.

"Okay, Lord, I won't have it. But that better be You speaking to me! If it isn't, You'd better let me know. Don't You dare let me die and get to heaven and then shake Your head back and forth and say, 'No, no, Candy, that wasn't Me.' Lord, this isn't even logical. Are You aware that six doctors have said that I should have it? Of course You are."

My decision was made. I got out of the shower, dried off, and put on my robe, which had been hanging on the back of the door. Lee was sitting in bed watching television when I walked into the bedroom. The children were already asleep.

"Lee, I'm not having radiation." I knew he could tell by the tone of my voice that I was confident in my decision.

"And what happened that makes you know that? Three hours ago you still weren't sure what you'd do."

"Three hours ago God hadn't told me." I was relieved the decision was made, it was final, and I knew it was *right.*

Eyeing me as if he were a psychiatrist addressing his patient, Lee asked, "And what exactly did God say?"

"He said if He'd taken care of the cancer, why would I want to be radiated?"

I took the Bible off the end table and held it up in front of me. "See this Bible? I'm going to open it, and whatever chapter it falls on is a confirmation for you." I'd only done that one other time, but somehow I knew God would do that for Lee. I already knew I'd heard God's voice, but I wanted my husband to know it too.

I opened the Bible and pointed my finger to Jeremiah 17:5-8, a passage I wasn't familiar with, and then read it out loud.

"Cursed is the man who trusts in man and makes flesh his arm, whose heart turns away from the Lord. He is like a shrub in the desert, and shall not see any good come. He shall dwell in the parched places of the wilderness, in an uninhabited salt land. Blessed is the man who trusts in the Lord, whose trust is the Lord. He is like a tree planted by water, that sends out its roots by the stream, and doesn't fear when heat comes, for its leaves remain green, and is not anxious in the year of drought, for it does not cease to bear fruit."

My insides were jumping with joy. I knew He'd do it!

"That's good enough for me," Lee said.

From then on, I never wavered, even when friends looked at me with that "Oh, dear, Candy, you're making a huge mistake" look.

"Nope," I'd assure them. "I'm not having it. God said I didn't have to."

Two weeks later I boarded the Northwest plane to Rochester. I changed planes in Memphis and then again to the small prop plane in Minneapolis for the last quick leg of flight. I liked studying the other passengers and trying to guess why they were going to Rochester. The only big things there were the clinic and an IBM headquarters. My fellow passengers were either IBM executives, or patients, physicians, or workers at the clinic.

The man next to me, wearing a khaki suit, white shirt, tie, brown socks, and brown shoes, was reading an oncology book.

"Are you a doctor?" I asked, talking loudly enough for him to hear me over the roar of the propeller.

"Yes, I am." He smiled and continued to read.

"At the Mayo Clinic?"

He looked at me and nodded, then turned back to his book.

"Really?" I mentioned Dr. Creagan's name and asked if he knew him.

"Yes, very well. He's a medical oncologist, and I'm a radiation oncologist."

"I just made the decision not to have radiation."

"Oh, really? And how did you come to that decision?"

"The Lord led me not to have it." I waited for his reaction, knowing he wouldn't be a radiation oncologist if he didn't believe in its importance. *He probably thinks I'm one of those religious nuts, but I don't care.*

He smiled. "Well, if the Master has led you, then you can't do better than that."

I was shocked. "I beg your pardon?"

"God gives us as physicians just so much knowledge, but only He knows what's right for each individual patient. If that's how you've made your decision, then you can't do better than that." He smiled again and went back to his book.

He continued to read for the remainder of the flight, but I was overwhelmed and astounded. *God, I didn't need a confirmation, but thank You for it! What are the chances of this happening, God?* I laughed to myself. *You're always doing stuff like this!*

When we landed, the oncologist picked up his briefcase, put his book in it, and stood up. He let me get in front of him, and when I was almost to the bottom of the steps, I turned back.

"By the way," I said, wanting to remember this detail, "what's your name?"

"Leonard Gunderson."

My eyes widened. *God, how'd You do that?*

I wanted to scream with excitement. I couldn't wait to tell Dr. Jackson.

◇　　　◇　　　◇

When Dr. Jackson picked me up at the Kahler Hotel to take me to their house for dinner, I felt like I was about to explode with excitement. "Guess what, Dr. Jackson!"

"I don't know," he laughed. "Is this one of those divine intervention stories?"

"Just listen, and I'll let you decide."

I told him about my "divine appointment" with Dr. Gunderson, and then went on to confirm my decision not to have the radiation. To his credit, Dr. Jackson stuck to his promise to support me in whatever I decided and didn't try to change my mind.

When I met with Dr. Creagan, however, he wasn't quite as supportive or comfortable with my decision. "Would you like to go speak with someone in radiation oncology?"

"Why would I want to do that? I already talked to God!"

The next day was July 3, and I had a late flight back to Birmingham after a picnic at the Jacksons' house. They invited several guests, and I was pleased to be included. A croquet course had been set up on the right side of the long driveway, and a fiercely competitive game was already going on among the adults when I arrived.

The children swam, and there were plenty of hamburgers and hot dogs for everyone. Nothing was said about my decision, and I relaxed and enjoyed myself, knowing I'd be back in a few months for routine tests.

23

◇　　◇　　◇

THE FIRST MAJOR WARNING SIGN POPPED UP TWO MONTHS AFTER MY last surgery in 1985. Determined not to let cancer rob me of anymore time and not wanting my senses dulled by medication, I prematurely stopped taking the prescribed amount of pain medicine, and I paid the price.

Throughout that summer, my head, especially the right cheek, throbbed, but I pressed on. I didn't miss the children's events or time at the pool with them, Lee's tennis matches, or time with my friends, and I pushed to finish the makeup and hair-loss video. I was antsy and stressed but disregarded it, reaffirming my commitment to make the most of each moment.

During that time I went to see a counselor. After detailing my busy schedule to her, she challenged me with the question, "Who are you angry with?" I couldn't imagine what she was talking about, so I asked God to show me if I really was angry at someone, but otherwise I simply ignored the counselor's challenge and went on about my business.

On Saturday following my appointment with the counselor, Lee and the children went to the country club for the day, and I planned to join them later after doing some things around the house.

By then people in our neighborhood and city were aware of the "Candy Wood story" and that I'd had another surgery at the beginning of the summer. Churches and Bible study groups prayed, and I received dozens of letters from people I didn't even know, wishing me the best.

Such a young person to have to deal with so much, they'd say, marveling at my cheerful attitude. And they were right. I wanted everyone to know how faithful God had been, how His grace was sufficient, and how I could be joyful in my circumstances. I wanted people to know I considered myself blessed to be alive and to be able to raise my children, and to understand that the headaches were a small price to pay to be cancer-free.

That was the persona I willingly modeled as I walked through the house that Saturday morning, tidying up before leaving to join my family. Then something happened that shattered the calm exterior I'd worked so hard to maintain. Seemingly out of nowhere, I felt intense anger, rising up from deep inside, yet I couldn't imagine what set it off.

I climbed the stairs to the playroom—a long, open room that extended almost the depth of the house, with skylights allowing the summer sunshine to fall on the brightly decorated room filled with toys and games. Lee had even added a fireplace for the winter months, making it a lovely retreat.

That day I looked at the two lamps Lee had bought while I was away at the clinic, and I realized I hated them. My eyes fell on Lee's favorite recliner, a huge monstrosity that didn't match the room at all. The game table and chairs didn't match either.

My insides boiled. At that moment, I hated the room and everything in it, including Elliott's Star Wars spaceship and the Matchbox cars and the Fisher Price little people that were supposed to be on the shelves but were instead strewn across the middle of the floor.

"God, I've had it!" I screamed—twice, to be sure He heard me—and then I yelled, "I'm *tired*—of everything! I'm tired of being Miss Susie Sweet Christian because the truth is, I'm *not sweet!*"

When no booming voice answered me from the heavens, I hollered, "I'm *not,* I said!" Then I methodically began to pick up one toy at a time and toss it across the room. "How's that, God? Just watch! I'm gonna do it again!"

I continued to toss toys across the room, as I screamed out my frustrations. "I'm tired of this constant headache that won't *ever* go away! And I'm *not* joyful!" My logic was telling me to obey the Scriptures and be content in my circumstances, but I wasn't content—and I wasn't happy.

I continued tossing toys until I'd thrown them all, and then I started on the games. Monopoly pieces flew across the sofa. Candy Land figures landed at the other end of the room. Elliott's spaceship cracked when it hit the floor. I didn't care. I was on a tirade, and I wasn't through yet. Boxes of puzzles opened midair and scattered on the grass-green carpet. Playing cards quickly followed.

When I looked around and found nothing left to throw, I spotted my straw sewing box. It was as if I had a personal vendetta against that sewing box, as spools of thread, ric-rac, and even scissors sailed across the room.

"God! Do you see what I'm doing? I know You don't like it, but I'm mad! I don't even know what I'm mad at—or who!"

I tossed a game table chair, and then another, until all four were out of the way so I could turn the table over.

"God, I'm so sorry," I screamed, "but you'll have to forgive me later!"

The room looked like pictures I'd seen of tornado damage, but it felt so good to let the anger out. And I wasn't finished yet.

I went downstairs, calmly took the end table drawer by my bed, walked back upstairs, and dumped the drawer and its contents in the middle of the room. I repeated that action three times until everything in the bed-side table drawers was strewn across the floor.

Finally, standing there with my hands on my hips, I surveyed the room. I thought my tantrum was over, so I walked downstairs and into the kitchen. Then it hit again. I took each kitchen drawer and dumped it into the middle of the kitchen. The brick linoleum was soon covered in kitchen utensils, flatware, dishtowels, and anything else that once occupied a drawer. Then I opened each cabinet and swept the contents out in one full sweep—Tupperware, pots, pans, skillets … everything.

When there was nothing left to dump or toss or throw, I stepped over the pillage and said, "God, I'm so sorry. I know this is not how You like people to handle being mad. Will You please forgive me?" Then I walked into our bedroom and pulled my swimsuit out of a dresser drawer and went to the linen closet for a beach towel and a beach bag. "Well, God, now I'm going to the pool."

It was over. When I arrived at the pool, I was completely conscious of what I'd left behind, but I didn't care.

"Lee," I said, smiling when I found him sitting in a lounge chair, "don't get mad, but I want to warn you that I had a temper tantrum at home."

He frowned, wondering what I was talking about. He found out when we arrived home that afternoon.

That's when I felt remorse. The children surveyed the destruction, their eyes wide as they cried and asked if they had to clean it all up, as they began to re-gather their toys one at a time. Lee stood in the middle of it in obvious disbelief.

I sat down on the floor and cried with Colley and Elliott. "I'm so, so sorry," I sobbed. "That was so wrong of me. Will you please forgive me? I've asked God to forgive me, but will you two forgive me? Please?"

I hugged them, and we cried together. They promised to forgive me but were still concerned about who would clean up the playroom, since that was typically their job. I assured them that I would take care of it.

All this took place two weeks after my meeting with the counselor, two weeks after I asked God to show me if I was angry—and at whom.

What was that all about? I asked the Lord. *You showed me I was mad, but You didn't show me who I was mad at. Was it You? Surely not! Was it Lee? Why? Was I mad at people thinking I was more spiritual than I obviously was?* I never successfully figured out the who or the why, but at least I knew the anger was there. Maybe I'd just had enough and finally decided to let it out. Whatever the reason, after that one episode, life went back to normal—whatever that was.

◇　　　◇　　　◇

It shouldn't have come as a surprise, since the problem had been building for years. Red flags were everywhere, but I was determined to ignore them. Having a life-threatening illness made it easier to do that, as it demanded all my energy and focus. Once I started feeling better, those red flags flapping in the wind became more difficult to ignore.

One morning I heard Lee screaming about something. Because these episodes were becoming more frequent, I didn't tune in to the specifics of his complaints, but I noticed his voice was more intense than usual.

I was wrapped in my favorite turquoise chenille bathrobe, the one he'd given me for Christmas. I didn't know exactly where Lee was in the house, but I knew I didn't want to be in the same room with him, so I made my way as nonchalantly as possible to the breakfast room. If he spotted me, I didn't want him to suspect I was afraid, but I wanted to be near a door leading outside. I also wanted to get the handheld Dictaphone I was using to write my book. My intent was to turn it on and put it in the pocket of my robe. That way, if he killed me, it would be on tape.

Too late. He came through the door of the kitchen and saw me as I picked up the recorder.

"What are you doing in here?" he demanded, his voice at a lower volume than it had been a moment earlier but his tone definitely interrogating.

"Oh, just picking some stuff up," I said, trying to inconspicuously lay down the recorder and edge my way toward the sofa, closer to the door.

Then I brought up something light, hoping to distract Lee from his anger. It seemed to work, as he settled down and appeared to forget what he'd been screaming about earlier. Once again, the storm had passed and everything was okay. There was no need to tell anyone of these instances because he never actually hit me. I don't know why I felt the need to record anything, since his rage always blew over and everything was fine—until the next time.

But when it happened again, I left. It was late at night, and the children were in bed. Lee and I had another confrontation, though I wasn't sure what it was about. When things calmed down, we went to bed, but my heart was still racing, as I lay there beside him in the dark. I wanted to cry, but he seemed to have fallen asleep and I didn't want to wake him and risk making him mad again.

When I was sure he was sound asleep, I slipped out of bed, always with a ready answer in case he awoke and asked where I was going. I put on my sweatshirt and pants and tennis shoes, grabbed the car keys, and sneaked out the side door from the dining room.

It was midnight. I passed our friends' houses, thinking how happy all their marriages were and wishing ours was, too. I reached the four-lane highway heading south, but I hadn't driven far when I realized I had nowhere to go. The night was dark, and the streets were bare. I surely couldn't go to Lee's parents' house, nor to Momma and Daddy's, as they would know something was wrong. What would I tell them? He hadn't really done anything to me. Besides, the children were at home asleep. What would they do if I wasn't there the next morning?

Oh, God, what do I do? I want to run away, but I can't. I decided Lee would probably sleep through until the next day and everything would be okay, so I went back home, making it back inside without our dog barking. Shaking with relief, I got to our room and slid under the covers. Lee never knew I was gone.

My escape seemed silly the next morning when everything appeared normal. What had I been thinking?

◇   ◇   ◇

The skin graft that covered half of the back of my head was paper thin and very delicate, and I had no feeling on the right side of my face. My custom-made human hairpiece was backed with rubber, and specially made two-way tape was attached to the hairpiece and then carefully positioned on the skin graft itself. It was a perfect fit, and after taking it off and putting it on for nearly two years, I could almost do it with my eyes shut.

For several evenings in a row, however, I noticed the hairpiece didn't come off as easily as usual, and the skin graft felt damp and slippery where the tape was placed. One night, after taking off the hairpiece, I looked at the back of my head with a mirror and was horrified to see three bloody areas where the tape had pulled the graft away. A sick rush of fear flowed through me, and I couldn't imagine what had happened, as the tape was specifically made for hairpieces and should never have caused a problem.

I went down the hall to our bedroom door, where Lee was propped up in bed watching television. "Lee, look at my head." On the verge of tears, I bent down to show him. Seemingly unconcerned, he asked what kind of tape I'd been using.

"The same kind I always use—my toupee tape."

"Go get it."

I found it in my medicine cabinet in the bathroom, right where it always was, and brought it to Lee. He examined the roll of white-backed tape and then tossed it back to me on the bed.

"Candy, you're so daft. That's carpet tape."

I was confused. "How would carpet tape get into my medicine cabinet? It looks like my toupee tape, and we don't even have carpet. Why would we have carpet tape?"

He shrugged. "How would I know? You probably didn't pay attention when you put it in there."

I still didn't understand, but Lee sounded so sure and he was almost always right. I decided I mustn't have been paying attention, just like he said. But what was that look on his face? I had seen it before. As always, I disregarded it.

I went to the doctor the next morning to make sure the area wasn't infected, and after he assured me it wasn't and told me to keep Neosporin on it and not to wear the hairpiece until it healed, I laughed with him about how stupid I was to use carpet tape on my head. I would definitely have to be more careful in the future.

◇   ◇   ◇

In the summer of 1986, we sold our house, leaving the familiar community of friends and shops and proprietors to move to a very nice house that sat back in the woods by itself. I couldn't put my finger on what it was about that place, but it wasn't a happy house. At least, it seemed that way to me.

We hosted a couples' Bible study in our new home, and I learned that a woman was to be submissive to and respectful of her husband, as he was the spiritual head of the household. I knew the Scriptures were true, but I was having a hard time applying these commands. Lee's treatment of the children and me was so unpredictable. At times he was gentle and giving, his baby face sweet and kind, and he seemed in control of his emotions. Then there were those raging outbursts that came out of nowhere.

We hadn't been in our new home long when Colley started being fearful at night. It seemed no matter what I did to try to maintain a happy home, it just didn't work. I remembered hearing a saying once that the mother was the barometer of a home, so I worked hard at helping everyone get along, but the underlying tension remained.

It was also about that time, soon after Colley started kindergarten, that she asked me to come to school and take my hair off for show-and-tell. Leave it to my Colleybug to come up with that one!

By now we'd joined the nearby evangelical, conservative Briarwood Presbyterian Church, and we were happy there. And yet, it was a season of living in denial. I smiled and said everything was wonderful, and medically it was. I'd had a few false alarms at the clinic when it appeared the tumor had recurred, but biopsies showed only scar tissue.

Each visit to the clinic, until my last in 1988, was a time of testing my faith, as with each trip I learned to more quickly surrender my fears, the results of the tests, and my life itself to the Lord and His will. By then, I knew with surrender comes peace. God, in His own way, allowed me to stop going to the clinic—and I was as certain of that as I was when He told me I didn't need to have radiation.

I was sitting in my club chair one day, gazing out of the three sets of French doors that opened onto the woods behind our house. "Lord," I prayed, "I don't know how to live without a crisis. But don't worry—I'll get it!" I laughed. "Just give me time!"

With surrender comes peace.

I thought the major trials in my life were over, but I soon found everything I'd been through so far had just been boot camp for what lay ahead.

24

◇   ◇   ◇

IN 1990 I RECEIVED A CALL FROM THE PRODUCER OF *THE SALLY JESSE Raphael Show.* She introduced herself as Karen and asked if I'd be interested in flying to New York City to be a guest on the show.

I was stunned. "How in the world did you get my name?"

"I read your story in the *Let's Face It* monthly newspaper. It was very impressive."

Let's Face It was a national support group for the facially disfigured. At the time I served on its advisory board, and my story had been featured on the front page several months before.

"Candy," she continued, "we're going to be doing a show with the topic of 'Beautiful Women Who Lost Their Looks.' I thought you'd be perfect. We'll fly you up here, and you'll be picked up at the airport where your driver will take you to your hotel in Manhattan. You'll be given a food voucher, film the show the next morning, and then fly home. What do you think? You're so brave, and your story would be so encouraging to others."

I'd gone from stunned to humbled, as I listened to her words. "First of all," I said, "I'm really not that brave. I'm actually pretty much of a wimp. The Lord just enabled me to persevere. My strength comes solely from Him, and if I was to be on your show, that's what I'd have to say. Would that be alright? Can I say anything I want?"

"Absolutely! That's what we want you to do."

I then asked for dates and other specifics, and told her I'd need to check with my husband and get back to her.

"We'd need you to fly up next Monday," she explained, apologizing for the short notice and then adding, "We'd film the show on Tuesday morning."

"Oh, I can tell you right now that I won't be able to do that. My family and I are going to Virginia Beach next Wednesday so I can appear on *The 700 Club*. I've already done their program before, but they want to do an update on the air."

"That's no problem. You'll be home Tuesday afternoon."

I then explained that the pressure in the plane was bad on my head and it took awhile for me to get acclimated again. Physically I couldn't fly home on Tuesday and then leave again on Wednesday. Besides, the children got out of school early on Wednesday for Thanksgiving holidays. We were going to make a vacation out of it and travel to Williamsburg.

"Okay," she conceded. "What if we film the show on Monday instead? That would give you enough time. Candy, we're working the entire show around you."

Why would they want to do that? "I'm so sorry. That's still not enough time between flights. Besides, my husband always travels with me when I'm out of town."

"That's alright. We'll pay his way, too, and fly you first-class, nonstop, if that will help."

I had to admit, she was persuasive. I finally told her I'd call her back after talking with Lee, since he was in charge of my schedule. As it turned out, his answer was anything but what I would have expected.

"Call them back, and tell them that if they'll fly both of us up there on Monday to tape the show on Tuesday and pay for us to stay Tuesday night too, we'll do it. That way we can see a Broadway show. Then, if they'll pay for us to rent a car to drive to Washington, D.C., and for Colley and Elliott to fly to meet us there, we can all drive through Williamsburg to Virginia Beach. *The 700 Club* can pay to fly us home."

It was the craziest idea I'd ever heard! Why would *The Sally Jesse Raphael Show* or *The 700 Club* agree to all that? Besides, I didn't think it was safe for the children to fly by themselves—especially Colley, who got scared easily.

But Lee was insistent, so I finally gave in. "Fine, if that's how you want to do it, but you'll have to call Karen and ask. I'm too embarrassed."

Lee made the call, and amazingly, they agreed to everything he asked. It looked as if we were going to the Big Apple!

◇   ◇   ◇

Once in New York, a driver picked us up at the hotel to take us to the studio. Sally's practice was to tape two live shows daily, and I was to be on the second show. Outside the green room (a theater term for the place actors wait until they go onstage), we waited for the previous guests to leave.

My sole purpose for doing the show was to share my faith in Jesus Christ, and despite assurances that I was free to do so, I was uncertain as to how much Sally would allow me to say.

Four other women had come to appear on the program with me. Three had been in automobile accidents, and one had been burned in a house fire. Sally briefly came into the green room to introduce herself. She was cordial but businesslike, as she shook each of our hands and thanked us for coming.

Then Karen, the producer who'd called me, pulled me aside. "We want you to go on first. Sally will ask you a lead-in question, and then we want you to talk for seven or eight minutes. Are you comfortable with that?"

"I can say anything I want? *Anything?*"

"Anything, as long as it pertains to your story. Can you do that?"

"Sure. No problem." There I had it—free reign to say whatever I wanted, and more time than expected.

I'd already prayed that God would give me the right words and the opportunity to say them, so I took a deep breath, prayed, and nearly laughed aloud from excitement. *Okay, Lord, let's go for it!* The next thing I knew, I was onstage.

Sally had me briefly share the circumstances of my story, and then she was respectfully quiet as I said, "That was a difficult time, but I grew to have a dependency on the Lord Jesus Christ that I never had before. I can honestly say that I wouldn't change one minute of the last eight years."

Amazed, Sally responded, "Wouldn't change one minute? Could I have done that, Candy? That's what we're all thinking right now."

"I had a peace that the Bible describes as beyond understanding."

Looking at me through her bright red-rimmed glasses, she slowly shook her head.

"After all that and you talk about peace." The camera stayed on her another second before cutting to a commercial break.

A man in the front row of the audience gave me a thumbs-up each time I mentioned Jesus Christ, and two black women seated in the center of the audience encouraged me by mouthing "You are beautiful" each time I looked at them. Since I was appearing on a show called "Beautiful Women Who Lost Their Looks," their silent affirmation meant a lot.

Everyone applauded when Sally went into the audience to introduce Lee. He was a hero because he was the only husband or boyfriend who hadn't abandoned the woman who had "lost her looks." Statistically, most marriages and relationships break up after disfiguring illnesses or accidents. Lee told Sally, "Candy is still beautiful."

When the show was over, Lee and I went to dinner and took in a Broadway musical, then watched the ice skaters and the Christmas tree at Rockefeller Center and walked through Chinatown and Times Square.

New York! I'm in New York! Skipping ahead of Lee, I threw my arms up in the air and began to sing from the musical *New York,* which starred Gene Kelly. Finally, we topped off the night with donuts and milk.

Car rented and bags packed, we left early the next day for Washington. I was anxious to get there as soon as possible, with no chance of being late to pick up the children at the airport. I'd already called home and talked to Colley, and I knew she was scared.

"Colley, you'll be with Elliott, and he'll take care of you," I'd assured her. "The stewardess will be with you the whole time, and we'll be right there at the gate when you get off the plane."

I finally convinced her and hung up, anxious to fulfill my promise to my children. According to the map, it would take about four and a half hours to get to the Washington airport. Their flight was scheduled to arrive at six-thirty that evening, but right outside of Washington, Lee mentioned we were low on gas—and continued to drive.

Finally I asked, "Are we going to get gas?"

"I'll stop when we need to." He didn't like to be questioned about his judgment on things, and the tone of his words reminded me of that fact.

We drove on, as I continually peeked at the gas gauge, hoping he wouldn't notice. I didn't want to make him mad, but I could see we were nearing empty. At last I said, "How much gas do we have now?"

"We're on empty." He laughed but made no attempt to exit the highway.

"You always do this!" I said, nervous but unable to remain quiet any longer. "We don't have time to run out of gas. We'll be late picking up the children. Please stop."

"Let me be the judge of how much time we have."

By that time I was begging. "Lee, please stop. If we run out of gas and aren't at the airport on time, Colley is going to be so upset. You're doing this on purpose!"

"I want to see how much farther we can go before we give out."

I was mad and on the verge of tears, but I knew if I said anything more or started to cry, it would just make it worse. I'd promised Colley we'd be there, and now I wasn't going to be able to keep my promise.

The car began to feel sluggish, and the light indicator was on empty. That was it. We coasted toward the nearest exit, down the ramp, and almost made it to the gas station before Lee had to push the car the rest of the way, while I anxiously stared at the clock.

Taking his time, Lee filled the tank and then announced, "We need to get something to eat."

"I want to eat at the airport," I said. "I don't want to risk being late."

"We're not eating at the airport," he informed me, and that was that. He found a Chinese restaurant and strolled in as if he had all the time in the world. I hurriedly ate some soup and was ready to leave, but Lee was still eating. Finally he finished his meal, paid the check, and followed me outside.

"Now I want to take a walk by the river," he announced, sauntering across the street to the banks of the Potomac and ignoring my protests.

We were already late and there was nothing I could do about it. When we finally arrived at the airport, the plane had landed and the passengers had deplaned. I spotted Colley and Elliott, sitting with an unfamiliar woman at the gate.

"Where were you, Mom?" Colley cried. "You promised to be here."

"I didn't want to leave them here by themselves," the lady said, and then introduced herself. Her daughter went to the same junior high as Elliott, but we'd never met.

I'd been told not to demean your spouse in front of the children, so I covered for him, but I knew no one believed me.

◇   ◇   ◇

It was fun to see everyone at *The 700 Club* again. They were taking stories they'd done in the past and giving updates to their audience.

After they taped Lee's and my interview section, they wanted footage of our family. The four of us walked through the fall leaves, the brilliant colored trees providing the backdrop for this perfect scene.

"Smile, everybody," they told us. "Talk to each other. Act playful. Look natural." I kept smiling, though it was anything but natural.

It took three attempts at walking through the leaves and clowning around to look like the happy family that had survived so much. Apparently we played the part well.

It was after the airing of *The Sally Jesse Raphael Show* that I asked Colley, "Weren't you proud of your daddy?"

Colley, as always, saw things as they were—and spoke accordingly. "Why? What else could he say on television?"

Maybe we didn't play the part as well as I'd imagined.

◇   ◇   ◇

I'd made it through the years of "cancer boot camp" without realizing it was essential for preparing for the real battle. The next five years were spent coming out of denial and facing the circumstances in our household. I was more determined than ever to focus on Lee and our relationship. No longer making the trips to the clinic made that easier. I vowed I'd do everything to be a submissive, loving wife. We'd had a seven-year "cancer interruption," but that was over.

Unfortunately, it seemed no matter how hard I tried to rebuild and strengthen our marriage, nothing worked. The more I tried, the worse things became.

One day in March I felt like God told me to give up the Junior Miss Program. It was the only thing I had left where I could use my theater and dance background, so I didn't understand, but I knew it was God making the request. I called the director and resigned, and within twenty-four hours, he had my replacement. I was brokenhearted and humbled that I could be replaced so quickly after doing the job for twelve years.

Still hurting from that incident and needing a little time to myself while the children were in school, I decided to drive to my maternal great-grandparents' farm in Equality, Alabama. The field next to the old home-place was abloom with wild daffodils. As I gathered a bouquet of the beautiful yellow flowers, tears ran down my cheeks and I prayed silently, *What else do I have to give up, Lord? It's all I had left of the things I love to do, and they gave it to someone else so quickly.*

As I picked another blossom to add to my bouquet, it was as if I heard Him say, "If I didn't fill it quickly, you may have taken it back." I'd walked with God long enough by then to know He had His reasons; my part was to just be obedient, even if doing so made me sad.

I soon found out, however, that I was going to need to spend all my time at home, as well as helping Lee at his office twice a week. I turned over the handling of my speaking schedule to him and only went out of town to speak if he could go with me. My older lady friends told me that was part of being submissive, and that he was being my protector and I should be grateful. I tried to look at it that way, but all I sensed from Lee was a resentful and controlling attitude. And it wasn't just my speaking schedule that brought out his resentful, controlling behavior; it was anything and everything that popped up in our day-to-day lives.

"How many times do I need to tell you to consult with me?" became a common question from Lee, and I soon found myself resorting to lies to avoid confrontation.

"Where's the cottage cheese that was in the refrigerator, Candy?" he asked one day. When I explained that I'd thrown it away because it had passed its freshness date, he responded with his "How many times do I have to tell you" question.

The next time he asked where something was that I'd thrown out, I told him I ate it. Then the interrogation began, as he tried to trip me up. When did I eat it? Why had I eaten that instead of something else? One day I realized he wanted me to think I'd pulled it off, even though I hadn't.

He knew I'd lied, but he let me play out the charade because he enjoyed watching me squirm.

That's crazy. Why would he do that? It doesn't make sense.

I soon began to think I was the crazy one. He had a way of turning things around—simple, insignificant things, like statements I'd make or everyday things I'd do, but in such a way that made me wonder what I'd really said or done. When we got into an argument, I'd agree with him, since he continually reminded me that he was always right.

One day, he asked, "Who's the one who's had head surgeries? Who's on pain medication?" That settled it. He was probably right since I was the one who was least likely to be thinking clearly—yet deep inside, I knew that wasn't true.

I soon found myself covering for him to the children and, by his instruction, calling in sick for him at work, an occurrence that was becoming more frequent all the time.

One night Colley confronted me on the situation. Lee had come in the door from work, and I cheerfully called out to him, asking about his day and telling him we were glad he was home. But the truth was that each time I heard the back door open, my stomach knotted up and the entire atmosphere of the house became tense. I'd heard in church that "feelings follow actions," so I did loving things for him, hoping the feelings would come. I showed respect for him in front of the children because all the Christian books said to do so.

That one particular evening Lee walked past Colley's room, grumbling about something, and I quickly reminded Colley, who was ten at the time, that he'd probably had a bad day.

"What about all the other days?"

"He works hard."

"Mom, stop covering for him. He doesn't love you, and he doesn't love us. He's a jerk, and you know it."

She was right, but I didn't let her know I agreed.

At the same time, I was taking a good look at my own heart. I was doing all the right things, but my heart was resisting every step of the way. I was angry and confused and wished I had someone to talk to about the situation. We had the couples' Bible study at our home every week, and Lee led another one at his office. He knew the Scriptures well, so why couldn't I trust him? Time and again, I asked God to forgive me for feeling the way I did.

"Cancer was a breeze," I announced one day at my ladies' Bible study, "compared to submission. Submission's going to kill me!" I laughed, but I was serious. No one noticed that I was trying to tell them something was wrong. I'm not sure I even realized that's what I was doing.

A ray of hope broke through when Lee began seeing a counselor at the church. For four years, he went from one counselor to another. He attended group meetings. He read books. Seeing him want to change was encouraging—and yet there was no change. Again I looked at myself. Surely it must be me!

I started praying for God to change me. I wasn't responsible for Lee— just me. I'd built a protective wall around my heart that nothing could penetrate. At one point, I decided I'd stay with him, since I had no biblical grounds for divorce, but I also decided that nothing he said or did was going to bother me anymore. I'd love him as the Scriptures instructed me, but I couldn't love him any other way.

◇　　　◇　　　◇

By 1994 everything was going downhill fast. The episodes had become like the firing of a machine gun—one after another and closer together. No one knew about them, other than the counselors Lee was seeing and my doctors, who were picking up on my symptoms of stress, stomach problems, and worsening headaches.

I thought I was handling the situation relatively well until one day, as I sat in the examining room, Doug, our friend and my internist said,

"I'm starting you on Elavil to help the nerve pain in your face—and also the depression."

Depression? Why, I was happy—and I told him so!

Apparently I wasn't too convincing because he said, "Candy, one dysfunctional person in the house is enough. There can't be two." I continued to argue that I didn't need medication for depression, but he finally persuaded me otherwise.

25

◇　◇　◇

When I awoke early one morning, I had the feeling Lee was watching me. I opened my eyes just enough to confirm I was right.

The drapes were still closed, but there was enough light around the edges to make out Lee's features. When our eyes met, I waited for him to speak, but he continued to stare silently.

"Is something wrong?" I finally asked.

He turned away and gazed up at the ceiling, pausing a moment before saying, "God's just dealing with me."

That's a good thing. If God's dealing with him, that means he's growing spiritually. "Dealing with you in what area?"

"My pride."

"Pride in what?"

"Oh," he said, and then paused. "For my pride in sticking it out."

His tone was indignant as he stressed the final three words, sticking it out, leaving them hanging in the air between us. Then he turned back to me and, deliberately emphasizing each word, added, "With such a *grossly disfigured, skinny* wife."

At one time his words would have devastated me, but that morning they fell to the floor as if they'd bounced off a suit of armor. My protective wall was doing its job.

Until that moment, no one had been cruel enough to refer to me as "grossly disfigured." It seemed everyone had loved me for who I was and had been happy I'd survived. Although I wished my husband could react the same way, I knew he couldn't. I'd accepted that, so I didn't get angry or cry. I simply responded as if I understood what he was saying—and why.

"Oh, Lee, that's so good that you're able to express your feelings instead of holding them in!"

When he didn't answer, I got up and went into the bathroom, flipping on the light and gazing into the mirror at my sunken forehead and the scar running down my face. *He's right, God. I am disfigured. But I'm so thankful to be here. And makeup helps! I know it's noticeable, Lord, but it's not that bad, is it?*

Before I could hear an answer, Lee came into the bathroom.

Still unemotional over his statement, I asked, "Does it bother you that much?"

"Of course it does. Think what I had when I married you."

Is that what was going through his mind when he was staring at me when I woke up? I wondered.

"Does it bother you to see me in the morning before I've put on my makeup and hairpiece?" I asked.

When he acknowledged that it did, I asked, "Does it make you sad, or do you just think it's ugly?"

"Both," he answered, not even trying to soften the blow.

Oh, well, Lord, I continued in silence, *You think I'm beautiful, and that's what really matters. But the way he said all that sounded mean.*

Another time Lee and I were watching a *National Geographic* program about a remote people with unusual customs, and I had said, "I sure wouldn't want one of those things sticking out of my lips and ears!"

"Yeah, you'd rather just have a torn-up face," Lee had replied.

In addition, he occasionally referred to me as "Scarface," though in my naïveté I refused to believe he meant it in a mean way. He had felt that way all along. I had just missed it, until now.

◇   ◇   ◇

One week later, the mail arrived, and I received a letter from a man who'd seen a rerun of me on television and had somehow obtained my address. As I read his letter, I was stunned. It was as if the Lord Himself had written through this gentleman to assure me I was indeed as beautiful— or more so—than ever.

Dear Candy Wood:

This is the first letter of its kind I've ever written. I met you first in James Dobson's Focus on the Family *magazine. I'm sixty-nine years old, but your story touched me more than anything has in a hundred years! You, specifically, your family, supportively, are absolutely the gutsiest children of God I've ever experienced in any way. This opinion was reinforced when I clicked on* The Sally Jesse Raphael Show *this week.*

I live alone, so imagine the dialogue sounds were weird. I saw your gorgeous smile and said, "I know her!" My immediate response was, "No, you don't. Don't be silly!" I'll save you the boredom of the rest of my dialogue, mostly referring to my sanity. But I was right. I watched your segment of the program—thank you! My heart sang! You are beautiful.

I haven't had much experience (lately) writing love letters, but this is one. I send you and Lee and your youngsters my prayer and my love and most profound thanks!

You are beautiful. The words would echo in my heart for years to come and sustain me through the incredibly difficult times that still lay ahead.

It was a Saturday morning in October, 1994. I thought I was immune to Lee's rages, despite the fact that I had no idea when they might occur. I'd tried to figure out what sparked them so I could avoid setting him off, but it seemed his behavior was becoming more erratic and unpredictable every day.

That morning I stood at the kitchen sink, unloading the dishwasher. I thought Lee was still asleep, but suddenly I heard him behind me. By the tone of his voice, I knew he wasn't happy. I turned on my appeasing attitude, hoping to pick up a clue about what was bothering him and then calm him down. Sometimes that worked; that morning it didn't.

He was seated at the kitchen table, his voice becoming louder and louder, as his tirade built in intensity. He began pounding his fist on the table, as the salt and pepper shakers jumped with each blow.

I pulled up my protective wall and could almost feel the thick, invisible barricade close in around me, blocking out his words.

Lord, look at this. It's not even bothering me anymore. I've come a long way, haven't I? He can call me whatever he wants. Those names don't even touch me anymore—nor do those hateful looks. Besides, I have You, and that's all I need.

I don't know why I didn't just walk out of the room. My counselor had told me I didn't have to stay and be verbally abused. Maybe I was afraid to walk away while Lee was still talking. But as soon as he finished, I left without saying a word. Whatever he was mad about wasn't worth my rebuttal, and it wouldn't have changed things anyway.

I went on about my business around the house as if nothing had happened. I got dressed, put on my makeup, and told Lee I was going out. Colley had spent the night at a friend's house the night before, so she wasn't there, and Elliott was away at college.

I didn't really have anywhere in particular to go, so I went to the Wright Center Concert Hall. My friend and director of the theater had made it clear I was welcome to watch rehearsals anytime, so I walked up the aisle and sat down next to him. The technical crew was busy with last-minute lighting changes and sound checks for the show that evening, and it felt good to be somewhere other than home.

I stayed until it was time to pick up Colley, but when I got there, she said she wanted to stay at her friend's another night. By then the morning's episode was history. Lee and I didn't speak when I got home, and that was fine with me. I'd already decided to go back and see the show.

Sometime during the show, my head started to hurt in a different way than normal. It felt like the scalp was tightening. By the time I got home, I was ready to take another pain pill and go to bed.

The next morning, during Sunday school, I couldn't stand the pain any longer, so I left church early. That afternoon I called Momma and Daddy and asked them to take me to the emergency room for a pain shot. Lee stayed home. Colley was at a friend's.

By Monday, when I still had no relief, Lee was forced to take me to the doctor's office for another shot. "If you aren't better by this afternoon," Doug said, "we need to admit you."

The pain was so bad by that afternoon that I was admitted to UAB Hospital in downtown Birmingham, where I was given a pain drip. Almost immediately, the pain began to ebb, and I fell into a deep sleep. It was Tuesday night before I awoke.

"Candy."

I opened my eyes and tried to focus on Doug. "We need to talk about your situation at home," he said. "I know what's going on. We may need to talk about a physical separation for you two."

I hadn't said a word to him about Lee and me, but just when I thought I'd finally be able to talk to someone about it, Lee walked in and curbed the conversation.

It was decided I could go home the next day. When the doctor came in on Wednesday to give me my discharge papers, he told me not to take the pain medicine I'd been taking before but to try another one for a while.

Lee took me home and then left for work, while I went to Elliott's bedroom and crawled into his twin bed. Sleeping in another room was about as much physical separation as I was willing to try for the time being. Besides, I was tired; I just wanted to sleep.

Momma picked up Colley from school, and by late afternoon, my head was getting worse. The new pain medicine wasn't helping, but I wanted to listen to my doctor and not resort to the old medicine, so I decided to hang on a little longer.

When Lee came home from work, he found me in Elliott's bed. Colley was in her room across the hall, doing her homework. It was Wednesday night, the night the youth group met at church. Lee asked Colley to see if she could get a ride to church, and then came into Elliott's room to talk to me.

"How do you feel?" He sounded irritated.

"My head hurts," I whispered.

"Have you taken your Esgic?"

"The doctor told me not to. He wants me to try this new medicine."

"Well, if it's not working, it seems you'd take something that does."

"I'm just doing what I was told. But I've called his office, and I'm waiting for him to call back."

"When is he supposed to call? Are you just going to lie there and hurt?" He kept firing questions at me, getting louder and louder until Colley came across the hall to the door.

"Dad, leave her alone. She just got back from the hospital."

Colley never seemed afraid of Lee, and she always spoke her mind, especially when it came to protecting me.

Lee exploded. "Look, Colley, you aren't the one that has to take her to the hospital if she gets worse, so don't *you* be telling *me* what to do!" Then he continued to badger me about taking my old prescription until I finally gave in.

"Okay, Lee, okay," I said, crying. "Go get it. Get me *two* if it'll make you happy. I don't care."

He went to get the medicine, while Colley came and stood beside me.

"It'll be alright, Mom," she said, putting her arms around me. "Don't cry."

Colley stayed while I took the two pills Lee gave me. When I calmed down, she went back to her room. Lee left, too, and I soon heard him in the kitchen.

"Colley!" he called.

"Yes, sir," she answered from her bedroom.

"Did you get a ride to Raiders?"

"Yes, sir."

"Come here!"

Oh, no, what's wrong?

"Why did you get a ride?" he demanded.

"You said to see if I could get one."

"That's right. I said to *see* if you could get a ride; I didn't say to *get* a ride."

Lord, he is so mean. He's just so mean! I began to cry, wishing I were strong enough to get out of bed and help her. Instead, I lay there, listening and praying....

"Well, I just assumed you meant—"

He cut her off before she could finish. "That's right. You *assumed.* Spell *assume* for me, Colley!" When she didn't respond immediately, he yelled, "I said, *spell* it."

I heard her mumble something, but it wasn't clear.

"You spell it *a-s-s-u-m-e,*" Lee bellowed. "What does that mean, Colley?"

Again, I couldn't hear her answer.

"*A-s-s-u-m-e*, Colley. Assume! It means you make an *ass* out of *you* and *me*. Do you understand?"

I heard a faint, "Yes, sir."

Oh, Lord, what do I do? What do we do?

Soon Colley slipped into Elliott's room and knelt down beside the bed. "Mom," she whispered, "I hate him."

I reached out to hug her. "Colley, I'm so sorry. I know."

We heard the footsteps coming down the hall from the kitchen. "I heard that!"

Stopping in the doorway, he demanded, "Go get the belt—right now!"

"Leave her alone," I pleaded, forcing myself into a sitting position.

"By God, Candy, you stay out of this!"

Colley ran around the end of the bed to the corner of the room, the bed and me between her and her out-of-control father. Colley and I were crying, and Lee was screaming.

"You aren't touching her," I told him with all the strength I could muster. "You won't touch Colley, do you hear me? You'll have to beat me before you touch her! You leave her alone, Lee. She hasn't done anything wrong."

"I love you, Dad. *We* love you!" Colley was sobbing, her pitiful little body tucked in the corner, while she said whatever she could to make things better.

The phone rang in the midst of all the tears and shouting, and I snatched up the receiver next to Elliott's bed. It was Doug, returning my call, and he heard what was going on in the background.

"We've got to do something about this," he said, his tone serious.

"I know." I couldn't say more with Lee in the room. I asked about my pain medicine, and he told me to go ahead and take my old medicine and he'd check on me the next day.

I hung up, just as Lee announced to Colley, "You got out of it this time, but you won't next time."

He stormed out of the room, and Colley came back to sit beside me on the bed. It was over—at least for that night.

◇   ◇   ◇

When Doug called the next morning to check on me, I assured him the pain had eased. They'd done a CT scan at the hospital, and I hoped they'd have some answers by then.

He explained that the muscles surrounding my head had tightened, causing something like a Charlie-horse effect. That's when I knew the events of the weekend had affected me more than I realized.

"We have to do something," Doug repeated. "I can't keep putting you in the hospital on a pain drip every time one of these episodes occurs."

"I know. It'll be alright, though. I'm sleeping in Elliott's room now."

"We need to talk about a physical separation," he continued. "It's admirable to try to stay in this marriage, and if you want to play Russian roulette with your life, that's one thing. But you're playing it with your children's lives, too."

I knew he meant what he said and I respected his opinion, but everything was alright now, especially since I was in Elliott's room. For some reason, I felt safe there, and I believed Colley was safe too, since she was just across the hall from me.

Two days later, Lee and I went to a friend's fortieth birthday party, and everything was back to normal.

◇   ◇   ◇

Things continued to progress smoothly over the next few weeks so I moved back into our bedroom. Lee stuck to himself now, going to work less and less and staying in our bedroom with the lights off and the draperies closed much of the time. He'd come out to eat and then go back to our room and close the door.

One day while he was sitting at the kitchen table, I tried to cheer him up, but his only response was, "Why can't you understand that I'm in a pit right now?"

"I'm just trying to help, Lee. I'm sorry."

"If you're really sorry and want to help, why don't you get in the pit with me?"

"What do you mean—crawl into bed in that dark room with you all day?"

"That would be nice." The look on his face made me uncomfortable, but I really wanted to help him, so I tried again.

"I'm sorry you're so down, but somebody has to run the household," I said, not daring to tell him that the last thing in the world I wanted was to lock myself away in that room with him. But he made me feel guilty, so I proposed that I'd make a point to go in and sit with him now and then—and I did. I sat right next to him, silent and still, while he hibernated under the covers.

There was just so much that I could take. It began to drag me down, which was the last place I needed to be. Colley was fourteen and needed me, too. Besides, Lee was becoming more empty looking and non-verbal, so there seemed little point to sit by him in silence.

Then, late one night, I was awakened by the sound of his voice— gravelly, deep, and scratchy sounding.

"Go ahead. Go ahead, Lee. Just die. Have a heart attack or something." He continued to talk while I lay on my side, motionless, my back to him.

Then his voice changed to a high-pitched, singsong tone, until he said, "Don't listen, Lee. What's going on, God? What's happening?" He'd ask questions in his own voice, and then the singsong voice would quote lengthy scriptures. Without missing a beat, he went back to the gravelly voice, then cackled like the witch in the *Wizard of Oz.*

Amazingly, I wasn't really frightened, but I didn't move or respond either. I didn't want him to know I was awake, as these various voices continued back and forth for at least ten minutes. Finally, he cackled even louder and then said in the deep, wicked voice, "I bet if Candy's awake, she's freaking out." And he laughed again.

I continued to lie there like a stone until he quieted. Eventually I went back to sleep.

The next morning, Lee asked, "Hey, uh, Candy, did you notice anything different last night? Did you hear anything?"

Trying to maintain the same nonchalant attitude as he, I said, "You were talking kind of crazy. I think it may be a good idea if you make an appointment with one of your counselors today."

Surprisingly, he didn't object. He even took me with him to the counselor, and I told him what I heard. When he asked Lee if he remembered anything, Lee laughed and said, "Yeah, I remember. I was trying to scare Candy. I was mad at her."

From there on, things got worse, escalating at an alarming rate, until I knew something—or someone—had to break.

◇   ◇   ◇

Lee and I were on our way to a Christmas party at a friend's house one evening in 1994. By then, Elliott was a freshman in college, and he often worked at the church in the audio-visual department when he came home for breaks. This was one of those nights he was at the church setting up for an event, and I'd told Elliott that we'd stop by on the way to the party. The plan was to meet him under the back portico, but when we got there, he wasn't there and the church doors were locked.

"Where is he?" Lee asked, looking at me as if I'd made yet another of my many mistakes. "Are you sure he's supposed to be at *this* entrance?"

"Pretty sure."

"Pretty sure? What do you mean *pretty* sure?" His voice was beginning to escalate. "Weren't the directions clear?"

I felt myself getting nervous, so I hedged. "Maybe we should try the other side."

Elliott wasn't there either. Had I misunderstand? *Oh, no, Lord—not tonight!*

Too late. Lee was in a rage before I knew it, calling me names that I always hoped I'd forget—but couldn't. He hammered down on the accelerator and wheeled around the empty parking lot, barely missing the light posts. I pressed my feet against the dashboard, preparing to crash or turn over at any moment. In my calmest voice and hoping to protect Elliott from any fallout, I said, "I'm sorry. It isn't Elliott's fault. I must have made a mistake."

We continued to swerve around the parking lot, and he continued to raise his voice, while I, as always, tried to calm him down. We finally went to our friend's house without speaking another word. Throughout that thirty-minute drive, I felt so guilty that I hated my husband, but when we emerged from the car and walked into our friend's home, it was as the perfect, happy Christian couple.

No one suspected a thing.

26

◇　　　◇　　　◇

As 1994 DREW TO A CLOSE AND 1995 BEGAN, I SENSED IT WAS ALSO the beginning of the end of the life Lee and I had shared. Soon after New Year's, Lee looked at me and said, "It's time for me to go somewhere." It was obvious Lee needed more help than he had found in Birmingham, whether in one-on-one counseling sessions or various group therapy times. He wanted to be an in-patient somewhere, so I helped him pack, and we left for a clinic in Atlanta.

Around eleven that evening, after checking Lee in to a reputable mental facility where he would be an in-patient for at least two weeks and then an out-patient for another two, he was escorted back to the patients' quarters. I was allowed to go with him as far as the door, where I took one last look into his blank face before the doors locked behind him. Then I began the long three-hour drive home.

Back in Birmingham, I crawled into bed after what had been an extremely emotional and draining day. My husband of twenty-two years was gone.

◇   ◇   ◇

I spent the next month juggling my time between Birmingham, where I took care of Colley, being careful not to miss any of her junior high basketball games in the evenings, and driving to Atlanta several times each week to see Lee and meet with his counselors. Often I didn't get home until at least midnight or later.

One of those meetings with his psychiatrist was especially difficult. The doctor suggested that Lee and I be separated for a minimum of four months when Lee returned home. Then the doctor exited the room, leaving Lee and me alone. It wasn't five minutes before Lee went into a rage, immediately bringing the nurse through the door.

"Oh, dear, I thought the doctor was still in here with you. I didn't know you were alone. I'm so sorry!" She continued to apologize profusely as she ushered me to safety.

"You've never seen him like that, have you?" I asked, stunned to realize how controlled he'd been to that point.

The nurse confirmed my suspicions. "Never. He's usually very quiet and passive."

I left Atlanta feeling confused and guilty. Was I the only one who caused Lee to react the way he did? Was it my fault?

I stopped at a pay phone fifteen minutes after I left the hospital and called to check on him.

"He's doing fine now," the nurse said. "He's out here in the patient lobby, laughing with the other patients."

The drive home was difficult. It really was my fault, I decided. Maybe separation was a good idea. Maybe, if I was out of the picture, he'd be better.

The realization made me sad that I might be the cause of Lee's problems, but I was also glad that we'd be separated for at least four months.

By the time I got to Birmingham it was nine-thirty, and I couldn't make sense of anything. I couldn't go home to Colley, as Momma and Daddy were staying with her, and I didn't want them to see me in such a fragile condition. Instead, I drove by Frank and Barbara's house. Their lights were on, so I went to the door. Barbara answered, and I went inside and collapsed in a chair, bursting into tears and crying that everything was my fault. I couldn't really explain what I meant because I wasn't sure myself. After all, I'd done what God asked. I'd been submissive—almost to a fault by allowing things into our household that I shouldn't have. But what else could I have done?

Looking back, I shouldn't have kept the children in that atmosphere. My doctor had been right. What was it going to do to them later in their lives? Was it my illness that caused Lee to be that way? What about some of his odd behavior before my illness? He was angry with his family, too. Sometimes he blamed them for all his troubles. According to him, it wasn't just me that had ruined his life.

Frank and Barbara had company that evening, but it didn't seem to matter that I'd interrupted their evening. They wanted to help—and they did, by their friendship and prayers. Their friend Jim sat quietly while Frank and Barbara were calming me down, but I continued to sob. I politely apologized for interrupting, but none of them seemed to mind. A couple of weeks later, Barbara received the following poem.

THE JOY BENEATH

◇　　　◇　　　◇

THIS POEM WAS INSPIRED BY CANDY, WHO HAS ENDURED MORE THAN most could stand, and whose faith knows no limitations.

Across the room while firmly placed,
　　my weary eyes beheld her face,
　　　　and noticed scars had left their trace,
　　　　　　and for a moment missed her grace,
　　　　　　　　which flourished like the blooms of Spring.
Then to my marvel and surprise,
　　I saw the joy beneath her eyes,
　　　　and though they'd cried a thousand cries,
　　　　　　they mirrored what she held inside,
　　　　　　　　the faithful love of Christ the King.
While others would have been depressed,
　　this woman spoke of being blessed,
　　　　and as His will 'twas for the best,'
　　　　　　a faith so perfect I confess,
　　　　　　　　must raise the hosts bove to sing.
Then what at first mine eyes did shield,
　　resplendent beauty now revealed,
　　　　and scars once there His love concealed,
　　　　　　"Behold the lilies of the field,"
　　　　　　　　this thought the sight of her did bring
She'd denied strife room to fetter,
　　God her salve to make things better,
　　　　great her pain, God much greater,
　　　　　　grew my faith for having met her,
　　　　　　　　faith in the Christ, my Lord and King.

Jim Hill

After a month Lee came back to Birmingham and moved into an apartment to give us the physical separation his doctor had suggested. I felt sorry for Lee, but not enough to ask him to move back in. We talked on the phone, however, and when I called one morning and he didn't answer, I knew something was wrong. I called 9-1-1. It was a suicide attempt. Elliott was home from college for spring break when it happened, so he and I met the ambulance at the hospital, where Lee was admitted to the psychiatric ward.

From that point on, Lee and I were in counseling, both individually and together. It was advised for safety purposes that we not be alone together, although we did occasionally go out to lunch in open, crowded places, and always with a third party present.

At the end of six months, Lee called and announced he was moving back into the house and that if Colley and I didn't want to live there with him, we'd better find someplace else to live. We packed our things and loaded up the furniture I

Trust the Lord with your future.

wanted to take with us and moved to a two-bedroom apartment not far from our house.

Lee had been working on getting psychiatric disability for some time. In the meantime, we had no income, so my dear daddy, wanting me to be able to stay home with Colley, supported Colley, Elliott, and me as he'd been doing for a long time and would continue to do as long as necessary. That included all our living expenses—cars, rent, insurance, and tuition for Christian school for Colley and college for Elliott.

Weeks turned into months, and there was no progress between Lee and me. If anything, our situation worsened. I sought wise counsel and prayed for guidance and discernment, knowing I didn't have biblical grounds for divorce.

"I could live the rest of my life separated, couldn't I, Tom?" I once asked one of our associate ministers. I'd made an appointment with him to help me understand things spiritually. I knew I couldn't fix Lee, and I couldn't fix us. I was legally married, yet a single mom with no income. My only skill was teaching dancing, and I couldn't do that anymore—at least not enough to provide a living for Colley, Elliott, and myself, and I certainly couldn't depend on Daddy forever.

Tom was a wise man, and I trusted his advice. "Candy," he said, smiling across his desk, "I know this has been a hard time and still is. But you needn't worry about those things now. Just trust the Lord with your future."

His words resonated in my soul. *Just trust the Lord with your future.* I left his office, repeating those words over and over, until it became so clear—and so simple. I'd trusted God with my past, and He'd always been faithful, just like He said He'd be. There was no reason I couldn't trust Him with my future too.

Of course, that didn't mean I'd sit back and do nothing; I'd certainly continue to do my part. But, ultimately, I gave it all to Him.

"God, it's up to you. I trust you," I declared. And I meant every word.

◇　　　◇　　　◇

Several months later Colley and I came home one day to find a phone message from Lee. In his tight, controlled, expressionless, and emotionless voice, he'd left this slow, methodical message: "Colley, this is Dad. I just wanted to call before everything hits the fan and let you know I'm divorcing your mom. She's a pagan, and at this point in my life I'm not going to be disobedient to the Lord."

Colley's eyes opened wide, as she stared at me in disbelief. "What?" she asked, as I tried to read her emotions.

"I'll play it again," I said, pushing the repeat button.

We listened again, then exchanged glances, silently acknowledging that we'd heard it correctly. Neither of us responded immediately, and then the one-word exclamation burst forth almost in a whisper: "Yes!" I felt my eyes widen, as the impact of Lee's words settled into my soul. "Yes!" I exclaimed again, my voice rising now. "Colley, I'm free! I'm finally free!"

There, in our tiny kitchen, we gave each other two or three high fives, celebrating my impending freedom.

Then, suddenly, the ramifications of the call hit Colley.

"Now I'm going to be one of those children with divorced parents," she said, her tone sober and yet relieved.

Despite my own happiness, I felt sad for her. It was never my desire or intention for my children to be victims of a broken home. "I know, Colley. I'm sorry." There was nothing else I could say. I gathered her into my arms and hugged her.

◇　　　◇　　　◇

One year and three months after that call in May 1997, I walked out of Birmingham's courthouse, across the grassy courtyard, past the fountain, and to my car. Pigeons nibbled tidbits thrown by people relaxing on park benches in the sun. The birds' wings fluttered as they flew away from me when I got too close.

Free as a bird. That's what I am—free as a bird!

I opened my car door, sat down, put the keys into the ignition—and started to cry. It was over. It was finally over! A myriad of feelings engulfed me—relieved, glad, tired ... and sad. Yes, I was sad things couldn't have been different.

"God, I'm so sorry. I really am sorry. I know You hate divorce." I wiped my eyes. I had no regrets. I'd done everything I could, and there'd be no looking back—only ahead, trusting God with my future.

I started the car, pulled out of the parking space, and drove around the corner, just in time to see a man holding a bright yellow placard with two words written on it in big bold letters: "Trust Jesus." I smiled.

27

◇ ◇ ◇

"So what's your story?" Keith asked, as we sat in the middle of the Town and Gown Theatre during a rehearsal.

It was February 2004, and I'd just met Keith. Puzzled, I replied, "What's my story?"

"Yes. Are you a dance instructor in town, or what do you do?"

"I used to be a dance instructor at Steeple Arts Academy of Dance—and a performer too. In fact, I began in this very theater when I was fifteen years old."

Keith was from New York—a choreographer, dancer, singer, and now the newly hired director of Birmingham's Summerfest Theatre Company. Actually, it wasn't just a summer theater company at all but a large, year-round organization, consisting of two main-stage shows performed at the historic Town and Gown Theatre and several cabaret shows performed at a cabaret in downtown Birmingham's historic district. It also included three children's groups, the cream-of-the-crop of talent. I'd been asked to choreograph five numbers for the group's annual February show.

"I noticed you're good with the children," he said.

"Thanks. I love the kids. It's fun."

"Would you consider teaching at the workshop this summer and being my assistant director/choreographer for the production of *Annie* in August?"

I laughed. "I haven't danced or taught dancing in twenty-two years. I've choreographed a couple of high school musicals and the Junior Miss Program, and this is the first time I've ever choreographed anything for Summerfest."

"Why so long in between?"

"I was diagnosed with cancer twenty-two years ago—in the center of my head. It ended my dancing career."

"Tell me about it."

When I finished, he again asked me to consider being his assistant. I was flattered but felt unqualified. But then …

Lord, You've done it again! Who would ever have thought? This is amazing!

That began a three-year job at the Summerfest Youth Program, one of the most fulfilling experiences of my life, where I worked with some of the most talented young people in the city.

◇   ◇   ◇

Slightly over one year later, in September 2005, I stood in the wings of the historic Town and Gown Theatre where I'd stood so many times before, waiting to go onstage. It had been thirty-eight years since the first time I'd appeared here, in the story of Fannie Brice. The show was called *Funny Girl,* and I was fifteen years old.

I was born to be onstage. I'd known it even then, nearly four decades earlier. It was in my blood.

I thought of one of the songs from that show, "Don't Rain on My Parade," and the words seemed appropriate for my life. Barbra Streisand sang that song in the movie version, and though I'd loved the words when I was fifteen, I was even more excited now. I'd thought I'd never be onstage again, that I'd lost that part of my life. True, that wasn't a big price, considering the circumstances, and I gladly paid it. But now, standing in the wings and waiting to go onstage for the first time in so long, I wanted to soak up every emotion. *Please, Lord, don't let me be nervous. I only have this one time, and I want to enjoy it—all three minutes of it.*

It was the "Faces of Broadway," the University of Alabama Children's Hospital fundraiser for the Craniofacial Department. Several Broadway stars were included in the gala event, including the lead in *Cats*, the female and male lead in *Phantom of the Opera*, and the male lead in the national tour of *Annie*. I, along with them, had been asked to perform a number.

Then I heard it—my introduction. "And now, let's welcome to the stage—Candy Wood!"

God, you've done it now—more than I've ever asked for! I'm performing again—and with Broadway stars! Oh, yes, more than I could ever think or ask!

I walked out to center-stage, the full skirt of my strapless black dress swishing as I moved. I felt so elegant. There were many in the audience that night who knew my story, and I knew they were happy for me. I wanted to embrace every second of their gracious applause.

When at last it died down, I took a breath and began to speak.

"Good evening. Thirty-eight years ago as a fifteen-year-old, I stepped onto this stage to perform in my first musical, *Funny Girl*. Twenty-three years ago I stepped out onto this stage in what I thought would be my last show. Two months later I was diagnosed with a baseball-sized tumor in the center of my head. Eight surgeries later, I was left facially disfigured but cancer-free. I speak for other craniofacial patients. Thank you, physicians and caregivers in the audience, for your commitment and diligence to patients like me."

I paused. "Now, to Him who gives exceedingly and abundantly more than we could ever think or ask ..." I shook my head and smiled. "Who would ever think I'd be on the same stage as these performers tonight?" I laughed. "If my friends could see me now!"

The lights went out. The spotlight was on me. The music began, and I started to sing "If My Friends Could See Me Now" from the musical *Sweet Charity.* I was soon joined by eight men in black ties and tails, who'd come to sing and dance the chorus with me. All the while the audience saw a slide show of my hospital pictures, along with pictures of other craniofacial patients. It was a very emotional and moving moment for everyone present.

The applause lasted long after I'd exited the stage. *Oh, God, thank You! That was just a gift—a one-time gift that You gave back for a moment.*

28

◇   ◇   ◇

IT WAS SPRING 2006, AND I WAS SITTING IN MY CAR ON A BUSY highway, staring at a red light. The day was sunny and warm, the radio was off, and I was using the quiet time to make an inventory of my life.

So much had happened since that May twenty-four years earlier when I'd walked through those hospital doors, leaving my little girl and my mother to drive back into that Birmingham rainstorm without me.

In a world obsessed with makeovers of every kind, I had discovered a different kind of makeover—a lasting one—a makeover of the heart. It would change everything about me that really mattered.

Over the years God began to give me a soft and tender heart that cared more about what He wanted for me than what I wanted for myself. He eventually gave me a heart of forgiveness and healed those broken places that only He could heal. He gave me a grateful heart for the things

I had—not focusing on the things I had lost. The process would never be over until I graduated from earth to heaven.

I continued with my inventory.

I'd raised my children. Elliott and Sara were married and settled in Franklin, Tennessee, with two little boys. Colley and Gilder were married and living in Atlanta. My children were happy. I'd lived to see my grandchildren.

Momma and Daddy still lived in the same house where I grew up. They were healthy and active and enjoyed being together. Daddy had finally retired at seventy-eight, after supporting us for so many years. Now he and Momma could do whatever they wanted.

Everyone in my family had somebody. Elliott had Sara. Colley had Gilder. Momma and Daddy had each other. Why was I still here? Surely there was a purpose.

I envisioned myself holding an empty white plate in my hand. "Lord," I prayed, "here's my empty plate. You fill it with whatever You want." The light changed, and I turned onto the highway to resume my errands. But the vision of the empty plate remained.

When I got home I wrote my thoughts in my prayer journal. *Lord, here I am with nothing on my plate. You've blessed my children, and I thank You. You've blessed my parents, and I thank You. You've blessed me that they love and care for me. You've blessed me with friends who love me. You've restored everything that was allowed to be taken from me. I've enjoyed a new house. I've enjoyed performing one last time on the stage. I've enjoyed a position in the theater again. The only thing You haven't restored is a husband, and that's okay. You're my husband, and that's good. And though all of those other things have been more than wonderful, they only give temporary satisfaction. There is really nothing on this earth that keeps me here—nothing that I live for—except You and what You have for me to do, though I don't know what that is.*

For the first time, I understood what the apostle Paul meant when he said "to live is Christ, and to die is gain." I wanted to be here if there was something for me to do for God, but other than that I might as well be in heaven with Him. I wasn't being morbid; I was simply assessing where I was. What on this earth was forever? Nothing.

So in May of 2006, my plate was empty.

◇   ◇   ◇

On a hot July day, two months later, my longtime friend Ginny, who was staying with me while her adult son recovered from surgery, asked, "Can you believe it's been thirty-six years since we met?"

We laughed, remembering that first meeting when we were taking a tennis course at Samford University in summer school. I needed a P.E. credit, and so did she, so there we were.

"Those awful P.E. uniforms!" she exclaimed, and we laughed again.

"And it was so hot," I added, remembering the eleven a.m. class in the middle of July. "A lot has happened since then," I commented. Ginny had gone through a rough divorce about the same time I did, and she'd only recently remarried.

"I'm glad you're so happy, Ginny. I don't want to be married again. I'd just like to have some nice, godly man in my life who'd take me places, places where people are typically with someone. I don't mind going by myself; I do it all the time. I've also gotten Daddy to take me to a few black-tie events or dances. But I'd love to have someone to talk and dance with. Oh, well, maybe it's just not meant to be."

◇   ◇   ◇

The next day Ginny was in the guest bath doing her hair, while I put dishes away in the kitchen.

"Hey, Ginny!" I called, as a thought struck me. "What about John Lindley?"

"What about him?"

I went to the bathroom door, which was open. "I wonder if he'd want to take me places now and then."

I hadn't seen John in eight years, and had never even had a conversation with him, but I knew he, too, had gone through a difficult divorce. For whatever reason, his name and face had popped into my head.

Now, as I thought about John, I got a little nostalgic, remembering the night Ginny had sensed God telling her to go to Birmingham and pray for me the night before I left to go to the clinic. She and her husband had come, along with Bob and Becka and a single friend of theirs named John Lindley. Lee had also known John because they'd been in the same college fraternity, but I'd never met him before that night.

I shook the memory loose and turned back to the present. "What about John? What do you think? And how is he?"

She said John still lived in Knoxville and was doing fine. One thing led to another, and two weeks later, John drove to Birmingham to take me on a date.

◇   ◇   ◇

That Friday evening, after attending a party, John and I went to a nearby lake and sat on some steps in front of a building overlooking the water. The night was clear and cool, and during the quietness of the next three hours, we caught up on one another's lives. After twenty-one years of marriage, John and his wife had divorced, and he had custody of their two adopted teenage children.

Then he shifted the direction of the conversation. "I was sorry to hear about Lee." He didn't ask for details, and I knew he wasn't just referring to the divorce. During the time since my marriage to Lee had legally ended, he had remarried twice, both ending in divorce. Lee had eventually committed suicide in 2005. Obviously John was aware of that horrible fact.

"Lee was a very troubled man," I told John. "His suicide was a tragic ending to a tragic life, though I wasn't terribly shocked. His counselors had warned me there was a possibility it would play out like that. I didn't realize how afraid I still was of him until he was gone. I'm just glad he didn't take anyone else with him when it happened."

We then talked about our children, and about how strongly each of us felt about the covenant of marriage. We also talked about college. He'd been in a fraternity, but had really been more into Jesus Christ and spending time with his friends, singing praise songs and praying.

"I guess I would have been called a Jesus freak," he explained, "but I didn't care."

That was definitely different than my college experience. Though I was moral, I was primarily there for the social scene and the theater. Sadly, I didn't think a whole lot about Jesus in those days, and I considered people who passed out the little yellow booklets called *The Four Spiritual Laws* a little different and odd.

Before we knew it, it was after midnight, and we had to call it a night because John needed to be back in Knoxville the next morning.

◇　　　◇　　　◇

On Saturday morning I was surprised when John called early to ask if I had plans for the day. When I said I didn't, he asked if I'd like to go to an art museum in Tuscaloosa and then to dinner with Bob and Becka and Ginny and her husband, Jerry.

I accepted and started getting ready for my second date with John. It was a perfect July day for Alabama—hot but beautiful. When I opened the door, John stood there with a big smile on his suntanned face, holding a small devotional book in front of him.

"When did you have time to get this?" I asked, impressed with his thoughtfulness as he handed the book to me.

"This morning," he answered, again flashing his contagious smile. "The bookstore was close to the motel."

The one-hour drive to Tuscaloosa flew by, as we discussed the many topics we enjoyed in common, including art and history, and Alabama football. We laughed as we listened to oldies music in the car, and later rode around the University of Alabama campus looking at all the changes that had taken place since those "hippie days" of the late sixties and early seventies. We remembered various classes in some of the old buildings that still remained, and joked about some of our professors.

Toward the end of the day, we met the rest of the group for dinner. The six of us all had stories to tell about each other, and the entire evening was comfortable and easy. As we got up to leave, Ginny pulled me aside and said, "Candy, ya'll are going to get married."

Astonished both by her comment and the immediate confirmation I felt in my spirit, I said, "I know," though John had said nothing to make me think that way.

By the time we got home that evening, I was sorry to see the day come to an end, but the next morning I was awakened by my ringing phone and John's voice asking if I'd like to go to church with him.

"You're not going back to Knoxville?"

"Not if you'd like to go to church together."

He hadn't missed a beat all weekend, and his perfect manners and charm continued through the day. He was right on time to pick me up. He opened the doors and held my elbow when I walked up the stairs to the church. He was courteous in an old-fashioned, Southern kind of way, which seemed to match his unique Montgomery accent. Dressed in khaki pants, a starched button-down collar shirt, a Navy sports coat, and a Rep tie, as well as his ever-present smile, John explained that he always carried a coat and tie when he went out of town.

When we left church to walk to the car, he slipped his hand into mine, and it felt as natural as if we'd been together for years. After lunch he came to my house, and we looked at old college pictures and discussed the possibility that we might have met when we were there, but eventually came to the conclusion that we hadn't.

As he gazed at the pictures, he said, "Candy, it's no doubt you were a beautiful girl back then, and I hope you don't take this wrong, but ... I think you're more beautiful today."

It was one of the sweetest and most sincere things anyone had ever said to me, and I was very touched. Before he left, I handed him a copy of the CD of my testimony. Four hours later, he called. "Candy, I know I prayed for you twenty-four years ago, but I'm sorry to say I really didn't know or keep up with your situation." He paused, and then continued. "I listened to your CD tonight, and I wept. I just wanted you to know that it was an honor and a privilege to be in your presence this weekend. Thank you."

◇   ◇   ◇

The evening of November 3 was cool and crisp, with a clear sky and full moon overhead. Just three months after my first date with John, we were gathered together with about forty friends and family members at Raleigh and Dottie's old English Tudor home, which sat back off the winding road in Mountain Brook, one of Birmingham's oldest and most beautiful neighborhoods. Copper lanterns lined the driveway to the front door, which was flanked with freshly planted flowers and ivy in old French planters. Softly lit lamps and candles glowed through the windows. We'd decided we wanted a small, intimate ceremony where we could make our commitment to one another, and Raleigh and Dottie's home was the perfect setting.

The staircase in the foyer led to their upstairs master bedroom, and an old English grandfather clock stood on the landing halfway up the stairs. Dottie made sure to make everything lovely and special. Their bedroom, warm with antiques and family pictures, was the bride's room where I dressed for the evening. Guests were to arrive at seven, and the ceremony was planned for eight. There, in Dottie's bathroom, I stood in my taupe satin robe, as Dottie hooked my grandmother's pearl necklace around my neck. It was a very emotional moment.

White roses adorned the white marble countertops that glistened in the mirror, showing the Belgian lace curtains in the background. "We've been through a lot together, haven't we?" Dottie said.

"I know," I agreed. "Who would have imagined twenty-four years ago that I'd even be here, much less this?"

"Oh, Candy, I could cry! I'm so happy for you."

I put the finishing touches on my hair, as we stood looking in the mirror.

"You look beautiful," she said.

"You said that one other time," I commented, referring to the hour after surgery in ICU when my head was shaved, my face swollen, and I could barely muster a smile.

"Well, you were," she said, and we laughed.

She zipped my simple taupe strapless floor-length dress, and I emerged from the bathroom into her bedroom to have pictures taken with "the girls" in the family: Momma and Colley, Elliott's wife, Sara, and John's daughter, Margaret.

Barbara, my longtime friend and Bible study leader, was also upstairs with us. I asked who else we could get to join us for prayer before we went downstairs, and Barbara quickly gathered a handful of people together to ask God's blessing. As we did so, I thought of how amazing it was that God had orchestrated the events and people in my life.

Momma, Colley, and I had a strong bond. We'd always been there for each other in the difficult and the joyful times, each playing different roles at different times. Now was the time for us to rejoice together.

Raleigh took on the part of wedding coordinator. At seven forty-five, he came to tell everyone it was time to go downstairs and be seated. Dottie and I exchanged a humorous glance, realizing Raleigh was once again in charge. What a stark contrast to twenty-four years earlier when he'd been ushering me around the Mayo Clinic!

After escorting the others downstairs, Raleigh returned to the bedroom. "Are you ready? The clock is about to strike eight, and you want to go down right after that."

I stood at the top of the stairs as the clock struck one, two, three … I wanted to soak in every emotion of the moment. God had done exceedingly, abundantly, more than I could ever have thought or imagined. We'd had that very verse printed on the laminated bookmarks we distributed to our guests as a reminder of the One who was to be glorified that night.

At the eighth strike, the two violinists began to play the beautiful hymn "To God Be the Glory," which was also written on the bookmarks. Slowly I walked downstairs to take Daddy's arm. He was in the foyer, and beyond him was the dining room, its rich red walls decorated with sterling trumpet vases full of white roses. Candles glistened in the two candelabras on the dining room table and buffet. The living room had been turned into a chapel, with an aisle between the lined-up chairs. There, in front of the warm, crackling fireplace, awaited Barbara's husband, Frank, who was also my minister and dear friend, as well as Don, another friend who was also my counselor and a priest. They would perform the ceremony together.

And, of course, there was John. His eyes twinkled, and his smile shone. He cherished me, and I knew it. I couldn't wait to stand by his side and become his bride.

Elliott and Colley joined me on my left, while Margaret and John, Jr., joined John on his right.

After taking our vows, we took communion together as one.

When Frank announced us as Mr. and Mrs. John Lindley, I expected John to give me a very sweet and delicate kiss, like in the movies. Instead, he hugged me so tightly that he lifted me right up off the floor. In fact, my left foot lifted into the air, and Momma later said I planned it to be dramatic. I didn't, of course, but everyone laughed and clapped and cried.

To God be the glory, for great things He hath done!

About Candy Wood Lindley

◇   ◇   ◇

WHEN DOCTORS TOLD CANDY WOOD LINDLEY THAT SHE HAD SIX
months to live, she prayed that God would allow her to see her two young
children grow up. That was 1982.

Candy was diagnosed with a baseball-sized tumor in the center of her
head. Eight surgeries and several years later, she was left facially disfigured
but determined to make the most of what she had. In 1987, she was one
of twenty-five recipients of Clairol's national "Take Charge Award," given
to women who have overcome obstacles and turned their lives around
after the age of thirty. This was awarded to her for the production of two
nationally released videos, together called *Let's Face It*. One dealt with
makeup techniques for the facially disfigured and the other with wig and
scarf applications for hair loss patients.

In 1997, she was given the Life Inspiration Award by the American Cancer Society. The American Society of Plastic Surgeons gave Candy their "Patients of Courage Award" in 2004, and she accepted the 2005 Legacy of Courage Award from Alabama's For the Cause.

During the past two decades, Candy has been asked to speak to more than 1,000 different groups, including the Mayo Clinic Nursing Conference, the Christian Medical and Dental Associations' national events, and American Society of Plastic Surgeons. She has spoken to many college classes, ministries, and organizations. She is at home in both secular and religious groups.

A favorite at women's retreats and youth meetings, she also has been featured on television and radio programs (both at the local and national level) including *The 700 Club, Heart to Heart* with Sheila Walsh, *The Sally Jesse Raphael Show, The Maury Povich Show,* and *Mother Angelica.*

Her story was told on the television program *It's a Miracle* with Roma Downy. She is frequently interviewed on national radio programs, most notably *Life Perspectives* and *Back to the Bible* with Don Hawkins.

Candy's story has been featured in newspapers across the country and other publications including *Focus on the Family* magazine, *Experiencing God* magazine, and *Stern* (a German magazine similar to *Life*).

Several books have picked up her story including *When Cancer Comes* by Don Hawkins, *Chicken Soup for the Christian Woman's Soul* ("You Are Beautiful" by Sandra P. Aldrich), *Tilling the Soul* by Denise George, and *Miracles of Hope* published by Guideposts.

Candy is no stranger to the stage. She received a B.A. degree in Speech and Drama from the University of Alabama. She has been a performer/dancer/choreographer in numerous musical productions. Candy served as assistant director of youth programs for Red Mountain Theatre Company in Birmingham, Alabama, from 2004–2006, where she was assistant director/choreographer for the musical *Annie* (2004). For twelve years, Candy was choreographer of Jefferson County, Alabama's Junior Miss program.

Because of her performing background, Candy brings an entertaining speaking style to her listeners. As evidenced by the diverse audiences to whom she has spoken, her presentation lends itself to people of all ages, backgrounds, and circumstances.

In 1996, her husband of twenty-four years filed for divorce, giving her new challenges.

Candy is the mother of two. Elliott, a graduate of Belmont University, and his wife, Sara, also a graduate of Belmont University, and sons Nathan and Calvin live in Franklin, Tennessee. Her daughter, Colley, and her husband, Gilder Hatchett, both graduated from Auburn University and now live in Atlanta with their daughter, Mallie Tate, and son, Davis. Colley is pursuing a master's degree in counseling.

Candy and her husband, John Lindley, live in Knoxville, Tennessee.

Formerly a member of the Briarwood Presbyterian Church PCA in Birmingham, Alabama, Candy is now a member of the Cedar Springs Presbyterian Church EPC in Knoxville.

ABOUT KATHI MACIAS

◇ ◇ ◇

KATHI MACIAS, POPULAR SPEAKER AND PROLIFIC AUTHOR, IS AN Angel-award–winning writer who has published twenty-two books and hundreds of articles. In 2008, she was honored at the Golden Scroll Awards as the Advanced Writers and Speakers Association member of the year.

Whether keyboarding her latest book, keynoting a conference, or riding on the back of her husband's Harley, Kathi is a lady on a mission to communicate God's vision. Her insightful words—filled with passion, humor, and soul nourishment—refresh audiences from all walks of life, and her Spanish devotionals, "Desde el Corazon del Padre" (with English translations), can be found on www.Crosswalk.com each Monday.

Her newest book, *Beyond Me: Living a You-First Life in a Me-First World,* was released in July 2008 from New Hope Publishers and was named "top pick" in the Christian Living category by *Christian Retailing Magazine.* Contact Kathi at www.KathiMacias.com.

ORDER COPIES FOR YOUR FRIENDS!

Date _____

Customer Name _____

Shipping Address _____

City _____ State _____ Zip _____

Telephone (___) _____

Email _____

Price: $19.95 x _____ (number of copies) $ _____

Sales Tax (use applicable tax in your state) $ _____

Subtotal $ _____

Shipping Costs: $5.00 for 1st book (allow 2 weeks) $ _____

$3.00 for each additional book $ _____

TOTAL $ _____

PAYMENT METHOD

☐ Check enclosed made payable to "Exclaim Publishing"

☐ VISA ☐ MasterCard ☐ American Express ☐ Discover

Name on Card _____

Billing Address (if different from above) _____

Account Number _____

CVV _____ Exp. Date _____

(3 digits on back of card near signature on Visa/MC/Discover - 4 digits on front of AmEx)

Cardholder's Signature _____

MAIL THIS FORM TO

Exclaim Publishing
c/o 4822 South 133rd St.
Omaha, NE 68137

Order online at: *www.FaceofFaith.com*
Order by phone (402) 884-5995